The Equality of the Two Sexes

The Equality of the Two Sexes

by

François Poullain de la Barre

Translated with an Introduction by

A. Daniel Frankforter
Paul J. Morman

Studies in the History of Philosophy
Volume 11

The Edwin Mellen Press
Lewiston/Lampeter/Queenston

Library of Congress Cataloging-in-Publication Data

Poullain de la Barré, Francois, 1647-1723.
   (De l'égalité des deux sexes.   English)
   The equality of the two sexes : a 17th-century French treatise on
the state of women / Poullain de la Barre ; translated with a
commentary by A.D. Frankforter and Paul Morman.
         p.   cm. —— (Studies in the history of philosophy ; vol. 11)
   Translation of: De l'égalité des deux sexes.
   Bibliography: p.
   Includes index.
   ISBN   0-88946-303-4
   1. Women--Early works to 1800.   2.   Equality--Early works to 1800.
3. Women's rights--Early works to 1800.   I.   Frankforter, A. Daniel.
II.   Morman, Paul J., 1942-   .   III.   Title.   IV.   Series: Studies in
the history of philosophy (Lewiston, N.Y.)   v. 11.
   HQ1201.P6613   1989
   305.42--dc20   89-33547
                                                                          CIP

This is volume 11 in the continuing series
Studies in History of Philosophy
Volume 11 ISBN 0-88946-303-4
SHP Series ISBN 0-88946-300-X

REF
RC00785 31444

A CIP catalog record for this book
is available from the British Library.

The Edwin Mellen Press   The Edwin Mellen Press
        Box 450   Box 67
     Lewiston, NY   Queenston, Ontario
     USA 14092   CANADA L0S 1L0

            The Edwin Mellen Press, Ltd.
            Lampeter, Dyfed, Wales,
            UNITED KINGDOM SA48 7DY

        Printed in the United States of America

Contents

Acknowledgments

The labor of preparing this volume was facilitated by the generosity of two institutions and shared by several friends and colleagues. A sabbatical leave granted by the Behrend College of the Pennsylvania State University and a fellowship awarded by the Virginia Center for the Creative Arts provided a block of uninterrupted time for pondering the problems of translation. Dr. Kathryn Wolfe and Ms. Claudette Bedard uncovered and corrected numerous mistakes in the typescript. (Those that remain are to be charged to the account of the authors.) Readers who derive pleasure from the attractiveness and legibility of the pages that follow owe a debt of gratitude to Dr. Roland E. Larson for his skill in transforming artless copy into print.

For

Louise Flickinger Myers

Introduction

LIFE

In 1647, when François Poullain[1] was born, Louis XIV (1638–1715) was a boy of nine and René Descartes (1596–1650) had only three years left to live. The king and the philosopher set in motion contrary currents that were to complicate the course of young Poullain's life. Poullain's problems were to stem from the difficulty of trying to be both Louis XIV's subject and Descartes' disciple. As Poullain's education developed, he accepted the argument that Descartes made for the right of each rational individual to discover truth for him or herself. Poullain's homeland, however, was ruled by a king who believed that God had given him absolute authority over his subjects. The king would never agree with the philosopher that individuals had a greater right to decide on questions of truth than their government. It was sometimes necessary, therefore, for a person who was both the subject of the king and the disciple of the philosopher to make hard choices.

Poullain was a forthright Cartesian. He made no sophistic distinction between freedom of thought and freedom of action, and he believed that if anyone had a right to such liberties, everyone did: male or female, rich or poor. But Poullain was a theoretician, not an organizer of revolutions. He understood that the ideas that were dawning with the "Age of Enlightenment" would create an appetite for reform. But he did not pause to provide his readers with anything more than a vague suggestion of the path they might take into the future. If he had been born a hundred years later, he probably would have leapt into the fray that became the French Revolution. But in his day the power of the French throne was nearing its apogee, and republican sympathizers were few and far between. Although Poullain lingered in his native land for a long time after publishing the books that

---

[1] Poullain did not add "de la Barre" to his name until he left France in 1688, and his reason for assuming the new name is unknown. See: Marie Louise Stock, "Poullain de la Barre: A Seventeenth-Century Feminist," Ph.D. Dissertation, Columbia University, 1961, pp. 1–2. The account of Poullain's life offered here follows Stock's outline.

publicized his point of view, he ultimately concluded that he could not live under Louis and enjoy the liberty that his Cartesian principles had led him to believe was his right. He fled France and the Catholic Church for the company of Geneva's Protestants.

To honor his principles, Poullain took great personal risks. He sacrificed his career, his citizenship, and his financial security—and dramatically altered the circumstances of his life. In any period of history when ideas grow faster than institutions, intellectuals are likely to suffer. Poullain endured no more than many others—and he came to a much happier end than some. His adventures did not make him more than an ordinary hero, but they do testify to the sincerity of the proposals he put forth in his books.

The violent upheavals of the Revolution of 1790 (to which Poullain may have made some small, unintentional contribution) destroyed the records of his birth. We only know that he was born in Paris in July of 1647 (the son of a Nicolas Poullain) because he recorded this information about himself when he emigrated to Switzerland. Nothing is certain about his family—except that it was able to educate him. During Poullain's childhood the peace of France was disturbed by popular uprisings called the *Frondes* (i.e., the "Slingshot Riots"), but the threat of civil disorder diminished as Poullain grew. While he attended school in Paris, Louis XIV schooled himself toward the autocratic system that was to make France a model absolutist monarchy. By the time that Poullain came of age, France was adjusting to the weight of an increasingly heavy royal hand.

Louis's wars and Louis's taxes were a great burden for his subjects, but the "Sun-King" inspired his countrymen to lay hold on what they believed to be their destiny. For centuries France had been a crippled giant. It had more resources and a better location than any of the other nations that aspired to the leadership of Europe, but it had long found it difficult to build on its strengths. Most of France's problems were of its own creation. An entrenched and powerful feudal nobility frustrated the efforts of kings to centralize the administration of the state. Consequently, civil war was always a possibility and frequently a reality. Hamstrung by confusion at home,

French kings could rarely make their country's full power felt abroad.

France's kings and nobles struggled together for most of the Middle Ages, but at the end of the fifteenth century the crown seemed on the verge of victory. In 1453 France brought a long war with England (the "Hundred Years War") to a victorious conclusion. The crises of that war did more than anything the royal government had ever done to unite the French behind their king. The French king emerged from the war with the right to levy taxes without consulting his subjects, and he used the emergency of the war to nip the evolution of the "Estates General" in the bud. In England, a "parliament" established itself as an instrument of popular government with the power to check the ambitions of kings (and queens). But no comparable institution arose to provide a counterweight to the authority of France's kings. In France the idea that God appointed kings—who were answerable only to God—triumphed.

The French aristocracy was alarmed at the growth of royal power. The gains of the central government were losses for the local governments through which the aristocratic families dominated the countryside. Factions developed within the nobility, and the king's vassals organized to fight what they considered to be royal encroachment on their traditional domain. It was one of the curious complications of history that this development in French politics should have coincided with the beginning of religious reform movements in neighboring Germany.

In 1520 Martin Luther destroyed the unity of European Christianity by taking a highly publicized, successful stand against the pope. Luther's trouble with the ecclesiastical authorities began when he protested one of the fund raising activities of the Church—the issuing of "indulgences," a practice that Luther believed contradicted the Bible on the vital point of how sins are forgiven. When the pope ordered Luther to change his mind, Luther refused. He argued that no one had the right to come between an individual and his or her reading of the word of God. Luther believed that in matters of faith the individual conscience ought to have complete freedom of self-determination.

The case that Luther made for the sovereignty of the
individual was seized on by reformers of all kinds, for the
arguments Luther mustered against the divine rights of popes
were also effective against the presumptions of kings and the
extortions of landlords. Germany, which had never been a
strongly unified nation, was further fragmented by dozens
of religiously inspired wars. For awhile it looked like every
minority in Europe intended to use the Reformation as an
excuse for taking up arms. Religion and politics melted
together, and combatants' motives were an inextricable
mixture of this-worldly and other-worldly causes. Uprisings
against entrenched authorities became a possibility in every
country, and every government had to reflect on the dangers
of this new source of threats to its stability.

France, at the time, was in the capable hands of Francis
I (1515–1547), a vigorous, intelligent, and ambitious man—
with a good head for intrigue. Francis realized that the
papacy feared further defections from a church that was
becoming less "Catholic" (i.e. "universal") with each passing
day. To frighten the pope into granting him a free hand with
the French church's resources, Francis professed an interest in
Protestantism. The king's strategy of seeming to teeter on the
brink of conversion enabled him to blackmail the pope into
making concessions. It also gave Protestants a free hand to
conduct their mission in France and allotted them ample time
to make converts among members of the politically influential
educated and propertied classes. The period of grace for
Protestantism was, however, short lived. Francis was far too
ambitious a king to be an advocate of Protestant liberties.
Once the pope yielded to his demands, Francis no longer had
anything to gain from tolerating an ideology that challenged
his divine right. Rome permitted a virtual nationalization
of the French church, and Francis renewed his commitment
to defend Catholicism. French Protestants went underground
or scurried for the frontiers. Under the leadership of John
Calvin, they established a stronghold in French-speaking
Geneva and made Geneva a kind of international capital for
the Protestant movement.

Despite official disapproval, Protestantism did not fade
away in France. The new religion flourished—particularly

among the urban classes and the nobility. Its championship of the rights of the individual appealed to those Frenchmen whose stations in life gave them reasonable hopes of trimming royal power and forcing the king to share his privileges. The growth of the "Huguenot" (Protestant) movement in France was assisted by the ineptitude of the kings who followed Francis to the throne. Francis's son, Henry II (1547–1559), was a man of limited ability whose premature death threw the royal house into confusion. Each of Henry's three sons became king in his turn, but none was strong enough to maintain order. The nobility split into Protestant and Catholic camps, and religious wars flared. In 1572 a plan to use a royal marriage to bring about a compromise among factions misfired horribly. During the wedding festivities an attempt was made on the life of a Protestant leader. The royal government—fearing a revolt by the enraged Protestants— hastened to get the jump on them. It ordered its army to kill all the Protestants that could be found. The result was a national disgrace remembered as the "St. Bartholomew's Day Massacre." France was plunged back into war, and peace was not achieved until all of Henry II's sons had died and their cousin, Henry IV (1589–1610) established a new dynasty. Henry IV had been raised a Protestant. Although he converted to Catholicism in order to become the king of a Catholic nation, he had no passion for religious wars. In a proclamation known as the Edict of Nantes (1598) he arranged a truce by giving Protestants a number of havens inside France.

The Edict of Nantes deprived France's religious parties of an excuse for war—which was fortunate, for the French monarchy had to struggle to cope with its minimal responsibilities through much of the seventeenth century. Henry was assassinated in 1610, and his throne passed to an under-aged son, Louis XIII (1610–1643). Richelieu, a gifted royal minister who was also a Catholic cardinal, managed the kingdom for the boy and stayed on after the prince grew to be a man. Shortly after Richelieu's death, Louis XIII died. Once again the crown passed to a minor: Louis XIV (1643–1715). Richelieu's successor, Mazarin, protected Louis XIV's interests during the years of the *Frondes* (1648–1653), and he

bought time for the young king to mature. Louis's childhood was clouded by the atmosphere of danger and confusion that civil wars create. By the time that Louis came of age, he had had many lessons to teach him the importance of being a strong leader. It is not surprising, therefore, that when he took charge of the government, he dedicated himself to making the king the absolute master of France. Louis insisted on universal conformity to his will, and in 1685 he took a step that was intended to head off any religiously motivated resistance to his plans. He revoked the Edict of Nantes and expelled the Protestants from France.

While these events were transpiring on the main stage of history, Poullain was growing up in the wings. His aspirations were modest. He intended to make a career for himself in the Catholic Church. He has told us little about the formative years of his life. He took a degree in theology and was attracted to the study of rhetoric and languages. Although he was well grounded in Latin and Greek and followed a traditional scholastic program of study, he developed a professional interest in vernacular languages that marked him as a thoroughly modern young scholar. His first book (*Les Rapports de la langue Latine à la Françoise pour traduire elegamment et sans peine*) was a text to guide students through the labor of translating Latin into French (1672). Later in life (1691) he published another volume that dealt with language. This one (*Essai des Remarques particulières sur la Langue Françoise pour la ville de Genève*) compared the French of Geneva with that spoken in France.

Somewhere along the line Poullain became disillusioned with the medieval scholasticism that, in his day, still dominated the curricula of the Parisian schools. Loss of confidence in the education he was receiving may have led him to give up the pursuit of a doctorate in theology.[2] Poullain was not alone in being depressed by the state of affairs in the academic world. Centuries of minute logic chopping had filled libraries with ponderous, unreadable tomes that did little to clarify the questions over which advocates of different

---

[2]Some of the early biographical dictionaries claim that he earned the degree, but Stock (pp. 10–14) presents convincing evidence to the contrary.

religions were passionately shedding blood. The scholastic method of elaborating subtle arguments by carefully defining the words of ancient texts could not cope with the debates that were tearing Europe apart. People on every side of every issue could use the scholastic technique to create rationales for their opinions, and no one could cut through the swirling haze of suppositions to the truth.

Poullain was only about 20 years old when he developed second thoughts about the wisdom of the course he had been pursuing. He sank into the kind of depression to which idealism makes bright youths vulnerable. While he was deep in this mood and wondering what direction his life should take, a friend invited him to hear a lecture by a Cartesian philosopher. The event, which probably took place in 1667, was the turning point of his life. As he reflected on the methods of argument used by Descartes, Poullain began to hope that he had found the intellectual instrument that would enable him to hack through confusion to certainty.

Descartes had been dead for seventeen years when Poullain first discovered Cartesianism, but Cartesianism was not stale news. As the 1660's unfolded Descartes became something of an academic cult figure. In 1663 the pope listed Descartes's works on the *Index of Forbidden Books*. This and other attempts to suppress Descartes's ideas only made them more delicious, not more inaccessible. Original people learn to cope with oppressive systems, and Descartes proved more difficult for the French government to deal with in death than he had been while he was alive. Descartes prudently spent much of his life breathing the air of liberal Holland, and he died in Sweden while a guest of its queen (1650). His flourishing reputation rescued him from an expatriate's grave, and in 1667 (despite the misgivings of Louis XIV's ministers) Descartes' remains were brought to Paris for internment in the church of Ste. Geneviève du Mont. The hostility of the ecclesiastical and the scholastic establishments failed to prevent an intellectual underground of Cartesians from recruiting converts like Poullain.

Descartes resembled other formative thinkers in that he strayed into philosophy from mathematics. He said that he was attracted to the study of mathematics because the

field seemed to offer more certainty than others. A thirst for certainty was a natural appetite in the early seventeenth century. The Reformation had divided Europe among hostile Christian groups. Each cited the same Word of God and used the same kinds of arguments to defend a point of view that was completely at variance with principles advocated by the others. Since reason failed to be convincing in this situation, violence proved to be the most effective means for settling differences. As a result, Europe was torn by interminable religious wars.

For the intellectuals who were forced to live in the midst of this confusion, mathematics had a compelling fascination. Within a very limited sphere, mathematics offered a kind of certainty that was available nowhere else. Rational human beings cannot disagree about the truth of valid logical inferences. Everyone admits that "a = a." There is something about the structure of the human mind that forces it to recognize certain propositions as self-evident. Mathematics, therefore, suggested to the scholars of the seventeenth century that (at least with respect to certain kinds of problems) it was possible to arrive at a universal consensus by peaceful means. Strife-weary thinkers were intrigued by this and dreamed of finding ways of thinking that would create in other fields the kind of certainty offered by mathematics.

In 1637 (ten years before Poullain was born) Descartes published the *Discourse on Method* and in 1644 the *Principles of Philosophy*. In these treatises he did for science what Luther had done for religion. Where Luther had made the individual's conscience supreme in the realm of faith, Descartes proclaimed the sovereignty of the individual's mind in the search for information about the world. Just as Luther had dismissed the traditions of the Church as a scrambled heap of worn customs that had no innate authority, Descartes insisted that all the opinions about the world that had been handed down from the past were so muddled that they ought to be tossed aside and a completely fresh start made in the pursuit of knowledge. Luther believed that the faith that welled up in the individual as he or she read the Scriptures provided the test of truth in religion. Descartes, too, looked inside the individual for a touchstone that would

validate truth. He believed that each human mind contained innate ideas whose certainty it intuited. Descartes set about demonstrating that by drawing valid deductions from these indubitable premises it was possible to acquire a clear and trustworthy understanding of how the world worked.

Descartes believed that if the proper method of research was followed, scientific facts presented themselves like the facts of mathematics. They could be defined with precision, analyzed for their implications, and every person (who cared to) could discover the necessity of the conclusions that followed from them for him or herself. Descartes knew that mathematics dealt with forms and models and most other sciences with empirical data, but unlike many of the philosophers who had gone before him, he did not think that research in different fields required different methods. Descartes believed that truth was one thing and that a sound technique of exploration would demonstrate that all sciences were but subdivisions of a "universal science."

Poullain, like others of his generation, was intoxicated by Descartes's vision, but not completely carried away by it. For reasons that may or may not have been connected with his conversion to Cartesianism, he gave up the study of scholastic theology. But he continued to contemplate a career in the Church. Poullain clearly hoped that he could stay within an authoritarian system while promoting greater freedom for individual consciences. As he later advised the readers of *De l'Egalité*, he saw nothing wrong with conforming to customs that he no longer believed in for the sake of public peace.

After discontinuing his formal studies, Poullain spent about ten years as a tutor in Latin at one of the Parisian colleges. From a literary point of view, this decade was the most productive of his life. In 1672 he wrote his textbook on translation (*Les Rapports de la langue Latine à la Françoise*). In 1673 he published *De l'Egalité des deux Sexes*, and in 1674 a treatise on the education of women (*De l'Education des Dames pour la conduite de l'esprit dans les sciences et dans les moeurs*). In the latter books Poullain used Cartesian principles to critique common assumptions about sexual stereotypes. Since he advanced unconventional ideas about women and defended their fitness to play the same

role in society as men, he expected his books to make a splash. When they did not, he was openly disappointed. In 1675 he tried a different strategy. In *De l'excellence des hommes contres l'égalité des sexes* he took on the duties of the devil's advocate, but his discussion of the arguments for male supremacy attracted little attention. Someone, however, was interested in what Poullain had to say, for in 1676 an anonymous translator (identified only as A.L.) brought out an English version of *De l'Egalité* (entitled: *The Woman as Good as the Man, or the Equality of Both Sexes*).

Disappointment at the reception his books received may have contributed to Poullain's belated decision to enter the career for which his early schooling had prepared him. In 1680, at the age of thirty-three, he was ordained to the Catholic priesthood and sent to serve a parish in the archbishopric of Laon. His experience as a priest could not have been pleasant. Having spent his whole life in Paris at the center of things, he was relegated in middle age to an obscure, poverty-stricken rural parish. There, at a time when (as his subsequent decision to flee to Geneva suggests) he must have been entertaining Protestant thoughts, he served an episcopal administration that was extremely hostile to Protestantism. Poullain's disillusionment with scholastic theology and his faith in the Cartesian idea that individuals should be the final arbiters of truth for themselves must have made it difficult for him to endure the authoritarianism of his bishop.

In October of 1685 events conspired to increase pressure on him. Louis XIV revoked the Edict of Nantes and expelled the Huguenots from France. Poullain may have got into some difficulty with his ecclesiastical superiors over his willingness to cooperate with the government's policy. In 1685 he appears to have been transferred to an even more remote parish than the one to which he had first been posted. Plainly his career in the Church was not flourishing and the points of view that he had advocated in his books were not congruent with those of the men who now had power over him.

At some point in 1688 Poullain made the decision to leave the priesthood and the Catholic Church. He returned to Paris for a brief period of time, but there was no future for him in the city of his birth. He prepared to leave France, and on 14

December 1689 he registered an application for a residency permit in Geneva. The Protestant city granted Poullain the status of a religious refugee, and Poullain embarked on a new and more promising phase in his career. His education, books, or connections won him admission to the circle of Geneva's prominent families, and early in 1690 he married a magistrate's daughter. Later that year they had a daughter, and Poullain renewed his literary activity. Second editions of *De l'Egalité* and *De l'excellence des hommes* were brought out. Six years later Poullain became the father of his only other child, a son. (Jean Jacques de la Barre grew up to become a Protestant clergyman and, like his father, a publishing scholar.)

Poullain supported his family by teaching Parisian French to Genevans who wanted to improve their provincial dialects. As part of this work Poullain published a second language textbook in 1691: *Essai des Remarques particulières sur la langue Françoise pour la ville de Genève.* At the same time he must also have been engaging openly in theological discussions, for the Swiss Protestant authorities let him know that they were not necessarily more open minded than their French Catholic colleagues. In 1696 they ordered Poullain to defend himself against the charge of harboring unitarian sympathies.

Poullain must have succeeded in proving his doctrinal soundness, for he remained in Geneva and in 1708 was assigned to teach classical languages at Geneva's college—a sensitive position he was to hold until his death in 1723. In 1716 his loyal service was rewarded by a decree of naturalization. Classroom duties would have taken up most of his time and energy as he grew older, but he exerted himself to write one more book. In 1720 Poullain published *La Doctrine des Protestans.* In it he remained true to the liberal causes and critical principles that he had espoused in his treatises on feminism.

During the course of his professional life, Poullain ventured opinions on many subjects: linguistics, education, social theory, history, women's rights, Biblical interpretation, and theology. He made personal sacrifices so that his deeds might conform to his professed principles. And he died

respected and honored by the people of Geneva. These were worthy achievements, but it is hard to know what kind of place in history they merit for Poullain. Poullain developed sound arguments for women's liberation, and he was an early advocate of some of the social and political theories associated with the great thinkers of the Enlightenment. But there is not much of a "paper trail" to prove that Poullain influenced the generations that brought the "Age of Reason" to full flower. He has had a very long wait for the appreciative audience he failed to find in the domain of the Sun-King.

]

THE CARTESIAN INFLUENCE

Poullain de la Barre was a Cartesian, but what does that mean? Just as the term "Marxist" has become a useful appellation to describe the intellectual proclivities of certain modern political theorists, so also the term "Cartesian" has been employed as a convenience for categorizing some seventeenth-century intellectuals. Marx and Descartes wrote on widely different issues. But they both had large groups of enthusiastic followers and, as a consequence, came to illustrate a common phenomenon—whereby the name of an influential historical figure takes on a life of its own as a descriptive label. In both cases the label provides an excuse for lumping together a disparate collection of thinkers who may have little more in common than the fact that they drew inspiration from the same intellectual precursor.

Such labels facilitate broad generalizations, but they often obscure reality. The intellectual historian's effort to trace the influence of ideas is problematical at best, and labels can be seductive where empirical data remains elusive. We know that people are influenced by ideas, but we also know that they do not all assimilate ideas in the same way. If Poullain was a Cartesian, so were countless other intellectuals of the late seventeenth century. Some were trained philosophers who may have read and accurately understood the works of Descartes; others were simply inspired by the great philosopher and took from him whatever served their own purposes. Cartesians ranged all along this continuum, and the trick is to ascertain the place occupied by Poullain.

The study of the Bible and the texts of classical antiquity served as the cornerstone for education in early modern Europe. However, by Descartes's day there had been a considerable erosion of faith in the absolute validity of these sources of information about the world. Although intellectuals and scholars continued to accept the Bible as the word of God, the Protestant Reformation had altered the equation. The Protestant Reformers placed a heavy emphasis upon the rights of the individual conscience—insisting that the word of God was accessible to individuals without benefit

of interpretation by an authoritarian church. Direct access to sacred Scripture inspired the Reformation. But by the middle of the seventeenth century it had also generated a variety of Christian sects, each with its unique version of the truth. Since church and state were often closely entwined, religious differences exacerbated political differences. Descartes and his contemporaries came of age in a society torn by religious and political strife. All might agree that the Bible was the word of God, but no scholar could avoid the discomforting fact that Biblical truth was expressing itself in hostile, incompatible movements.

The Greek and Latin classics were also failing as reliable sources for the study of physical phenomena. Nothing illustrates this more graphically than the erosion of the Ptolemaic view of the universe that took place at the end of the Middle Ages. Under challenge by Copernicus, Galileo, Kepler and a host of their followers, this venerable model of the cosmos lost its credibility when confronted by a growing body of evidence contradicting its fundamental assumptions. The fading of support for Ptolemy's geocentric world-view was only the most dramatic sign of a widespread retreat by ancient authorities that threatened (by the middle of the seventeenth century) to become a rout. Historians have called the intellectual upheaval of the period "the Scientific Revolution," for, when the dust settled, there emerged a fundamentally new vision of the physical universe and a new set of strategies for unlocking its secrets. The preconceptions and methods of modern science had established their hold on the western mind.

To understand the decline of confidence in the Bible and the classics as the sole, sufficient foundations for education in the western world is to understand how Descartes was driven to his philosophical positions and why he became the hero of lesser thinkers—such as Poullain. Descartes and Poullain received traditional educations that inculcated respect for the opinions of ancient authorities. But they, and others like them, grew up to discover that the wisdom accumulated in the schools led to confusion and doubt. Descartes, lamenting the quality of formal education, described—in his famous

Discourse on Method—a personal experience that struck a responsive chord for many of his readers:

> From my childhood I lived in a world of books, and since I was taught that by their help I could gain a clear and assured knowledge of everything useful in life, I was eager to learn from them. But as soon as I had finished the course of studies which usually admits one to the ranks of the learned, I changed my opinion completely. For I found myself saddled with so many doubts and errors that I seemed to have gained nothing in trying to educate myself unless it was to discover more and more fully how ignorant I was.[1]

This revealing passage not only captures the essence of Descartes's personal struggle in the pursuit of truth but also describes the climate of thought that prevailed in his world. The question that hung over the search for certainty in the seventeenth century was how the human mind, bereft of authority and left to its own devices, could arrive at truth. In short, how did one know that ideas about the external world actually conveyed dependable information about that world?

In many ways Descartes was a typical seventeenth century philosopher–an individual preoccupied with epistemological problems and disposed to find solutions in the certainty of mathematics. His inspiration welled from his theory that size, shape, motion and rest define the fundamental qualities of the physical universe. Since these qualities are susceptible to mathematical analysis, they equip mathematics to be the handmaiden of the mind and the mind's most important guide to the world outside itself. As ideas in the mind, mathematics brings certainty to human reasoning on the abstract level. If the physical universe is structured according to mathematical principles, it follows that mathematical ideas (*qua* ideas) convey truth about the external world. The mind can, therefore, arrive at certainty about external phenomena—if it follows a method that ensures careful deduction from first principles. Descartes, an accomplished geometrician, drew

---

[1] René Descartes, *Discourse on Method*, Translated, with an Introduction by Laurence J. Lafleur (New York: The Liberal Arts Press, 1956), p. 3.

his method from the deductive procedures used in geometry. Starting with self-evident axioms, he constructed proposition after proposition and assembled increasingly complex proofs. Each proof was the product of a rigorous rational method, and each in turn became a building block contributing to a complex edifice of certainty.

Descartes spent his life working out the implications of his fundamental convictions, and he published on a wide range of topics (touching fields as disparate as astronomy and medicine). His *Discourse on Method* (1637) was, however, the work above all others that captured the imagination of his contemporaries. Many of them were sympathetic with his advocacy of "systematic doubt" and his rejection of authorities as guarantors of truth. Descartes's claim that truth was not the exclusive prerogative of ancient authors was a proclamation of intellectual egalitarianism. Just as the Protestant Reformation had challenged the power of the Church by insisting that the individual could arrive at divine truth directly by reading the Scriptures, so also Descartes broke the intellectual monopoly claimed by the schools. Descartes inspired his followers with the faith that each individual rational mind can arrive at certainty for itself—by using a method of systematic doubt and rigorously logical inference that accepts as true only things that can be demonstrated by "clear and distinct" ideas.

By the late seventeenth century Cartesian ideas were infecting most intellectual circles in France, and the supporters of *"l'esprit geometrique"* were bringing the methods of systematic doubt and careful argument to bear on all fields of learning. Mechanical and mathematical models were used to explain the behavior of all physical phenomena. And even scholars who opposed the Cartesian method were forced to defend themselves with rational arguments rather than by making the appeals to authority that previously had swayed their audiences. There were many variations on the Cartesian theme, and there was no doubt that Descartes's example (i.e., his rejection of authority and his determination to strip old questions of accumulated prejudices) was engendering an exciting new era of intellectual endeavor.

As a youth of about twenty, Poullain was drawn into the Cartesian sphere of influence. From the meager biographical information that can be gleaned from his writings it appears that an invitation to a public lecture led him to convert to Cartesianism about 1667. Poullain expressed his new-found enthusiasm for the method of "systematic doubt" by designing a project that would demonstrate its utility. He embarked on an extensive study of human prejudice. The issue of sexual inequality was an ideal vehicle for this purpose. What better way to illustrate how social custom—reinforced by the learned opinions of the ancients—creates a heavy weight of prejudice that men (and women themselves) accept as unquestioned fact? If by rational deduction from "clear and distinct ideas" Poullain could demonstrate that the seemingly self-evident inequality of the sexes is nothing more than an unfounded prejudice, he could graphically illustrate the virtues of the new methodology he championed.

In 1673 Poullain presented his case by publishing *De l'Egalité des deux Sexes*. Poullain's approach in this treatise is an excellent example of the kind of applied Cartesian rationalism that was becoming popular in France in his day. Starting from a position of "systematic doubt," Poullain rejects the traditions and assumptions that customarily promote belief in the inequality of the sexes and accepts only those characterizations of men and women that are "clear and distinct ideas." Following the Cartesian method of rational deduction, he concludes that sexual inequality has no basis in nature. The female intellect, he maintains, is in no way inferior to the male. The sexes may differ in physical stature (reflecting their different roles in reproduction), but their difference does not constitute an argument for their inequality. Poullain attributes popular notions of female inferiority to social inertia and historical conditioning. He dismisses civil law's attempt to legitimatize male authoritarianism as an error that has no foundation in natural law. Boldly radical in his support for sexual equality, Poullain argues that women are intellectually and physically capable of serving as heads of state, clergy, military officers, lawyers, and (even) college professors.

Poullain maintains that women were relegated to an inferior role at some very early point in human prehistory, that this accident had its roots in the female's unique reproductive responsibilities, and that familiarity has given an arbitrary distinction between the sexes the feel of a natural gulf. As laws and states evolved, Poullain suggests, bad habits ossified into permanent institutions. Men, as well as women, began to believe that a situation of their own making was a product of natural law and divine will. High priests and intellectuals encouraged this by inventing justifications for male supremacy. Their declarations of female inferiority were reinforced by society and transformed into self-fulfilling prophecies.

For Cartesians, history and tradition carry little weight. They know that prejudices of all sorts try to validate themselves by appealing to the past. Clear thinking requires "systematic doubt"—which means that ideas that previously have been accepted can continue to be endorsed only if they withstand the critique to which each rational individual subjects them. Only "clear and distinct ideas," the products of careful, logical arguments, carry the weight of conviction. Poullain captures the essence of the Cartesian spirit in the following passage:

The most fortunate thought that can occur to people who work at acquiring sound knowledge (having previously been instructed in the ordinary way) is to wonder whether they have been well taught and to wish to discover the truth for themselves.

During the course of their research, these people will inevitably find that our minds are filled with prejudices. And they will find they must renounce these opinions absolutely before they can arrive at clear, distinct understandings.

With the intent of establishing so important a principle, we have believed it best to choose a specific, striking subject (in which everyone takes an interest) so that after demonstrating that an opinion as ancient as the world, as widespread as the earth and as universal as the human species itself is a prejudice or an error, knowledgeable people will finally be

convinced of the necessity of judging things (after having carefully examined them) for themselves and of not abiding by the opinions or the testimonies of others if they want to avoid being deceived.

Of all prejudices, none can be found more appropriate for this purpose than the commonly held belief in the inequality of the two sexes.[2]

Poullain's feminism is, therefore, first and foremost an illustration of the power of rational deduction. Throughout his treatise he uses reason to show how accepted "facts" about women are no more than deeply ingrained prejudices. He also mounts a campaign to heap reason's ridicule on the pronouncements of venerated experts—Plato and Aristotle being his main opponents. The whole exercise is designed to demonstrate how—if "clear and distinct" ideas are ignored—a false notion can (throughout the ages) be accepted without question by both the educated and the illiterate.

A willingness to reject accepted wisdom was fundamental to Poullain's program—and to that of any respectable Cartesian. He believed that proper training of the mind is the only trustworthy preparation for those who hope to pursue truth and find liberation. Since women are as capable of using the tools of reason as men, the key to woman's advancement and to the righting of the ancient wrongs of sexual discrimination is, in Poullain's opinion, education. Liberating education, however, has little in common with the kind of training offered by the schools—which are, Poullain charges, mere literacy factories that promote slavish dependency on the authority of classical Greek and Latin authors. A person must learn how to think, and, for Poullain, this means how to use Descartes's critical methods. Poullain developed this idea in a second book, *De l'Education des Dames pour la conduite de l'esprit dans les sciences et dans les moeurs* (1674). Here Poullain outlined the program of study for women that *De l'Egalité des deux Sexes* promised would equip women to use clear thought to cast off the heavy yoke of tradition and history.

---

[2] See authors' translation, p. 5

In his books, Poullain took care to distance himself from the witty and urbane feminist authors who were popular at court during the latter part of the seventeenth century. Their romanticized "feminism" lauded women for virtues that allegedly proved that females were superior to males in the spiritual things that really counted. This kind of feminist writing was flattering, but it did nothing to help women combat the fundamental inequalities institutionalized in Salic law and perpetuated by the custom of primogeniture. It offered no practical advice on rectifying situations that subjugated women to men. Poullain's arguments were set on a better intellectual foundation—one that could support a program for a radical feminist revision of law and society. The gallant compliments that aristocratic champions lavished on women were, by comparison, bits of fluff that retarded a fight for genuine equality.

The Cartesian perspective that led Poullain to grasp the essential equality of the sexes, also brought him to denounce the artificial constraints on individual freedoms imposed by Europe's traditional class structures. He saw the issue of female liberation in the broader context of a campaign for social justice and equality for men as well as women. Poullain anticipated the eighteenth century debates that enlivened the Enlightenment and the era of the French Revolution. His works, therefore, support the theory that there is at least a parallelism—and perhaps a vital connection—between Cartesian rationalism and the revolutionary ideologies of the Enlightenment.

De l'Egalité des deux Sexes suggested many ideas that were to be explored by later generations of feminists. It proposed a theory that linked the emergence of misogynistic attitudes in human cultures with the process by which the state evolved from the relationships of the primitive family. It indicted intellectual giants of the past for blatant sexism. It illustrated an effective reform strategy by skillfully using its opponents' arguments to undermine their positions— employing the Cartesian methods that many male scholars endorsed to weaken the confidence these men had in the superiority of their sex. It anticipated the modern debate about language and its role in subtly perpetuating the myth

of male supremacy. And it maintained that women had little hope of achieving equality of opportunity in society until they had won equal access to education.

Poullain anticipated many of the debates about social issues and reform techniques that still wax hot in our world. He was not a systematic philosopher like Descartes. He did not construct mathematical and mechanical models to explain his positions or advance the techniques of Cartesian argument. But he was a Cartesian in the sense that he grasped the potential of Cartesianism as an instrument for social reform. He did not lay out a detailed program for revolutionary action. But he sensed how the world of ordinary people might be opened up when the past no longer shackled thinkers and when people imbued with the habit of clear thinking entered on the race's ancient quest for certainty.

THE ARGUMENT

Poullain divided *De l'Egalité des deux Sexes* (243 pages) into two parts. The second (168 pages) is twice as long as the first (75 pages) and is broken down into six separately headed sections. A *Preface* (14 pages) explains the objectives that Poullain set himself in writing his treatise, and a concluding *notice* (2 pages) deals very briefly with an objection that Poullain anticipated from his critics.

Poullain was a theorist for feminism, but the raising of consciousness about the wrongs society inflicts on women was only part of what he hoped his book would achieve. His goal in writing was not just to dispel prejudices about women, but to convert his readers to a method of thinking that he was convinced would free them from all kinds of error. Poullain was a convert to Cartesianism. He hoped that *De l'Egalité* would vindicate his faith in Descartes by demonstrating the value of the Cartesian method. Poullain wanted to show that a straightforward analysis of facts, which reason and sense make obvious to every intelligent observer, rids people of the errors and prejudices in which tradition mires them.

The clergy and the university establishment in France were hostile to Cartesianism, and its advocates were suspected of being both religious and philosophical heretics. There is no doubt that Poullain was unusually sensitive to the injustices being done women in his world, but his concern for their liberation was not entirely devoid of self-interest. Poullain's campaign for women was also a campaign for freedom of thought in France. The women's issue was tailor-made for the case that Poullain wanted to make for Cartesianism. Prejudice against women was one of the strongest, oldest, and most widespread systems of belief known to Poullain. He concluded, therefore, that if the Cartesian method could lead people to revise a set of assumptions as ancient and deeply entrenched as those they held about women, there could be no greater demonstration of Cartesianism's power to dispel the confusion that clouds our minds.

To speak out in favor of women was, however, to invite misunderstanding. Debate about the relative merits of males

and females had a long history in western literature. The Bible and the works of the ancient Greeks and Romans were full of it. And at the end of the fifteenth century the argument about woman's place in the world had become heated—fueled perhaps by the appearance of an unprecedented number of queens reigning over European states. Hundreds of authors (particularly in France and England) took up their pens to participate in the "*querelle des femmes*"—a lengthy and wide-ranging argument about the capacities of women.

Much of the literature on the allegedly feminist side of the *querelle* would be offensive to modern feminists. It was flattering, but condescending. Its aim was to praise women, not to create new opportunities for them in public life. It consoled women for their lack of political power by assuring them that they were too refined for the burdens that coarse males bore in running the world. It taught women that it was their privilege and duty to stand above the fray and witness to the higher values of which men often lost sight. Much of this "feminist" writing was a mere amusement for courtiers—an opportunity to demonstrate the wit and gallantry that were the hallmark of the manners cultivated by the upper classes.[1]

Poullain designed the *Preface* to *De l'Egalité* to make sure that no one would confuse him with the "courtly feminists." The *Preface* advised the book's readers not to let a mere title prompt them to a hasty conclusion about a volume's content. Poullain knew that he was likely to be misunderstood, for he confessed at the start that nothing required more care than laying out thoughts about women—particularly for male authors taking up the feminist cause. Poullain worried that the man who defends women is always assumed to be acting from self-interest (i.e., pursuing a reputation for gallantry that will win him sexual prizes). Poullain insists that *De l'Egalité* has a much more serious purpose. By dispelling prejudices against women it teaches people how the mind should work. This ought to promote improvements in woman's condition,

---

[1]Michael A. Seidel, "Poulain de la Barre's *The Woman as Good as the Man*," *The Journal of the History of Ideas*, XXV (July/Sept., 1974), p. 501, offers a brief survey of this literature.

but Poullain is not particularly concerned with the practical implications of his argument for sexual equality.

Poullain said that the best thing that can happen to people who seek truth is doubt—doubt about whether they can trust what they have been taught. Suspicion of what they have been told prompts them to acquire a taste for working things out for themselves. And if they step back and take an unbiased look at themselves, they will discover (Poullain insisted) that their minds are cluttered with all kinds of unfounded opinions. Since these "prejudices" keep them from recognizing the clear and obvious truths that reason and experience hold out to them, the first step toward enlightenment is a decision to renounce unfounded opinions.

The value of the Cartesian program of pursuing clear and distinct ideas could be demonstrated in any field of knowledge, but Poullain proposed to show how it worked by taking on one of the most difficult subjects he could imagine: the sexes. He promised to demonstrate that what has been taught about men and women since the beginning of the world—and held to be true everywhere on earth—is nothing but prejudice.

Poullain pointed out that his readers should be suspicious of what they have been taught about men and women, for even at first glance popular opinion does not make sense. When we look at men and women, we see that they do not differ much in the way their bodies are put together. Yet we are told (with such certainty that women themselves believe it) that women are inferior beings who deserve the handicaps in education, career opportunities, and civil rights that society imposes on them. In which physical structures is the alleged incapacity that is said to be innate in females grounded?

Poullain believed that when we break through the prejudicial opinions that society perpetuates about women to the clear and distinct ideas of nature, we discover that the sexes are equal. But to do this, we must confront two different kinds of defenses against the truth: the assumptions made by ordinary people and the theories defended by professional scholars. In the first part of his treatise Poullain dealt with the common person, and in the second he took on the

arguments of experts. The conclusion he came to in both cases is that a woman's failings are a result of the inadequate education she is given.

Poullain predicted that many readers would not like what he had to say, but he eschewed any responsibility for where the chips fall in the pursuit of truth. Truth establishes itself by its own clarity and obviousness. We can either reconcile ourselves to it or throw up smoke screens of prejudice to protect ourselves from it. When we opt to stand with the truth, we have to change our ways. But Poullain felt that there was little to fear from reform. Many of his contemporaries were contemptuous of arrogant women (the *sçavantes* of the salons) who made a great show of their learning. And many people believed that women's minds were likely to be unbalanced by education.[2] Poullain, however, was confident that society's potential gains outweighed the risks. He noted that by educating women we put their idle time to productive use, and he insisted that liberated women would have to be unnatural monsters to turn against the men who helped them to freedom.

In the first part of his book Poullain examined "ordinary beliefs"—with the intent of demonstrating that when we take an unbiased look at the behavior of men and women we find no difference in their abilities. He began by reminding his readers that untrained people harbor all kinds of erroneous ideas: e.g., that the sun revolves about the earth or that animals have the capacity to reason. These opinions rise from our failure to examine things that at first glance seem self-evident—or which serve our vanity and self-interest. Ask any man what he thinks of women (Poullain wrote), and he will tell you that women are made to serve men and to care for the home and children. Some women are brighter than others, but all are unmistakably female in their lack of intellectual depth and conviction. For this reason society has wisely excluded them from positions of authority. And the fact that women have always been in a state of submission to

---

[2] Anxiety about "uppity" women was sufficiently widespread for Molière to exploit it as a theme for one of his popular plays: *Les Femmes Sçavantes.*

men proves that they have no capacity for leadership—for if things could be different, at some time they would have been.

Poullain warned that the fact that a practice is established is no proof of its rightness, but he admitted that it is hard for us to imagine that a prejudice that is as ancient and universal as the one against women could not have a grounding in nature. Everywhere in the world (From China to Turkey to Africa and the Americas) women are treated like servants. It has been this way for so long that it is difficult to imagine how things could be otherwise. And the tendency of the law-givers of all nations to deny women equality with men almost makes it look like men have entered into a universal conspiracy against women. Custom is so powerful that women themselves assume the inferiority of their sex.

Reflection on the probable course of humanity's social evolution led Poullain to conclude that the dominance of the male was a historical accident—not a conscious plot or a dynamic of nature. Poullain assumed that men have always struggled among themselves for dominance and that this behavior eventually spilled over into family relationships. Poullain was a pioneer in a field that might be dubbed "speculative anthropology." He thought that it was possible, using reason alone, to infer what life was like before civilization and historical records appeared. He assumed that, without institutions to establish pecking orders, men and women had an equal start in the state of nature. Primitive people played at dominating each other, but they shared the work of survival equally and they automatically honored him or her the most who made the largest contribution to the community.

Over the long haul, however, the burden of pregnancy disadvantaged women. Poullain theorized that pregnancy limited a woman's ability to work and made her dependent on a man for help. As more children were born to her, her need for a mate to help support them increased. The result was the evolution of the family. And as the family increased in size, it forced a more elaborate system of organization on society.

Children naturally honored their fathers, but, when fathers died, younger brothers would not inevitably accept the yoke of an older brother's authority. Power struggles

might emerge within families. These would result in one male establishing dominance over the females and some of the younger males of a kinship group. But a few of the new leader's siblings would choose exile rather than submission. Possessing no patrimony, they would form warrior bands with other outcasts and prey on the property of their neighbors. These associations of brigands laid the foundations for states—the next step in social organization beyond the family. Despising those whom it conquered as weaklings, the new warrior class enslaved its victims and created societies where soldiers were supported by serfs.

Poullain believed that women had no role to play in the rise of the military state, for they were not physically adapted to warfare and were innately "too humane" to enter into the fight to dispossess their neighbors. (Poullain was not immune to infection by the prejudices of "gallantry.") The fact that women did not fight put them at a great disadvantage in competition with men. For when armies became essential to the survival of states, males came to be preferred to females. And militaristic societies, which needed efficient leadership and rigid organization, naturally assumed that authority was a male prerogative. Kings and social classes appeared. Formal religion was established. Men took control of all the institutions that ran communities. Women were confined to the home and so burdened with domestic responsibilities that they had no leisure for anything else.

Most portentous for the future, Poullain believed, was what the values and structures of early states did to prevent women from participating in the rise of science and the birth of formal education. Poullain claimed that science began in the conversations and inquiries of Egyptian priests, whose light professional responsibilities left them with a lot of free time on their hands. Priests set up schools and research institutions, but the jealousy of husbands prevented women from leaving their homes to study with the priests. The occasional, exceptional woman who did educate herself received no recognition and had no way to hand on her learning to other females.

Men permitted women to lead in only one area of life: fashion. Men enjoy beautiful women, and women who must

live in a male-dominated world discover advantages in being beautiful. It was, therefore, mutually pleasing that women should become experts in self-adornment. The result was a nurturing of female vanity that Poullain considered to be so firmly entrenched as to be ineradicable.

Poullain concluded from his theory of evolution that, although the system of male dominance was universal, it was rooted in history, not nature. He bolstered this point by noting that no one could claim that power had shifted to men simply because males were best adapted to handle it. If that were the case and the world were that rational, then only the men who are best suited to rule would rise to power in each generation. No one who has any knowledge of how things operate could argue seriously that this is the case. Power does not come to those who have the best natural capacity to wield it. It is in the hands of those whom the accidents of history have best situated to seize it. Woman's exclusion from positions of leadership is no argument against woman's ability to handle the responsibilities of power. It is a function of a chain of events that would have been different if society had taken another path of evolution.

Poullain's conviction that one's station in life depended more on chance than talent led him to anticipate some of the rhetoric of the revolutionaries who stormed the Bastille a century after *De l'Egalité* was published.[3] Poullain (with a sense of outrage that suggests that he had some personal experience with the situation) noted that a lack of alternatives almost always forces children to follow in the footsteps of their parents—and that all the talent in the world will not win a man a position unless he has the money or influence needed to buy it. Poullain insisted that there were many peasants who could have been brilliant scholars if they had been given a chance—and many in the ranks of the upper classes who had little aptitude for the important offices they occupied. Social handicaps, not natural traits, prevent women and poor people from becoming leaders.

---

[3] See: Stock, p. 198-212, where she recaps arguments for Poullain's influence on Montesquieu and Rousseau—writers whose works helped stimulate the appetite for reform that grew into the French revolution.

Poullain hastened to add that he did not believe that every women was equipped to handle a position of public responsibility. He only meant to point out that the community of females probably had as many gifted individuals as the community of males. But, in reality, Poullain was willing to venture a little further than this. He suggested that if woman's nature is what it is popularly believed to be, women are more likely than men to possess the traits that we want in our leaders. Poullain pointed out that little girls are often found to be cleverer, quicker to learn, more diligent, and more self-controlled than little boys. Although these are the qualities that supposedly equip young men to become leaders, nothing is done to educate young women who show the same signs of promise. All attention is focused on their brothers, and girls are allowed to languish in ignorance. (Poullain confessed—with more than a little note of sarcasm in his voice—that reflection convinced him that in many cases young women who were deprived of educations were better off than their brothers. The educations boys are given, Poullain said, rarely make them better men. They are still such barbarians when they leave school that, before they can be introduced into society, they must be turned over to women for training in manners and decent conduct.)

Since women are not spoiled by bad educations, women at least have a chance to follow whatever good impulses nature has rooted in their characters. As a result, Poullain believed that women tend to be more morally fastidious, more naturally graceful, and of sounder opinions than men. Poullain objected to the kind of training available in the schools of his day. He felt that it burdened men with a welter of prejudices, muddled their thinking, and confused their speech with meaningless jargon. Women were better off relying on common sense. As proof of this, Poullain claimed to have quizzed women from all walks of life on several of the scientific and theological questions debated in the schools. He reported that he had never found a woman who professed any opinions as outlandish as those defended by experts in scholastic philosophy. Poullain said that women tend to be less disputatious, more open-minded, and quicker

to penetrate to the heart of a matter than a man who has been taught the logic chopping and hair-splitting of the university.

By relying on their unspoiled natural gifts, women do quite well at the tasks they set themselves—and Poullain noted that they are particularly famous for fluency and eloquence of speech. They may not know much about scientific theory, but they have a great deal of practical experience (e.g. in nursing or farming) from which they make accurate inferences. If women occasionally lapse into superstition, it is no wonder—given the ignorance to which society condemns them.

Chance has situated a few women so that by dint of great exertion they can acquire formal educations. These privileged women have achieved remarkable things, and, at the very least, their existence refutes the assumption that women are incapable of higher learning. Since many uneducated women are more virtuous and more sincerely Christian than men, it would also seem that with very little training women do a better job than men of realizing some of the most important goals of education.

Since, in the first part of his book, Poullain was addressing the ordinary man, he concluded his remarks with an invitation to his reader to make some practical observations. He asked his reader if he[4] could think of a nobler model of humanity than that provided by the nuns who served the sick and the poor. He asked the reader to consider the record of the many large monastic establishments that are capably run by women. And he asked him to reflect on woman's role in marriage. Marriage is the natural state in which human beings are made to live, but women are better at it than men. They can rise to the challenge of managing a household at an age when boys should not be trusted with much responsibility. And it is generally said that the best way to settle a young man down is to get him a wife. Women put up with a great deal from their husbands, and they are more faithful to the marriage vow than their mates. Women

---

[4]Although Poullain said that women would read his book—and possibly not agree with all of it, in several places he assumed the reader to be a male like himself.

have demonstrated their competence so consistently that the state has surrendered the important tasks of caring for the home and training the young to unsupervised women. The unprejudiced observer, Poullain noted, can scarcely avoid seeing what daily life reveals about the sexes: i.e., that men have no virtues they do not share with women—and many vices that are especially their own!

In the second and longer part of his treatise Poullain undertook a more carefully targeted defense of his hypothesis about the equality of the sexes. He examined the arguments that various authorities have advanced against gender equality, and in each case he concluded that the experts did nothing but cite the prejudices of the past to justify those of the present.

Poullain said that poets are the least trustworthy guides to truth, for their primary intent is to amuse, not enlighten, and their facility with words obscures plain facts. Poets frequently employ the logical fallacy of inferring the characteristics of a whole class of people from the behavior of a few aberrant individuals. We should, therefore, never take the striking images they invent literally. And the best way to break the spell of their entrancing language is to turn poems into prose to see what their ideas look like without rhetorical trappings. When we do this, we find that poets acquire their ideas about women in the same way that ordinary people do. Poets' minds, like those of "average men," are shaped by prejudice and tradition.

Poets, like most of us, leap to the conclusion that women are innately inferior because females are rarely seen in positions of authority. To warrant this conclusion, however, those who assert it have to demonstrate that women are excluded from high office because of some inadequacy of their nature, not simply by force and custom. This, Poullain claimed, would be very difficult to do. Even if women remained confined to the humble occupations they have traditionally followed, rational observers must esteem their services to society more highly than those of men. We could (and once did) do without the princes and soldiers who are the most respected of men, but we could never dispense with women. Governors and protectors are needed only when there

is disorder in the world, but women are always necessary for the survival of the species. Logically, therefore, women must be judged to be at least as important as men. Also, it is manifestly absurd, Poullain pointed out, for us to praise a man who can train a horse or an elephant and never give a thought to the skill that women devote to the much more important task of shaping the minds of children. The fact that what women do is so ordinary (and ordinarily so well done) causes us to take their services for granted, but no rational person can be comfortable with such a prejudice.

At first glance, Poullain observed, historians seem to be more trustworthy than poets, for they seek truth and claim to have no preconceptions about their subject matters. But all that historians usually do is to confirm modern opinions by reporting on ancient prejudices. Poullain was thoroughly modern in his belief that ancient authors were not to be trusted unless there was independent evidence to confirm what they said. He believed that the study of history could be useful to the feminist cause, however, for it turns up many stories of women who did not conform to our expectations about their gender. It shows us that women have led nations, commanded armies, defended fortresses, and mastered sciences. The historical record of their achievements gives the lie to those who claim that women are inferior creatures.

Since lawyers deal in justice—giving each person his or her due—their opinion of women carries great weight. But Poullain warned that we must be wary of what lawyers teach. All laws have been made by males for their own convenience, and it has never been necessary for men to grant women equal rights in order to achieve the primary goal of the law (the preservation of order). The first lawyers found male dominance established in society and simply leapt to the unsubstantiated conclusion that it was "natural"— and, therefore, just. The world for which the law invents rules is characterized by relationships of subordination, and the function of the law is to find explanations for these relationships. Poullain's potentially radical position on human rights made him highly critical of the law's record. He claimed that, with the exception of children, subservience

is not a natural condition. The only rational basis for subjecting one person to the authority of another, Poullain insisted, is some difference between their natural endowments of reason and experience. Since neither of these things is the prerogative of the male, Poullain concluded that the law must treat men and women as equals. The idea that the female should be subject to the male because of his greater physical strength is so morally flawed that Poullain said that it was unworthy of serious consideration by civilized people. Might does not make right.

The words of philosophers are respected, for philosophers have a reputation for examining things very closely. But, with respect to gender roles, Poullain believed that philosophers do little more than drag prejudices from the streets into the schools. Poullain doubted that the peculiar logical and metaphysical problems that preoccupy philosophers have much relevance to the real world of the sexes.

As a Cartesian, however, Poullain had a deep interest in the branch of philosophy known as epistemology, and he set down a brief exposition of what he thought the "science of knowledge" implied about the relationship between men and women. Poullain argued that since all people have the same physical form, they receive sense impressions and shape their ideas about things in the same way. Knowledge comes to everyone by a common path, and gender has no effect on how people learn. In a passage reminiscent of John Locke, Poullain asserted that all knowledge comes down to comprehending the relationship between a thing and the impression a thing makes on us. Teachers of philosophy can help us to become more aware of what we are experiencing, but we can only appropriate a truth by confronting it personally. Learning is a matter of using reason to correct common sense. Once we catch on to how to do it, we discover that clear thinking requires far less skill than women employ in doing needlework. If they can excel at the latter—as they so obviously do, it is all the more certain that they are fit for the former.

Poullain devoted a separate section of his book to arguing this point, for it was an important one. Most men believed that it was obvious that, as a thinking instrument, the male brain was superior to the female. Poullain insisted that a true

philosophical understanding of the mechanics of knowledge dispelled this illusion.

Poullain believed that examinations of male and female bodies demonstrate that they differ only in the organs of reproduction. Since these organs have nothing to do with thought or with the process of reasoning, Poullain concluded that there is no basis for the claim that males and females think differently. He maintained that the contrast between male and female minds—like that between informed and uninformed minds—springs from environmental factors (like education, exercise, and stimulation), not physical structures. A woman's mind occupies her body in the same way that a man's mind inhabits his. Poullain insisted that a careful study of anatomy could document no differences in the construction of male and female brains. Sense, memory, imagination, and feeling operate in the same way for persons of both genders.

Since women have brains, Poullain believed that there was nothing to prevent women from discovering and thinking through all the sciences for themselves. By reflecting on how their minds operate, Poullain said that women could intuit the nature of logic and metaphysics—just as men do. Since women have the same kinds of hands that men have—to gather information that can be fed to their brains, nothing prevents women from conducting scientific research. Like men, they can dissect bodies and acquire medical skill. They can conduct experiments and comprehend the principles of physics. They can analyze their experiences and note how physical stimuli excite the emotions.

This activity is enough to set a woman on the path to comprehending the highest and most abstract of academic subjects. If a woman allows her thoughts to be guided by the order of nature, she will see the principles of logic inherent in the structure of the world. From these she can progress to mathematics and engineering. Mathematics and engineering can help her to understand the movements of heavenly bodies and "the whole mechanism of the universe."

Poullain assumed that all fields of knowledge were related—springing from a "universal science." Therefore, if a woman mastered something of logic and physics, she could do equally well at the study of the "humanities." For

Poullain, this term encompassed languages, rhetoric (the art of "persuasion"), ethics, political science, civil and canon law, geography, secular and ecclesiastical history, and theology. Although Poullain believed that women had always been excluded from the professions that teach and practice these things, he insisted that there is no justification in nature for society to perpetrate such injustice. Men and women have identical minds, pursue knowledge by common means, and arrive at the same truths.

If either gender has a natural disposition toward learning, Poullain suggested that it is the female. Among males roughness is associated with stupidity and refinement with intelligence. Since women are innately more delicate than men, Poullain concluded that they are better equipped for learning.

Poullain insisted that not only were women educable, but they had a natural right to education. Every human being (male and female) has the same need for knowledge, for knowledge is our only route to happiness—which, Poullain said, is the end of all human actions. True knowledge teaches us to distinguish good from evil, and happiness exists in knowing that we are doing good. If we behave virtuously without being conscious of what we are doing, we derive little satisfaction from our virtue. Human fulfillment depends on knowing the good and knowing that we are achieving it.

Poullain acknowledged that not everyone agreed with him. There are many—among whom was Poullain himself—who worry that learning can corrupt character, for they know highly educated people who are morally reprehensible. They fear, therefore, that women are not strong enough to profit from education and that education would make women "wicked and arrogant." Poullain tried to quiet such fears by reminding his readers that only "false enlightenment" leads to a bad end. Since true knowledge helps us to see ourselves in perspective, it can never make us arrogant. It forces us to recognize that our lordly intellects are enslaved to our bodies and that they are thrown into confusion by the slightest indispositions of the flesh. It frees us from prejudice, but leaves us with a memory of our former stupidity and willful ignorance that beats down any impulse to pride. We

experience its flashes of insight as free gifts, not treasures that we have earned through our own merits. Knowledge makes us compassionate toward those who have not yet travelled as far as we have or been given the opportunities for growth that we have enjoyed. Poullain believed that the few educated women who give their species a bad name are victims of a system that makes education difficult for a woman to acquire. Many learned men are puffed up with pride at their achievements, and a woman who has overcome all the obstacles that society puts in the way of her pursuit of knowledge has reason to think highly of herself. If education were freely available to women, the cause of this character disorder would be done away with.

Poullain was contemptuous of the argument that because women do not have jobs that require formal training they have no need for education. He insisted that education is more than preparation for a career. It is essential for the pursuit of happiness and virtue. Without it, a just and full human life is impossible—no matter what one does for a living.

Poullain expressed amazement at the niggardliness of educated men and their unwillingness to admit everyone to their academies. He accused them of treating knowledge as if it were a finite treasure that was diminished by sharing. In reality, he insisted, knowledge was quite a different kind of wealth than that which is dissipated by sharing. If women get more of it, men do not have to make do with less. Quite the contrary. The more people who work at truth, the more rapidly truth is uncovered and the greater grows the store of wisdom laid up for everyone.

Having made a case for education as a universal good and an end in itself, Poullain raised the question of why educated women should not be given access to all the jobs that educated men do. Since knowledge equips us to govern ourselves and to govern others, why should educated women not be promoted to positions of responsibility in our communities?

The most natural use that can be made of an education is to pass it on to others, and women who acquire academic degrees could easily become teachers—posts for which their natural facility with words especially fits them. The skills that

make them good teachers also equip them for the ministry. Women could preach and provide spiritual counselling just as well as men. Women could interpret justice, maintain order, and rule nations. A woman's uniquely compassionate nature might even, Poullain suggested, make her a better monarch than a man. Since governmental posts require nothing that is markedly different from the kinds of thinking that women do everyday in running their homes and pursuing their entertainments, Poullain saw no reason why women could not lead armies, preside over courts of law, and handle any office in the state.

Poullain's usual habit was to assume that his readers were male and to address them as an insider—"one of the boys." But on a few occasions he excluded men and appealed directly to women. He knew that many women were alarmed at the prospect of liberation and intimidated by the thought of seeking an education. He pleaded with them to consider the advantages of education. He promised them that education would provide them with protection against deceivers. It would enrich the conversations with which they ordinarily divert themselves. It would make them more appealing to men—permitting women who were not beautiful to acquire at least one attractive feature. Education would make women better judges of the men who have authority over them and give women a stronger hand in partnership with their husbands. Poullain also assured women that learned subjects would not be all that difficult to master if a few reforms were made in the educational system. What makes study so difficult, Poullain said, is the insistence on the part of teachers that we learn everything that everyone in the past has thought about a subject. We would master truth much more easily and quickly if we dispensed with ancient prejudices and thought things through for ourselves. (Like many reformers, Poullain had many causes. He was extremely dissatisfied with the scholastic training he had received and hoped that the Cartesian method would sweep the schools clean of a great deal of medieval rubbish.)

Poullain encouraged women to hope that they might be designed by nature to be better students than men, for he believed that women were more verbally proficient,

more imaginative, and had better memories than men. Any assertion of female superiority was, however, likely to be met with skepticism, for many "authorities" claimed that women were imperfect imitations of men. Poullain, therefore, tried to defend his position by embarking on a brief exploration of the concept of perfection. He argued that the perfection of a thing should not be judged by comparing it to some other thing, but by reflecting on its purpose. The fact that men and women are different does not imply that one must be less perfect than the other. It only reminds us that we must appreciate each gender for its unique function. Everything is perfect that does what it is supposed to do.

Poullain was too sophisticated a thinker to claim that all value judgments are purely pragmatic. He pointed out that our feet may be as perfect as our brains (in that both do what they are supposed to do), but we account our brains to be "nobler" than our feet—for they perform a function for which we have greater respect. Judgments of this kind are, however, relative. They assume a set of values that differs from culture to culture, and they are not dictated by the nature of things.

To explore the question of the relative "nobility" of males and females, Poullain devoted a separate chapter of his book to explaining the difference between the sexes. He maintained that each gender is perfect, for each does what God designed it to do: each has a unique contribution to make to the perpetuation of the species. Women's biological functions, therefore, cannot be considered faults or weaknesses. They are essential to feminine identity. Since they define the female, it is illogical to think of them as imperfections in her. If women did not have feminine features, they would be men. There would then be no sexes, and the human race would be something other than it is. Women carry a greater burden in reproduction than men do, but this ought to earn them greater respect and gratitude, not contempt.

The only difference between the sexes that Poullain acknowledged is the distinct contribution each makes to reproduction. Apart from that, he claimed that men and women are identical in body and mind. (Poullain was not even certain that women constitutionally have less "strength and vigor than men." He pointed out that strong and weak

are to be found in both sexes. And since weak men can be strengthened by training, he speculated that women might develop as much strength as men if they exercised as men do.) Poullain argued that woman's biology does not constitute a justification for imposing civil liabilities on her, for there is no rational reason why the ability to conceive a child—any more than the ability to sire one—should disqualify someone from attending school or entering politics.

Poullain had a modern feminist's sensitivity to the power of language. He believed that figures of speech perpetuate the sex role stereotypes that are entrenched in a culture and make it difficult for people to think rationally about male and female potentials. He pointed out that the term "effeminate" implies things that are as degrading to women as the term "manly" is complimentary to men. If we were rational about it, he maintained, we would compliment a man for his virtue and decency by telling him that his conduct was "womanly."

Despite his musings on woman's potential for physical development, Poullain did not consider questions of strength to be relevant to the point he wanted to make. Brute strength may be a basis for making distinctions in the animal world, but it ought not to carry much weight in a civilized society. Since, Poullain observed, the strongest men are more likely to be chosen to dig ditches than to preside over courts and nations, men have no justification for using woman's alleged weakness as a reason for excluding her from public office.

Poullain admitted that the average female disposition is probably different from the average male character, but he saw no problem in this. Since differences in personality (like differences in strength) are not used to exclude males from public life, a range of degree between males and females (with respect to traits of character) cannot be held against women. Things tend to balance out. If men have an advantage of strength, women win the contest for beauty. Each of these attributes is as real as the other, and each is as deserving of respect and reward. In addition, Poullain insisted, women are known to excel in many admirable qualities (e.g., compassion) that are of great use to leaders.

There are differences between men and women, but Poullain believed that they are not as great as most people

assume them to be. He was convinced that the contrast between men and women that looms large in daily life owes more to education than nature. Poullain warned that people frequently credit to nature behaviors that spring from custom—and they fail to appreciate how strong an effect the environment has on us. Poullain did not deny that there are differences in natural capacities among individuals, but he claimed that they have a greater effect on the rate at which people learn than on what people can learn. If the women around us (Poullain warned his male readers) show little interest in serious study, we should not assume that this is because they are women. Instead we should consider what we have conditioned them to think about themselves. We should take into account how we have trained them to avoid serious pursuits.

Poullain pointed out that society does everything possible to persuade women that God and nature forbid them to aspire to equality with men. Young girls are given no independence and chastised for exercising any initiative. They are taught to be fearful and timid. They are praised for their beauty rather than their intellect. They are encouraged to spend their time on amusements and frivolities. They are given no serious books to read. And if one of them shows an inclination to study, she is ridiculed by her sisters and accused of putting on airs. Girls of humble station have no more freedom than those of the privileged classes. They are put to work as young as possible, and endless toil prevents their acquisition of educations. They are forced into marriage at the earliest opportunity or confined in a cloister. They have no freedom to grow, explore, or develop their talents.

Since the limited educations that women are given undercut self-confidence and promote frivolity, Poullain suggested that we ought to have nothing but compassion for women when they behave in a less than admirable fashion. If we are disappointed in a woman's conduct, we should remind ourselves that women are not taught much that prepares them for the challenges of life. There are, therefore, good reasons for the personal shortcomings commonly imputed to them.

We believe, for instance, that women are naturally timid creatures, but we do not reflect on the fact that women should be fearful. We do nothing to equip them to defend themselves. We do not allow them to develop either strength of body or mental acuity, and we leave them defenseless before men—who behave with less self-control than animals. Vulnerability also encourages women to become greedy and avaricious. Women have to horde resources, for society provides them with few means for earning money and for guarding against want.

If women are sometimes credulous and superstitious, we must recall that their minds have not been trained to think clearly. The inadequacies of their educations also explain why women are accused of being garrulous. If women are talkative, they are simply exercising an untrained gift for self-expression—a talent that could be profitably developed by education. (It is also likely, Poullain pointed out, that the gossip of male journalists and pedants is far more damaging to society than women's conversations about clothes and fashions.) Poullain suspected that male impatience with female chatter reveals an insensitivity in males to women's attempts to learn. Men who do not believe that women should be educated are offended when women ask to have things explained to them, and these men condemn in women the curiosity and persistence they praise in boys.

If women can be accused (with some justification) of being fickle, Poullain insisted that men are no less unfaithful. Men simply assume that they ought to be able to play by a different set of rules than women do. Anyway, Poullain added (with a touch of Gallic sophistication), fickleness is a basic human trait. We constantly change our minds about all kinds of things, and the difference between loving and hating a thing is no more than a matter of timing. We love something if we meet it when we are in a good mood and hate it if we encounter it when we are out of sorts.

If women are said to be craftier than men, Poullain suggested that they should take this as an unintended compliment. Craft is a sign of intelligence. Likewise, if women are accused of being more malicious and making more trouble than men, they can turn this charge to their

advantage. Since they cannot obtain the kinds of posts that give men the power to do harm to others, society prevents them from doing any real damage. And if they still succeed in creating problems—given the limited realm over which they have sway, this is yet more proof of their intelligence. A mind that can overcome obstacles for an evil purpose can—if it is properly directed by education—accomplish great good.

Poullain concluded from his survey of the failings that are commonly said to be characteristic of women that women's faults are neither very serious nor very difficult to eradicate. They are all defects of education, not ineradicable traits rooted in nature.

Poullain warned scholars that by rejecting his plea for the education of women they revealed the inadequacies of their own educations. He claimed that most academics are products of a system that enslaves them to the past. They are taught that they cannot improve upon the opinions of the ancient "authorities" whose works dominate the curricula of universities, so instead of thinking for themselves, they parrot and defend antique prejudices. Their ideas about women come from reading old books, not from observing women and thinking critically about what they see.

As a convert to Cartesianism, Poullain was contemptuous of the medieval methods of debate in which he had been trained at the Parisian schools. He believed that common sense sufficed to permit a person to see through the absurdities of scholastic arguments, and he had little reverence for the great philosophers who were worshipped by the scholastics. Poullain came to the end of his book without once bothering even to invoke the names of Plato and Aristotle. In a few concluding pages he dismissed them (and the other ancient philosophers who had laid up ammunition for misogynists) as a minor inconvenience. For Poullain it was obvious that the manifest absurdities that infected ancient pronouncements on women ought to prevent their authors from being taken seriously by any modern person of average intelligence.

Plato's speculation that women were less human than men and deserved to be classed with the animals was silly enough, Poullain said, to deprive Plato of any credibility on the issue of women. Aristotle's claim that women were travesties of

men—monsters—is likewise, in Poullain's opinion, a piece of nonsense. Who, he asked, is shocked or surprised at the sight of a woman—as he would be if he encountered a monster? Women have been around as long as men, and it makes as much sense to criticize Aristotle for being different from women as to complain that women are different from Aristotle. Although Poullain had not mentioned Philo earlier in his text, he had already offered his refutation of Philo's theory that women were imperfect men. Since both sexes are equally necessary to the act of reproduction, each one is imperfect when judged according to the functions of the other—but perfect in terms of its own mission. Poullain dismissed Socrates as a man angered by a shrewish wife and made resentful by an ugly face that robbed him of luck with the ladies. Diogenes's malicious epigrams were nothing more than expressions of spleen and attempts to get a rise out of an audience. Democritus was a comedian whose specious arguments can easily be turned against him. And Cato condemned women for failing tests of self-control that men could not pass.

Poullain concluded from his brief survey of the literature that there was nothing in this ancient twaddle of profit to the modern world. The true wonder, he remarked, was that "serious men" could try to make "serious use" of old jokes. Their behavior, Poullain suggested, was but another proof of the blindness that prejudice inflicts on people who ought to know better.

At this point Poullain abruptly laid down his pen and ended his book. A little more reflection, however, must have convinced him that some of his readers would be unimpressed by what he had written. He had not employed a traditional method for making his case. Most books on serious subjects took the form of commentaries on ancient texts. Poullain had virtually ignored the "wisdom" of the past. Only at the end of his volume did he condescend even to mention the great philosophers. And there was one major ancient source of truth that he had not referred to at all: the Bible. Most people believed that the Bible had a great deal to say about men and women and gender roles. In their opinion, Poullain

had sidestepped some of the most important evidence that could be brought against the points he wanted to make.

Poullain, therefore, attached a very brief "notice" to the end of his book. In it he defended his decision to ignore the ancient philosophers and the Bible. With respect to the first, he proposed that the only human authorities that anyone should pay attention to are those whose opinions conform to "reason and common sense." He had, therefore, no need to quote the words of other men—ancient or modern—to support his own. If the points he had made were true, they would automatically establish their own validity as "clear and distinct ideas" in unbiased minds. Each person could judge for him or herself if Poullain's arguments were correct, and no one should accept or reject them simply because of what someone else thought.

In regard to the sacred authority of the Bible, Poullain was more circumspect. He said that he ignored the Scriptures because he did not think that they had anything to say that was relevant to his topic. His intent was to argue for the equality of the sexes, and he maintained that there is nothing in the Bible about inequality. Further, he explained that the Bible is intended to be read as an ethical guide that leaves each person free to judge "the nature and true state of things." Poullain accused those who use the Bible to denigrate women of doing violence to the Word of God. He said that they develop sophistic arguments to twist the meaning of Scripture. They lift passages out of context and apply to all women injunctions that were meant only for a few in particular situations. Or they assume that nature and divine law are the causes of things that, in reality, spring from custom and education.

A few brief sentences—no matter how advanced they were in anticipating the canons of interpretation used by modern textual critiques—were inadequate to lay the Bible to rest. It was not long, therefore, before Poullain was at work on a second book (*De l'Excellence des hommes*) that dealt extensively with Scriptural material. *De l'Excellence des hommes* and *De l'Egalité des deux Sexes* supplemented each other so neatly that in 1690 they were published in one volume.

Text
and
Translation

De L'Egalité des Deux Sexes
Discours Physique et Moral

(Où l'on voit l'importance de se défaire des Préjugez.)

A PARIS

Chez Jean Du Puis, ruë Saint Jacques à la Couronne d'Or

C. LXXIII

Avec Privilege du Roy

The Equality of the Two Sexes: A Discussion of Physical and Moral Attributes

(Which Demonstrates the Importance of Ridding Oneself of Prejudice)

Paris

Printed by John Du Puis

Avenue Saint James, at the Crown of Gold

1673

With Royal Permission

PREFACE

Contenant Le Plan & le but de ce Discours.

[i][1]Il n'y a rien de plus délicat que de s'expliquer sur les Femmes. Quand un homme parle à leur avantage, l'on s'imagine aussitost[2] que c'est par galanterie ou par amour: & il y a grande apparence que la pluspart jugeant de ce discours par le Tître, croiront d'abord qu'il est l'effet de l'un ou de l'autre, & seront bien-aises [ii] d'en sçavoir au vray, le motif & le dessein. Le voicy.

La plus heureuse pensée qui puisse venir à ceux qui travaillent à acquerir une science solide, aprés avoir esté instruits selon la Methode vulgaire, c'est de douter si on les a bien enseignez, & de vouloir découvrir la verité par eux-mêmes.

Dans le progrez de leur recherche, il leur arrive necessairement de remarquer que nous sommes remplis de préjugez [C'est à dire de iugemens portez sur les choses, sans les avoir examinées.][3] & qu'il faut y renoncer absolument, pour avoir des connoissances claires & distinctes.

[iii] Dans le dessein d'insinuër une Maxime si importante, l'on a crû que le meilleur estoit de choisir un sujet determiné & éclatant, où chacun prist interest; afin qu'aprés avoir démontré qu'un sentiment aussi ancien que le Monde, aussi étendu que la Terre, & aussi universel que le Genre humain, est un préjugé ou une erreur, les Sçavans puîssent estre enfin couvaincus de la necessité qu'il y a de juger des choses par soi-même, aprés les avoir bien examinées, & de ne s'en point rapporter à l'opinion ni à la bonne foy des autres [iv] hommes, si l'on veut éviter d'étre trompé.

De tous les Préjugez, on n'en a point remarqué de plus propre à ce dessein que celuy qu'on a communément sur l'Inégalité des deux Sexes.

---

[1]Numbers in brackets within the text refer to pages in the original edition.

[2]Original spellings have been retained: note the appearance of "v" for "u", "oi" for "ai", "ez" for "es", "y" for "i", "an" for "en" and "th" for "t".

[3]Words within brackets within the text contain material printed in the margins of the original edition.

PREFACE

(Stating the plan and the goal of this Treatise)

[i][1] Nothing requires more care than the presentation of one's theories about women. When a man takes up their cause, the immediate assumption is that he is motivated by gallantry or love. There is a great likelihood that many readers (judging this treatise by its title) will assume at the start that it is the result of one or the other of these things. [ii] They will be pleased to learn its true motive and intent—as follows:

The most fortunate thought that can occur to people who work at acquiring sound knowledge (having previously been instructed in the ordinary way) is to wonder whether they have been well taught and to wish to discover the truth for themselves.

During the course of their research, these people will inevitably find that our minds are filled with prejudices. And they will find they must renounce these opinions absolutely before they can arrive at clear, distinct understandings.

[iii] With the intent of establishing so important a principle, we have believed it best to choose a specific, striking subject (in which everyone takes an interest) so that after demonstrating that an opinion as ancient as the world, as widespread as the earth and as universal as the human species itself is a prejudice or an error, knowledgeable people will finally be convinced of the necessity of judging things (after having carefully examined them) for themselves and of not abiding by the opinions or the testimonies of others-[iv]-if they want to avoid being deceived.

Of all prejudices, none can be found more appropriate for this purpose than the commonly held belief in the inequality of the two sexes.

Indeed, if the sexes are examined in their present condition, we notice that they differ more in social functions and in things that relate to the mind than in things that pertain to the body. And if we look for an explanation of this in ordinary conversation, we find that all people—those

---

[1]Numbers in brackets within the text refer to pages in the original edition.

En effet, si on les considere en l'état où ils sont à présent,
on observe qu'ils sont plus differens dans les fonctions Civiles,
& qui dépendent de l'Esprit, que dans celles qui appartiennent
au Corps. Et si on en cherche la raison dans les Discours
ordinaires, on trouve que tout le Monde, ceux qui ont de
l'étude, & ceux qui n'en ont [v] point, & les Femmes même
s'accordent à dire qu'elles n'ont point de part aux Sciences ny
aux Emplois, parce qu'elles n'en sont pas capables; qu'elles
ont moins d'Esprit que les hommes, & qu'elles leur doivent
estre inferieures en tout comme elles sont.

Apres avoir examiné cette Opinion, suivant la regle de
verité, qui est de n'admettre rien pour vray qui ne soit
appuyé sur des idées claires & distinctes; d'un costé elle a
paru fausse, & fondée sur un Préjugé, & sur une Tradition
populaire, & de l'autre on a trouvé que les [vi] deux Sexes
sont égaux: c'est à dire, que les Femmes sont aussi Nobles,
aussi parfaites, & aussi capables que les hommes. Cela ne
peut estre étably qu'en refutant deux sortes d'Aversaires, le
Vulgaire, & presque tous les Sçavans.

Le premier n'ayant pour fondement de ce qu'il croit, que la
Coûtume & de legeres apparences, il semble qu'on ne le peut
mieux combattre qu'en luy faisant voir comment les Femmes
ont esté assujetties & excluës des Sciences & des Emplois;
& aprés l'avoir conduit par les états & les ren-[vii]-contres
principales de la vie, luy donner lieu de reconnoître qu'elles
ont des avantages qui les rendent égales aux hommes; & c'est
ce qui comprend la premiere Partie de ce Traité.

La seconde est employée à montrer que les preuves
des Sçavans sont toutes vaines. Et aprés avoir établi le
sentiment de l'Egalité, par des raisons positives, on justifie
les Femmes des défauts dont on les accuse ordinairement, en
faisant voir qu'ils sont imaginaires ou peu importans, qu'ils
viennent uniquement de l'Education qu'on leur donne, &
qu'ils marquent [viii] en elles des avantages considerables.

Ce sujet pouvoit estre traité en deux façons, ou galam-
ment, c'est à dire, d'une maniere enjoüée & fleurie, ou bien en
Philosophe & par principes, afin d'en instruire à fond.

Ceux qui ont une idée juste de la veritable Eloquence,
sçavent bien que ces deux manieres sont presque inalliables,
& qu'on ne peut gueres éclairer l'Esprit & l'égayer par la

who have studied and those who have not [v] and women themselves—agree in saying that women have taken no part in the various fields of learning or the professions because women are not fit for these things. They claim that women are less intelligent than men and that they ought to be subordinate to men in everything—as they are.

After having tested this opinion by the rule of truth (which is to admit nothing as true that could not be supported by clear and distinct ideas)—on the one hand, it appeared false and founded on prejudice and popular tradition and, on the other, it was discovered that the [vi] two sexes are equal (i.e., that women are as noble, perfect, and competent as men). This can only be proven by refuting two kinds of adversaries: the common man and almost all the experts.

Since the first of these has for the support of what he believes mere custom and casual observation, the best way to fight him seems to be to force him to see how women have been kept in subjugation and excluded from education and the professions and, after leading him through an explanation of the situations [vii] and principal opportunities offered by life, to give him a chance to realize that women have attributes that make them the equals of men. This project takes up the first part of this essay.

The second part is used to show that the proofs of woman's inferiority offered by experts are all worthless. After we have established the principle of equality by positive arguments, we will explain away the faults of which women are ordinarily accused by demonstrating that these shortcomings are imaginary or of little importance—that they derive entirely from the education that women are given or that they [viii] are really signs of a woman's considerable advantages.

This subject can be dealt with in two ways: either dashingly (i.e., in a playful, florid manner) or else in philosophy and by principles that provide thorough instruction.

Those who have an accurate understanding of true eloquence know well that these two styles are virtually incompatible and that the mind can scarcely be enlightened and amused by the same approach. Not that elegant discourse cannot be combined with reason, but this mix often impedes the goal that we must [ix] propose for this treatise—which is

même voye. Ce n'est pas qu'on ne puisse joindre la fleurette avec la raison; mais ce mélange empêche souvent la fin qu'on se doit [ix]proposer dans les Discours, qui est de convaincre & de persuader; ce qu'il y a d'agreable amusant l'Esprit, & ne luy permettant pas de s'arrêter au solide.

Et comme l'on a pour les Femmes des regards particuliers, si dans un ouvrage fait sur leur sujet, on méle quelque chose de galant, ceux qui le lisent poussent leurs pensées trop loin, & perdent de veuë ce qui les devroit occupe.

C'est pourquoy n'y ayant rien qui regarde plus les Femmes que ce dessein, où l'on est obligé de dire en leur faveur ce qu'il y a de plus fort & de vray, autant [x] que la Bizarrerie du Monde le peut souffrir, on a crû qu'il faloit parler serieusement & en avertir, de peur que la pensée que ce seroit un ouvrage de galanterie ne le fasse passer legerement, ou rejetter par les personnes scrupuleuses.

L'on n'ignore pas que ce discours fera beaucoup de mécontens, que ceux dont les interests & les maximes sont contraires à ce qu'on avance icy, ne manqueront pas de crier contre. Pour donner moyen de répondre à leurs plaintes l'on avertit les personnes d'Esprit, & particulie-[xi]-rement les Femmes qui ne sont point la Dupe de ceux qui prennent authorité sur elles, que si elles se donnent la peine de lire ce Traitté, avec l'attention, que merite au moins la varieté des matieres qui y sont, elles remarqueront que le Caractere essentiel de la verité, c'est la clarté & l'évidence. Ce qui leur pourra servir à reconnoistre si les objections qu'on leur apportera sont considerables ou non. Et elles pourront remarquer, que les plus specieuses leur seront faites par des gens que leur profession semble engager aujourd'huy à renoncer à [xii] l'experience, au bon sens & à eux-mêmes, pour embrasser aveuglément tout ce qui s'accorde avec leurs préjugez & leurs interests, & à combattre toutes sortes de veritez, qui semblent les attaquer.

Et l'on prie de considerer que les mauvais effets qu'une terreur Panique leur feroit apprehender de cette entreprise, n'arriveront peut-estre pas à l'égard d'une seule femme, & qu'ils sont contrepesez par un grand bien qui en peut revenir; n'y ayant peut-estre pas de voye plus naturelle ny plus sure pour tirer la pluspart des Femmes de [xiii] l'oisiveté où elles

to convince and to persuade. (Agreeable things that amuse the mind do not allow it to settle on a solid foundation.)

And, as we have a particular regard for women, if in a work devoted to them we include some gallantry, those who read it can be carried away by their thoughts and lose sight of what they ought to concentrate on.

Consequently, there being nothing that concerns women more than this project (in which it is necessary to state in their favor what is most powerful and true—so far [x] as the caprice of the world can endure it), we believe that we must speak plainly and alert the reader—for fear that the assumption that this treatise is to be a work of flattery might cause it to be passed over lightly or rejected by serious people.

We are not unaware that this discourse will displease many—that those whose interests and principles are contrary to the ideas that we advance here will not hesitate to speak out against it. As a defense against their complaints, we warn people of intelligence (particularly [xi] women who are not the dupes of those in authority over them) that: if they take the trouble to read this treatise with the attention that at least the variety of the materials that it contains merits, they will notice the essential character of truth: clarity and obviousness. This could help them discover whether the charges laid against women are substantial or not. And it could help them to realize that the most specious arguments are made by people whose profession today seems to require them to renounce [xii] experience, common sense and themselves to embrace blindly everything that accords with their prejudice and self-interest and to combat all kinds of truths that seem to attack these things.

And we pray them to consider that the bad outcome that panicky terror might make them fear from this enterprise will perhaps not materialize in the case of a single woman—and that the dangers are counterbalanced by a great good that could accrue to women. There is, perhaps, no more natural nor more certain way to rescue the majority of women from [xiii] the idleness to which they are reduced and the disadvantages that result from it than to turn them to study (which is almost the only thing with which ladies can at

sont reduites, & des inconveniens qui la suivent que de les
porter à l'étude, qui est presque la seule chose à quoy les
Dames puissent à present s'occuper, en leur faisant connoistre
qu'elles y sont aussi propres que les hommes.

Et comme il n'y a que ceux qui ne sont pas raisonnables
qui abusent au préjudice des Femmes des avantages que leur
donne la Coûtume? [*sic*] Il ne pourroit y avoir aussi que
des Femmes peu judicieuses, qui se servissent de cét ouvrage
pour s'élever contre les hommes, qui les traitteroient comme
leurs égales [xiv] ou leurs compagnes. Enfin si quelqu'un se
choque de ce Discours pour quelque cause que ce soit, qu'il
s'en prenne à la verité & non à l'Autheur: & pour s'exempter
de chagrin qu'il se dise à luy-même, que ce n'est qu'un jeu
d'Esprit: Il est certain que ce tour d'Imagination ou un
semblable, empéchant la verité d'avoir prise sur nous, la rend
de beaucoup moins incommode à ceux qui ont peine à la
souffrir.

present occupy themselves) by making them realize that they are as fit for it as men.

And as only unreasonable persons employ the advantages that custom gives women to their detriment, women would be just as unfair if they were to avail themselves of this book to rise up against the men who treat them like equals [xiv] or companions. Finally, if anyone is shocked by this essay for whatever reason, let him blame the truth and not the author—and relieve his annoyance by telling himself that the book is nothing but a joke. It is certain that this trick of the imagination (or some similar one that prevents the truth from taking hold of us) will render the truth much less inconvenient to those who can scarcely endure it.

[1]   De l'Egalité des deux Sexes

Premiere Partie

Où l'on montre que l'opinion vulgaire est un préjugé,
& qu'en comparant sans interest ce que l'on peut
remarquer dans la conduite des hommes & des
femmes, on est obligé de reconnoitre entre les deux
Sexes une égalité entiere.

Les hommes sont persuadez d'une infinité de choses dont ils ne
sçauroient rendre raison; parceque [2] [Que les hommes sont
remplis de préjugez.] leur persuasion n'est fondée que sur de
legeres apparences, ausquelles ils se sont laissez emporter, &
ils eussent crû aussi fortement le contraire, si les impressions
des sens ou de la coûtume les y eussent determinez de la
même façon.

Hors un petit nombre de sçavans, tout le monde tient
comme une chose indubitable, que c'est le Soleil qui se meut
autour de la terre: quoyque ce qui paroist dans la revolution
des jours & des années y porte également ceux qui y font
attention, à penser que c'est la terre qui se meut autour
du soleil. L'on s'imagine qu'il y a dans les bêtes quelque
connoissance qui les conduit, par la même raison que les
Sauvages se figurent qu'il y a un petit demon dans les horloges
& dans les machines qu'on leur montre; [3] dont ils ne
connoissent point la fabrique ni les ressorts.

Si l'on nous avoit élevez au milieu des mers, sans jamais
nous faire approcher de la terre, nous n'eussions pas manqué
de croire en changeant de place sur un vaisseau, que c'eussent
esté les rivages qui se fussent éloignez de nous, comme le
croient les enfans au depart des bateaux. Chacun estime que
son païs est le meilleur, parce qu'il y est plus accoûtumé; que la
religion dans laquelle il a esté nourri, est la veritable qu'il faut
suivre, quoy qu'il n'ait peut-estre jamais songé à l'examiner
ni à la comparer avec les autres. On se sent toûjours plus
porté pour ses compatriotes que pour les étrangers, dans les
affaires où le droit même est pour ceux-cy. Nous nous plaisons
davantage avec ceux de nô-[4]-tre profession, encore qu'ils
ayent moins d'esprit & de vertu. Et l'inegalité des biens &

[1]   The Equality of the Two Sexes

Part One

In which it is demonstrated that ordinary belief is a
prejudice and that, when the conduct of men and of
women is compared without bias, a complete equality
between the two sexes must be recognized.

People are persuaded of an infinity of things that they do not
know how to prove, for [2] their convictions are based solely
on flimsy appearances which they allow to carry them away.
They would have accepted contrary ideas just as quickly if
their senses or custom had swayed them to these notions in
the same way.

Apart from a small number of educated people, everyone
accepts it as obvious that the sun moves around the earth—
even though the revolution of days and years brings everyone
alike (who pays attention to it) to the realization that the
earth moves about the sun. Some people imagine that there is
some understanding in beasts that guides them—for the same
reason that savages, who do not comprehend the construction
or the workings of the watches and the machines that are
shown [3] them, assume that such objects contain little
demons.

If we had been raised in the middle of the sea without
ever having approached land, we would not have failed to
assume—when moving from place to place on a boat—that it
was the shore that retreated from us (as children think when
boats set out). Each person assumes that his homeland is
the best (because he is most accustomed to it) and that the
religion in which he was raised is the true one that he must
follow (although he has perhaps never dreamed of examining
it nor comparing it with others). Everyone senses himself
always more disposed to favor compatriots than strangers—
even in situations where strangers are in the right. We take
special pleasure in the company of people who belong to our
[4] profession—even if they have less intelligence and virtue

des conditions fait juger à beaucoup de gens que les hommes ne sont point égaux entr'eux.

Si on cherche surquoy sont fondées toutes ces opinions diverses, on trouvera qu'elles ne le sont que sur l'interest, ou sur la coûtume; & qu'il est incomparablement plus difficile de tirer les hommes des sentimens où ils ne sont que par préjugé, que de ceux qu'ils ont embrassez par le motif des raisons qui leur ont paru les plus convaincantes & les plus fortes.

L'on peut mettre au nombre de ces jugemens celuy qu'on porte vulgairement sur la difference des deux Sexes, & sur tout ce qui en dépend. Il n'y en a point de plus ancien ni de plus univer-[5]-sel. Les sçavans & les ignorans sont tellement prévenus de la pensée que les femmes sont inferieures aux hommes en capacité & en merite, & qu'elles doivent estre dans la dépendance où nous les voyons, qu'on ne manquera pas de regarder le sentiment contraire comme un paradoxe [Opinion contraire à celle du public.] singulier.

Cependant il ne seroit pas necessaire pour l'établir, d'employer aucune raison positive, si les hommes estoient plus équitables & moins interessez dans leurs jugemens. Il suffiroit de les avertir qu'on n'a parlé jusqu'a present qu'à la legere de la difference des deux Sexes, au desavantage des femmes; & que pour juger sainement si le nôtre a quelque préeminence naturelle par dessus le leur il faut y penser serieusement & sans interest renonçant à ce qu'on en a cru sur le simple [Ce qu'il faut faire pour bien iuger des choses.] [6] rapport d'autruy, & sans l'avoir examiné.

Il est certain qu'un homme qui se mettroit en cét état d'indifference & de desinteressement, reconnoîtroit d'une part que c'est le peu de lumiere & la précipitation qui font tenir que les femmes sont moins nobles & moins excellentes que nous: & que c'est quelques indispositions naturelles, qui les rendent sujettes aux deffauts & aux imperfections qu'on leur attribuë, & méprisables à tant de gens. Et de l'autre part, il verroit que les apparences mêmes qui trompent le peuple sur leur subject, lorsqu'il les passe legerement, serviroient à le détromper s'il les approfondissoit un peu. Enfin, si cet homme estoit Philosophe, il trouveroit qu'il y a des raisons Physiques qui prou-[7]-vent invinciblement que les deux Sexes sont égaux pour le corps & pour l'esprit.

[than others].[2] And inequity in goods and situations causes most observers to conclude that there is no equality among people.

If we search out the bases for all these diverse opinions, we will find that they consist only in self-interest or custom. [We will also discover] that it is incomparably more difficult to draw people away from feelings to which their prejudices alone dispose them than from ideas they have embraced for reasons that have appeared to them to be strong and convincing.

We can number with these assumptions those that we commonly make (and all that depends on them) about the difference between the two sexes. There is nothing more ancient nor more universal. [5] The educated and the ignorant are so predisposed to the idea that women are inferior to men in capacity and merit and that women must be in the subservient state in which we see them that these people cannot fail to consider the contrary belief a strange paradox.

However, it would not be necessary to employ any supportive argument to prove the contrary if men were more just and less self-interested in their opinions. It would suffice to warn them that we have always spoken casually of the difference between the two sexes to the detriment of women and that in order to judge clearly whether our gender has some natural superiority to theirs, it is necessary to think seriously and without self-interest—renouncing ideas that we have accepted on the simple [6] testimony of others without examination.

It is certain that if a man were to put himself into this state of detachment and disinterestedness he would recognize, on the one hand that lack of understanding and haste have led to the opinion that women are less noble and less excellent creatures than we are. [He would see] that there are a few natural indispositions that render women liable to the faults and imperfections attributed to them and [make women] contemptible to so many people. On the other hand, he would see that even the appearances that deceive people about the

---

[2] Words enclosed by brackets have been added to the text to improve the clarity of the English translation.

Mais comme il n'y a pas beaucoup de personnes en estat de pratiquer eux seuls cét avis, il demeureroit inutile, si on ne prenoit la peine de travailler avec eux pour les aider à s'en servir: & parceque l'opinion de ceux qui n'ont point d'étude est la plus generale, c'est par elle qu'il faut commencer nôtre examen.

Si l'on demande à chaque homme en particulier ce qu'il pense des femmes en general, & qu'il le veüille avoüer sincerement, il dira sans doute qu'elles ne sont faites que pour nous [Ce que les hommes croyent des femmes.], & qu'elles ne sont gueres propres qu'à élever les enfans dans leur bas âge, & à prendre le soin du ménage. Peut-estre que les plus spirituels àjoûteroient qu'il y a [8] beaucoup de femmes qui ont de l'esprit & de la conduite; mais que si l'on examine de prés celles qui en ont le plus, on y trouvera toûjours quelque chose qui sent leur Sexe: qu'elles n'ont ni fermeté ni arrest, ni le fond d'esprit qu'ils croient reconnoître dans le leur, & que c'est un effet de la providence divine & de la sagesse des hommes, de leur avoir fermé l'entrée des sciences, du gouvernement, & des emplois: que ce seroit une chose plaisante de voir une femme enseigner dans une chaire, l'éloquence ou la medecine en qualité de Professeur: marcher par les ruës, suivie de Commissaires & de Sergens pour y mettre la police: haranguer devant les Iuges en qualité d'Avocat: estre assisse [*sic*] sur un Tribunal pour y rendre Iustice, à la teste d'un Parlement: conduire une armée, livrer [9] une bataille: & parler devant les Republiques ou les Princes comme Chef d'une Ambassade.

J'avoüe que cét usage nous surprendroit: mais ce ne seroit que par la raison de la nouveauté. Si en formant les états & en établissant les differens emplois qui les composent, on y avoit aussi appellé les femmes, nous serions accoûtumez à les y voir, comme elles le sont à nôtre égard. Et nous ne trouverions pas plus étrange de les voir sur les Fleurs de Lys, que dans les boutiques.

Si on pousse un peu les gens, on trouvera que leurs plus fortes raisons se reduisent à dire que les choses ont toûjours esté comme elles sont; à l'égard des femmes: ce qui est une marque qu'elles doivent estre de la sorte: & que si elles avoient

subject of women (when it is casually considered) would serve to undeceive him if he were to ponder these things a little. Finally, if this man were a philosopher, he would find that there are arguments based on physical attributes [7] that offer invincible proof that the two sexes are equal in body and mind.

But as there are not many people in a condition to practice this advice by themselves, it would remain useless if we did not take the trouble to work with them to help them avail themselves of it. Because the opinion of persons who have not studied is the most widespread, we must begin our investigation by considering it.

If you ask any male individual what he thinks of women in general (and he is willing to speak his mind sincerely) he undoubtedly will say that women have only been created for us men and that they are scarcely fit for anything but the nurture of young children and the care of the home. Perhaps the more thoughtful will add that there are [8] many women who have intelligence and deportment—but if the best are examined closely, there is always something that betrays their sex. They have neither firmness nor judgment, nor the depth of mind that at first glance seems to be theirs, and it is an act of divine providence and the wisdom of men to block their entry into academic fields, politics, and the professions. [These men might add that] it would be an amusing thing to see a woman lecturing from a university chair ([teaching] rhetoric or medicine at the rank of professor), marching along the streets followed by commissioners and sergeants to provide police protection, haranguing before judges in the office of an advocate, sitting on a tribunal rendering justice at the head of a high court, leading an army, fighting [9] a battle, and speaking before republics or princes as the leader of an embassy.

(I confess that this practice would surprise us, but only by reason of its novelty. If in setting up states and establishing the different offices that compose them, women had been appointed to them, we would be as accustomed to seeing women there as they are to see us. And we would not find it stranger to see them on the "Fleurs de Lys" [i.e., "the throne"] than in shops.)

esté capables des sciences & des emplois, les hom-**[10]**-mes les
y auroient admises avec eux.

Ces raisonnemens viennent de l'opinion [Fausse idée de
la coûtume.] qu'on a de l'équité de nôtre Sexe, & d'une
fausse idée que l'on s'est forgée de la coûtume. C'est assez
de la trouver établie, pour croire qu'elle est bien fondée. Et
comme l'on juge que les hommes ne doivent rien faire que
par raison, la pluspart ne peuuent s'imaginer qu'elle n'ait pas
esté consultée pour introduire les pratiques qu'ils voyent si
universellement reçuës; & l'on se figure, que c'est la raison
& la prudence qui les ont faites, à cause que l'une & l'autre
obligent de s'y conformer lorsqu'on ne peut se dispenser de
les suivre, sans qu'il arrive quelque trouble.

Chacun void en son païs les femmes dans une telle
sujettion, qu'elles dépendent des hom-**[11]**-mes en tout, sans
entrée dans les sciences, ni dans aucun des états qui donnent
lieu de se signaler par les avantages de l'esprit. Nul ne
rapporte qu'il ait veu les choses autrement à leur égard. On
sçait aussi qu'elle ont toûjours esté de la sorte, & qu'il n'y
a point d'endroit de la terre où on ne les traite comme dans
le lieu où l'on est. Il y en a même où on les regarde comme
des esclaves. A la Chine on leur tient les pieds petits dés leur
enfance, pour les empescher de sortir de leurs maisons, où
elles ne voyent presque jamais que leurs maris & leurs enfans.
En Turquie les Dames sont resserrées d'aussi prés. Elles ne
sont gueres mieux en Italie. Quasi tous les peuples d'Asie, de
l'Afrique, & de l'Amerique usent de leurs femmes, comme on
fait icy des servantes. Par tout on ne les oc-**[12]**-cupe que de
ce que l'on considere comme bas; & parce qu'il n'y a qu'elles
qui se mélent des menus soins du ménage & des enfans, l'on
se persuade communément qu'elles ne sont au monde que
pour cela, & qu'elles sont incapables de tout le reste. On a
de la peine à se representer comment les choses pourroient
estre bien d'une autre façon; & il paroist même qu'on ne les
pourroit jamais changer, quelque effort que l'on fist.

Les plus sages Legislateurs, en fondant leurs Republiques,
n'ont rien êtabli qui fust favorable aux femmes pour ce
regard. Toutes les Loix semblent n'avoir esté faites que pour
maintenir les hommes dans la possession où ils sont. Presque
tout ce qu'il y a eu de gens qui ont passé pour sçavans & qui

If these men are pressed a bit, it will be found that their strongest arguments come down to saying that, with regard to women, things have always been as they are now—which is a sign that they must be so—and, that if women had been capable of education and the professions, men **[10]** would have admitted women to these as partners.

These arguments spring from the belief we have in the righteousness of our sex and from a false notion that we have conjured up from custom. (It is enough to find that this notion is established to conclude that it is rightfully established!) And since we believe that people ought do nothing but what reason dictates, most of us cannot conceive that reason has not been consulted in establishing practices that we see are so universally accepted. We assume that reason and prudence have shaped these practices, because (since we must conform to both [reason and prudence]) we could not dispense with their guidance without some trouble developing.

In his homeland everyone sees women in such a state of subjection that they depend entirely on **[11]** men—cut off from access to education or any of the posts that give a person an opportunity to distinguish himself by the gifts of the mind. No one claims to have seen things different for women. We know also that the situation has always been as it is now and that there is no place on earth where women are not treated as they are here. There are even some countries where women are regarded as slaves. In China their feet are kept small from infancy in order to prevent them from leaving their houses—where they see almost no one but their husbands and their children. In Turkey ladies are confined just as strictly. They are scarcely better off in Italy. Almost all the people of Asia, Africa, and America use their women as we do servants. In particular, they **[12]** only assign women tasks that are considered inferior; and because there is no one but women to trouble about petty house chores and the care of children, women are usually persuaded that they are on earth for this purpose alone and that they are incapable of anything else. It is difficult to conceive how things could be right another way; and it even seems that things could never be changed—no matter what effort was made.

ont parlé des femmes, n'ont rien [13] dit à leur avantage: &
l'on trouve la conduite des hommes si uniforme à leur endroit,
dans tous les siecles & par toute la terre, qu'il semble qu'ils y
sont entrez de concert, ou bien, comme plusieurs s'imaginent,
qu'ils ont esté portez à en user de la sorte, par un instinct
secret; c'est-à-dire, par un ordre general de l'autheur de la
nature.

On se le persuade encore davantage en considerant de
quelle façon les femmes mêmes supportent leur condition.
Elles la regardent comme leur estant naturelle. Soit qu'elles
ne pensent point à ce qu'elles sont, soit que naissant &
croissant dans la dépendance, elles la considerent de la même
maniere que font les hommes. Sur toutes ces veuës, les unes
& les autres se portent à croire, que leurs esprits [14] sont
aussi differens que leurs corps, & qu'il doit y avoir entre les
deux Sexes autant de distinction dans toutes les fonctions de
la vie, qu'il y en a entre celles qui leur sont particulieres.
Cependant cette persuasion comme la pluspart de celles que
nous avons sur les coûtumes & sur les usages n'est qu'un pur
préjugé, que nous formons sur l'apparence des choses, faute
de les examiner de prés, & dont nous nous détromperions,
si nous pouvions nous donner la peine de remonter jusqu'à
la source, & juger en beaucoup de rencontres de ce qui s'est
fait autrefois, par ce qui se fait aujourd'huy [Comment il faut
iuger des Coûtumes Anciennes.], & des Coûtumes Anciennes
par celles que nous voyons s'établir de nostre temps. Si on
avoit suivi cette regle en une infinité de jugemens; on ne seroit
pas tombé en [15] tant de méprises & dans ce qui concerne
la condition presente des femmes, on auroit reconnu qu'elles
n'ont esté assujetties que par la Loy du plus fort, & que ce n'a
pas esté faute de capacité naturelle ni de merite qu'elles n'ont
point partagé avec nous, ce qui éleve nôtre Sexe au dessus du
leur.

En effet quand on considere sincerement les choses
humaines dans le passé & dans le present, on trouve qu'elles
sont toutes semblables en un point, qui est que la raison
a toûjours esté la plus foible: & il semble que toutes les
histoires n'ayent esté faites, que pour montrer ce que chacun
void de son temps, que depuis qu'il y a des hommes, la force a
toûjours prévalu. Les plus grands empires de l'Asie ont esté

The wisest legislators, in founding their republics, have established nothing that helps women with respect to this situation. All laws seem to have been made only to maintain men in the position where they are. Almost all the men who have passed for experts and who have spoken about women have said nothing [13] in their favor. The behavior of men towards them is found to be so uniform through the centuries and across the whole earth that it seems that men have formed a pact—or better, as many have imagined, that men have been led to use women in this way by an unconscious instinct (i.e., by a universal mandate of the Creator).

Additional persuasive arguments emerge when we consider how women themselves endure their condition. Women regard it as their natural state. Whether they never think about what they are or, being born into and growing up in subservience, they think of it in the same way men do. All these views lead women to believe that their minds [14] are as different as their bodies, and that there must be as great a difference between the two sexes in all aspects of life as there is between those things that are particular to each gender. However, this conviction (like most of those that derive from custom and habit) is nothing but a pure prejudice that we acquire from the appearance of things when we fail to examine them closely. And we would free ourselves of it if we could take the trouble to trace it to its source and to determine in many instances what was done formerly from what is done today (i.e., [understanding] ancient practices from those that we see established in our time). If we had followed this rule in an infinity of judgments, we would not have fallen into [15] so many errors. And in those things that concern the present condition of women, we would have recognized that women have only been held in subjugation by the law which favors the strong and that no lack of natural capacity or merit has kept them from sharing with us whatever activities elevate our sex above theirs.

Indeed, when we seriously reflect on human affairs past and present, we find that they are all similar in one way: reason has always been very weak. And it seems that all histories have been written simply to demonstrate what each of us sees in his own time: since men have existed, force

dans leur commencement l'ou-[16]-vrage des usurpateurs &
des brigands: & les débris de la monarchie des Grecs & des
Romains, n'ont esté recüeillis que par des gens qui se crurent
assez forts pour resister à leurs maîtres & pour dominer sur
leurs égaux. Cette conduite n'est pas moins visible dans
toutes les societez: & si les hommes en usent ainsi à l'égard de
leurs pareils, il y a grande apparence qu'ils l'ont fait d'abord
à plus forte raison, chacun à l'égard de la femme. Voicy à peu
prés comment cela est arrivé. [Coniecture historique.]

   Les hommes remarquant qu'ils estoient les plus robustes,
& que dans le rapport du Sexe ils avoient quelqu'avantage de
corps, se figurerent qu'il leur appartenoit en tout. [Comment
les hommes se sont rendus les maistres.] La consequence
n'étoit pas grande pour les femmes au commencement du
mon-[17]-de. Les choses estoient dans un état tres different
d'aujourd'huy, il n'y avoir point encore de gouvernement,
de science, d'employ, ny de religion établie: Et les idées de
dépendence n'avoient rien de tout de facheux. Ie m'imagine
qu'on vivoit alors comme des enfans, & que tout l'avantage
estoit comme celuy du jeu: les hommes & les femmes qui
estoient alors simples & innocens, s'employoient également à
la culture de la terre ou à la chasse comme font encore les
sauvages. L'homme alloit de son côté & la femme alloit du
sien; celuy qui apportoit d'avantage étoit aussi le plus estimé.

   Les incommoditez & les suites de la grossesse diminuant
les forces des femmes durant quelqu'interualle, & les em-
peschant de travailler comme auparavant, [18]l'assistance de
leurs maris leur devenoit absolument necessaire, & encore plus
losqu'elles avoient des enfans. Tout se terminoit à quelques
regards d'estime & de preferance, pendant que les familles
ne furent composées que de pere & de la mere avec quelques
petits enfans. Mais lors qu'elles se furent aggrandies, & qu'il
y eut en une mesme maison, le pere & la mere du pere, les
enfans des enfans, avec des freres & des soeurs, des aînez & des
cadets; la dépendence s'étendit, & devint aînsi plus sensible.
On vid la maistresse se soûmettre à son mary, le fils honorer
le pere, celuy-cy commander à ses enfans: & comme il est
tres-difficile que les freres s'accordent toûjours parfaitement,
on peut juger qu'ils ne furent pas long-temps ensemble qu'il
n'arrivast entr'eux quel-[19]-que different. L'aîné plus fort

has always prevailed. The greatest empires of Asia were at their start the [16] work of usurpers and brigands, and the spoils of the kingdom of the Greeks and the Romans were claimed only by those who believed themselves strong enough to resist their masters and dominate their fellows. This [kind of] conduct is no less apparent in any society. And if men display it with regard to their peers, there is a great likelihood that each has first behaved the same way (with all the more reason) with respect to his wife. Here, approximately, is how this came about.

Men, noticing that they were the strongest and that with regard to sex they had some physical advantage, imagined that a similar superiority prevailed for them in all things. This had no great consequence for women at the world's [17] birth. Things were then in a very different state than they are today, for no government, education, profession, or religion was yet established—and the concept of subservience implied nothing very troublesome. I imagine that early people lived like children and that all the dominance behavior that was displayed seemed like play. Men and women, who were at that time simple and innocent, labored equally at cultivating the earth or hunting—as savages still do. Man went his way, and woman went hers. The one who produced most was also most honored.

Since the inconveniences and the consequences of pregnancy sapped the strength of women from time to time and prevented them from working as they otherwise would, [18] the assistance of their husbands became absolutely necessary to them. [This was] even more the case when they had children. Everything was limited to a few signs of respect and rank while families were composed only of a father and a mother with several small children. But when they expanded and the father, and the mother of the father, the children of the children—with brothers and sisters, elders and juniors—occupied the same house, subordination increased and, consequently, became more obvious. We would see the mistress submitting to her husband, sons honoring their father, he ruling his children. And since it is difficult for brothers always to be perfectly in agreement, we may assume that they were not together long before a dispute developed

que les autres, ne leur voulut rien ceder. La force obligea les petits de ployer sous les plus grands. Et les filles suivirent l'exemple de leur mere.

Il est aisé de s'imaginer qu'il y eut alors dans les maisons plus de fonctions differentes; que les femmes obligées d'y demeurer pour élever leurs enfans, prirent le soin du dedans: que les hommes estant plus libres & plus robustes se chargerent du dehors, & qu'aprés la mort du pere & de la mere, l'aîné voulut dominer. Les filles accoûtumées à demeurer au logis, ne penserent point à en sortir. Quelques cadets mécontens & plus fiers que les autres refusant de prendre le joug, furent obligez de se retirer & de faire bande à part. Plusieurs de mesme humeur s'estant rencon-[20]-trez s'entretinrent de leur fortune, & firent aisément amitié: & se voyans tous sans bien, chercherent les moyens d'en acquerir. Comme il n'y en avoit point d'autre que de prendre celuy d'autruy, ils se jetterent sur celuy qui estoit le plus en main; & pour le conserver plus surement, se saisirent en même temps des maistres ausquels il appartenoit.

La dépendance volontaire qui estoit dans les familles cessa par cette invasion. Les peres & les meres furent contrains d'obeïr; avec leur enfans à un injuste usurpateur: & la condition des femmes en devint plus facheuse qu'auparavant. Car au lieu qu'elles n'avoient épousé jusque-là que des gens de leur famille qui les traittoient comme soeurs; elles furent aprés cela contraintes de prendre pour maris des étrangers [21] inconnus qui ne les considererent que comme le plus beau du butin.

C'est l'ordinaire des vainqueurs de mépriser ceux d'entre les vaincus, qu'ils estiment les plus foibles: Et les femmes le paroissant, à cause de leurs fonctions qui demandoient moins de force, furent regardées comme étant inferieures aux hommes.

Quelques uns se contenterent d'une premiere usurpation mais d'autres plus ambitieux, encouragez par le succés de la victoire voulurent pousser plus loin leurs conquétes. Les femmes estant trop humaines pour servir à ces injustes desseins, on les laisa [*sic*] au logis: & les hommes furent choisis comme étant plus propres aux entreprises où l'on a bésoin de force. En cét estat l'on n'estimoit les choses qu'autant

among them. [19] The elder, being stronger than the others, would not want to yield anything to them. Force would compel the lesser to submit to the greater, and daughters would follow the example of their mother.

It is easy to imagine that at this point a greater variety of specialized functions developed within the household: that women, forced to remain at home to raise their children, took care of the indoors; that men, being freer and more vigorous, assumed responsibility for the out-of-doors. After the deaths of the father and the mother the eldest son would want to rule. Daughters, accustomed to stay at home, would not think of leaving. Some malcontent younger sons (more assertive than others and refusing to remain under the yoke) would be forced to depart and to set up a separate band. Many men of like mind (joining forces [20] to provide for their futures) would easily strike up a friendship. Seeing themselves totally without property, they would look for ways to acquire some. As there was no other way but to take it from someone else, they would throw themselves on those who were closest at hand. And to secure [their booty] more firmly, they would (at the same time) seize the owners to which it had belonged.

The voluntary subservience that was customary in families ended with this invasion. Fathers and mothers, with their children, were forced to submit to an unjust usurper, and the condition of women became more unfortunate than before. For whereas up until that time they had married only men of their own family, who treated them like sisters, women were forced to take strangers as husbands-[21]-men who viewed them only as the most beautiful of spoils.

Conquerors ordinarily despise the weakest among their victims. And women, appearing weak because their activities required less strength, were viewed as men's inferiors.

Some men would be content with their first conquest, but others—more ambitious [and] encouraged by the success of victory—would push their conquests further. Women, being too humane to participate in these unfair projects, were left at home, and men were drafted—as being more fit for enterprises where strength is needed. In this situation, things were valued according to how they were believed to serve the end [22] sought. The lust for dominion having become one

qu'on les croyoit utiles à la fin qu'on se **[22]** proposoit; & le
desir de dominer estant devenu une des plus fortes passions,
& ne pouvant estre satisfait que par la violence & l'injustice,
il ne faut pas s'estonner que les hommes en ayant esté seuls
les instrumens, ayent esté preferez aux femmes. Ils servirent
à retenir les conquêtes qu'ils avoient faites: on ne prit que
leurs conseils pour establir la tyrannie, parce qu'il n'y avoit
qu'eux qui les pussent executer: & de cette sorte la douceur
& l'humanité des femmes fut cause qu'elles n'eurent point de
part au gouvernement des Etats.

L'exemple des Princes fut bien-tost imité par leurs
sujets. Chacun voulut l'emporter sur son compagnon: Et
les particuliers commencerent à dominer plus absolument sur
leurs familles. Lors qu'un Seigneur se vid maistre **[23]** d'un
Peuple & d'un Païs considerable, il en forma un Royaume;
Il fit des loix pour le gouverner, prit des Officiers entre les
hommes, & esleva aux Charges ceux qui l'avoient mieux servy
dans ses entreprises. Une preferance si notable d'un sexe à
l'autre fit que les femmes furent encore moins considerées: &
leur humeur & leurs fonctions les éloignant du carnage & de
la guerre, on crut qu'elles n'étoient capables de contribuer à
la conservation des Royaumes, qu'en aydant à les peupler.

L'etablissement des Etats ne se pût faire sans mettre de
la distinction entre ceux qui les composoient. L'on introduisit
des marques d'honneur, qui servirent à les discerner; & on
inventa des signes de respect pour témoigner la difference
qu'on reconnois-**[24]**-soit entre eux. On joignit ainsi à l'idée
de la puissance, la soûmission exterieure que l'on rend à ceux
qui ont l'authorité entre les mains.

Il n'est pas necessaire de dire icy comment Dieu a esté
connu des hommes: mais il est constant qu'il en a esté adoré
depuis le commencement du monde. Pour le culte qu'on luy a
rendu, il n'a esté regulier que depuis qu'on s'est assemblé pour
faire des Societez publiques. Comme l'on estoit accoûtumé
à reverer les puissances par des marques de respect, on crût
qu'il falloit aussi honnorer Dieu par quelques ceremonies,
qui servissent à témoigner les sentimens qu'on avoit de sa
grandeur. [Comment les femmes n'ont point eu de part aux
ministeres de la religion parmi les payens.] On bâtit des
Temples; on institua des Sacrifices: & les hommes qui estoient

of the strongest passions (one that can only be satisfied by violence and injustice), it is not surprising that men (having been its only instruments) were preferred to women. They helped to retain the conquests that they had made. Their counsel was all that was needed to establish tyranny, for they were the only ones who could carry out tyrannical acts. And, thus, the gentleness and humanity of women was the reason that they had no share in the government of states.

The example set by princes was quickly imitated by their subjects. Each wanted to impose his will on his companions, and private individuals began to dominate their families more thoroughly. When a lord saw himself master [23] of a people and a considerable country, he formed a kingdom. He made laws to govern it, chose officers from among his men, and elevated to positions of authority those who had best served him in his projects. So notable a preference for one sex over the other caused women to be even less appreciated. Since their personalities and duties distanced them from carnage and war, women were believed to be capable of contributing to the preservation of kingdoms only by adding people to them.

States could only be established by making distinctions among the persons who formed them. Badges of honor, which helped people discern ranks, were introduced. Tokens of respect were invented to witness to the differences that were recognized [24] among people. Thus the idea of power was united with the external signs of submission that are displayed before those who hold authority.

It is not necessary to explain here how God came to be known by men, but it is certain that God has been worshipped since the beginning of the world. The ritual by which He is served was regularized only after formal societies were set up. As it was customary to revere authorities by displaying marks of respect, it was believed to be necessary to honor God by certain ceremonies that served to testify to our sense of His grandeur. Temples were built; sacrifices were instituted, and men, who were already heads of governments, [25] did not fail to busy themselves with a concern for the things that related to religion. Women, having already been predisposed by custom to the idea that everything was in the hands of

déja les maistres du Gouvernement [25] ne manquerent pas de
s'emparer encore du soin de ce qui concernoit la Religion: & la
coûtume ayant déja prévenu les femmes, que tout appartenoit
aux hommes, elles ne demanderent point d'avoir part au
ministere. L'idée qu'on avoit de Dieu s'étant extrémement
corrompuë par les fables & par les fictions poëtiques, l'on se
forgea des Divinitez mâles, & femelles: & l'on institua des
Prestresses pour le service de celles de leur sexe, mais ce ne
fut que sous la conduite & sous le bon plaisir des Prestres.

   L'on a veu aussi quelques fois des femmes gouverner de
grands Estats: mais il ne faut pas pour cela s'imaginer, que
c'est qu'elles y eussent esté appellées, par esprit de restitution,
c'est qu'elles avoient eu l'adresse de disposer les affaires, de
sorte qu'on [26] ne pouvoit leur oster l'authorité d'entre les
mains. Il y a aujourd'huy des états hereditaires où les femelles
succedent aux mâles, pour estre Reines ou Princesses; mais
il y a sujet de croire, que si on a laissé d'abord tomber ces
Royaume-là [sic] en quenoüille, ce n'a esté que pour éviter
de tomber en guerre civile: & si l'on a permis les Regences,
on ne l'a fait que dans la pensée que les meres, qui aiment
toûjours extraordinairement leurs enfans, prendroient un soin
particulier de leurs états, pendant leur minorité.

   [Pourquoy elles n'ont point eu de part aux sciences.] Ainsi
les femmes n'ayant eu à faire que leur menage, & y trouvant
assez dequoy s'occuper, il ne faut pas s'étonner qu'elles
n'ayent point inventé de sciences, dont la pluspart n'ont esté
d'abord, que l'ouvrage & l'oc-[27]-cupation des oysifs & des
faineants. Les Prestres des Egyptiens qui n'avoient pas grand
chose à faire, s'amusoient ensemble à parler des effets de la
nature, qui les touchoient davantage. A force de raisonner,
ils firent des observations dont le bruit excita la curiosité
de quelques hommes qui les vinrent rechercher. Les sciences
n'étans encore qu'au berceau, ne tirerent point les femmes
de leurs maisons: outre que la jalousie, qui broüilloit déja
les maris, leur eût fait croire qu'elles eussent esté visiter
les Prestres plûtost pour l'amour de leur personne, que des
connoissances qu'ils avoient.

   Lorsque plusieurs en furent imbus, ils s'assemblerent en
certains lieux pour en parler plus à leur aise. Chacun disant
ses pensées, [28] les sciences se perfectionnerent. On fit des

men, did not ask to share the ministry. Since the concept of God was extremely corrupted by fables and poetic fictions, male and female divinities were fabricated. Priestesses were instituted to serve the gods of their sex—but only under the supervision and with the consent of priests.

From time to time, women have been seen as rulers of great states, but it need not be supposed that they were called to this honor in a spirit of fairness. [They rose to office because] they have had the ability to rule—such that no [26] one could rip authority from their hands. Today there are hereditary states where females succeed males to become queens or princesses, but there are grounds for believing that when kingdoms have been allowed to fall to the distaff side, the only reason has been to avoid a lapse into civil war. If female regents were tolerated, they were only established with the assumption that mothers (who always love their children extraordinarily) would take particular care of their children's legacies during their minorities.

Since women were not permitted to work anywhere but at home and found enough to occupy them there, it is not surprising that they did not invent the sciences (most of which were, at the start, simply the work and [27] occupation of loafers and idlers). Egyptian priests, who did not have a great deal to do, amused themselves by talking together about the phenomena of nature that impressed them most. By dint of reasoning [together], they made observations—the news of which excited the curiosity of various men who joined them in research. The sciences, which were still only in the cradle, did not draw women from their homes. Besides, jealousy, which already agitated their husbands, would have made men believe that women visited priests rather for love of their persons than for the knowledge that these men possessed.

When many men had been imbued with learning, they congregated in certain places where they could talk at their ease. Each spoke his thoughts, [28] and the fields of knowledge were perfected. Academies, to which women were not called, were set up. And, in this way, women were excluded from learning as they were from everything else.

The constraints binding women would not prevent some of them from gaining access to the conversation or the writings

Academies, où l'on n'appella point les femmes; & elles furent
de cette sorte excluës des sciences, comme elles l'étoient du
reste.
    La contrainte dans laquelle on les retenoit, n'empécha
pas que quelques-unes n'eussent l'entretien ou les écrits des
sçavans: elles égalerent en peu de temps les plus habiles: &
comme on s'étoit déja forgé une bien-seance importune, les
hommes n'osant venir chez elles, ni les autres femmes s'y
trouver, de peur qu'on n'en prist ombrage, elles ne firent
point de disciples ni de sectateurs, & tout ce qu'elles avoient
acquis de lumiere mouroit inutilement avec elles.
    Si l'on observe comment les modes s'introduisent &
s'embellissent de jour en jour, on juge-[29]-ra aisément qu'au
commencement du monde, on ne s'en mettoit gueres en
peine. Tout y étoit simple & grossier. On ne songeoit qu'au
necessaire. Les hommes écorchoient des bêtes; & en attachant
les peaux ensemble s'en ajustoient des habits. Le commode
vint aprés: & chacun s'habillant à sa guise, les manieres qu'on
trouva qui seoient le mieux, ne furent point negligées: & ceux
qui étoient sous le mesme Prince ne manquerent pas de se
conformer à luy.
    [Pourquoy les femmes se sont iettées dans la bagatelle.]
Il n'en fut pas des modes comme du gouvernement & des
sciences. Les femmes y eurent part avec les hommes: & ceux
cy remarquant qu'elles en étoient plus belles, n'eurent garde
de les en priver: & les uns & les autres trouvant qu'on avoit
meil-[30]-leure grace & qu'on plaisoit davantage avec certains
ajustemens, les rechercherent à l'envy: mais les occupations
des hommes estant plus grandes & plus importantes, les
empêcherent de s'y appliquer si fort.
    Les femmes montrerent en cela leur prudence & leur
adresse. S'appercevant que les ornemens étrangers les
faisoient regarder des hommes avec plus de douceur, qu'ainsi
leur condition en étoit plus supportable, elles ne negligerent
rien de ce qu'elles crûrent pouvoir servir à se rendre plus
aimables. Elles y employerent l'or, l'argent, de les pierreries,
aussi-tost qu'elles furent en vogue: & voyant que les hommes
leur avoient osté le moyen de se signaler par l'esprit, elles
s'appliquerent uniquement à ce qui pouvoit les faire paroî-
[31]-tre plus agreables. Elles s'en sont depuis fort bien

of learned men. In short order these women would equal the most adroit men. [But] as an unfortunate code of propriety had already been established—men not daring to come to their homes nor other women to seek them out for fear that someone might take offence, they did not attract disciples nor followers, and all the enlightenment they acquired died uselessly with them.

If we notice how fashions are introduced and embellish themselves from day to day, we may **[29]** readily infer that at the beginning of the world people scarcely took any trouble with such things. Everything was simple and crude. Only necessity was attended to. Men would skin beasts and, by attaching the pelts together, fit themselves with garments. Comfort came later. Each person dressed himself in his own way, and the styles that were found to fit best were adopted. (People who were subject to the same prince did not fail to conform to him.)

Fashion did not develop like government and science. Women shared it with men. Men, who noticed that style rendered women more beautiful, did not care to deprive them of it. Both men and women, finding that **[30]** certain adjustments would give a person more grace and make one more attractive, (competing to be envied) sought those things, but the greater and more important duties that occupied men prevented them from applying themselves to fashion as vigorously [as women].

In this area women showed prudence and skill. Perceiving that exotic ornaments would cause men to view them with greater tenderness (that their condition would thus be more supportable), they neglected nothing that they thought would serve to make them more appealing. They used gold, silver, and stones—as soon as these became popular. And seeing that men had deprived them of the means to distinguish themselves through their intellects, they applied themselves uniquely to things that could make them appear **[31]** more attractive. They have, subsequently, been very successful at this, and their trappings and their beauty have brought them more consideration than all the books and all the learning in the world would have. This custom was too well established to permit any subsequent change. The practice has been

trouvées, & leurs ajustemens & leur beauté les ont fait
considerer plus que n'auroient fait tous les livres & toute la
science du monde. La coûtume en estoit trop bien établie
pour recevoir quelque changement dans la suite; la pratique
en a passé jusques à nous: & il semble que c'est une tradition
trop ancienne pour y trouver quelque chose à redire.

Il paroist manifestement par cette conjecture historique &
conforme à la maniere d'agir si ordinaire à tous les hommes,
que ce n'a esté que par empire qu'ils se sont reservé les
avantages exterieurs, ausquels les femmes n'ont point de part.
Car afin de pouvoir dire que ç'a esté par raison, il faudroit
qu'ils ne les communicassent entr'eux qu'à ceux [32] qui en
sont les plus capables: qu'ils en fissent le choix avec un juste
discernement; qu'ils n'admissent à l'étude que ceux en qui
ils auroient reconnu plus de disposition pour les sciences;
qu'ils n'élevassent aux emplois que ceux qui y seroient les
plus propres, qu'on en exclust tous les autres, & qu'enfin on
n'appliquast chacun qu'aux choses qui leur seroient les plus
convenables. [Ce que devroient faire les hommes pour iustifier
leur conduite à l'égard des femmes.]

[Comment les homes entrent dans les emplois.] Nous
voyons que c'est le contraire qui se pratique, & qu'il n'y
a que le hazard, la necessité, ou l'interest, qui engage les
hommes dans les états differens de la societé civile. Les enfans
apprennent le métier de leur pere, parce qu'on leur en a
toûjours parlé. Tel est contraint de prendre une robe, qui
aimeroit mieux une épée, si cela étoit à son choix; [33] & on
seroit le plus habile homme du monde qu'on n'entrera jamais
dans une charge, si l'on n'a pas dequoy l'acheter.

Combien y a-t-il de gens dans la poussiere, qui se fussent
signalez si on les avoit un peu poussez? Et des païsans qui
seroient de grands docteurs si on les avoit mis à l'étude? On
seroit assez mal fondé de prétendre que les plus habiles gens
d'aujourd'huy soient ceux de leur temps qui ont eu plus de
disposition pour les choses en quoy ils éclatent; & que dans
un si grand nombre de personnes ensevelies dans l'ignorance,
il n'y en a point qui avec les mêmes moyens qu'ils ont eu, se
fussent rendu plus capables.

Sur quoy donc peut-on assurer que les femmes y soient
moins propres que nous, puisque [34] ce n'est pas le hazard,

passed down to us, and it seems to be a tradition too ancient to be contradicted.

It appears clear from this historical conjecture (and consistent with the kind of behavior so common to all men) that men have, by mastery alone, reserved to themselves public privileges that women have not shared. To be able to claim that this discrimination has been rational, it would have to be the case that men would never share their advantages among themselves except with males [32] who are most fit for them—that men would have been chosen [for places in society] with accurate discernment: that they would have admitted to education only those in whom they recognized a superior disposition for academic work, that they would have elevated to the professions only those who would be most fit for them, that all others be excluded, and, finally, that each man be assigned only things that be most appropriate for him.

We see that the contrary is customary and that only chance, necessity or influence enlists men into society's different posts. Children take up their father's vocation because they are raised hearing about it. Someone is forced to don the gown who, if given a choice, would prefer the sword; [33] and be he the most competent man in the world, he would never win a post unless he has what it takes to buy it.

How many people sprawl in the dust who would have distinguished themselves if they had had a little push? And how many peasants would have been great doctors if they had been given an education? We have little basis for pretending that the most highly capable people of the day are those of their generation who have the greatest natural aptitude for the things in which they shine—and that among such a great number of people engulfed in ignorance there is none who would excel them if given the same means that others have had.

On what then can we base the claim that women are less competent than we are—since [34] it is not chance but insurmountable necessity that prevents them from participating in things? I do not maintain that all women are fit for academic life and the professions nor that any one

mais une necessité insurmontable, qui les empesche d'y avoir
part. Ie ne soutiens pas qu'elles soient toutes capables des
sciences & des emplois, ni que chacune le soit de tous:
personne ne le prétend non plus des hommes; mas [*sic*] je
demande seulement qu'à prendre les deux Sexes en general, on
reconnoisse dans l'un autant de disposition que dans l'autre.

[Comparaison des ieunes enfans de l'un & de l'autre Sexe.]
Que l'on regarde seulement ce qui se passe dans les petits
divertissemens des enfans. Les filles y font paroître plus de
gentillesse, plus de genie, plus d'adresse; lorsque la crainte ou
la honte n'étouffent point leurs pensées, elles parlent d'une
maniere plus spirituelle & plus agreable. Il y a dans leurs
entretiens plus de vivacité, plus d'enjoüement, & plus de
liberté: elles appren-[35]-nent bien plus vîte ce qu'on leur
enseigne; quand on les applique également: elles sont plus
assiduës, & plus patientes au travail, plus soûmises, plus
modestes & plus retenuës. En un mot, on remarque en elles
dans un degré plus parfait, toutes les qualitez excellentes, qui
font juger que les jeunes hommes en qui elles se trouvent, sont
plus propres aux grandes choses que leurs égaux.

Cependant, quoique ce qui paroist dans les deux Sexes,
lors qu'ils ne sont encore qu'au berçeau, suffise déja pour faire
juger que le plus beau donne aussi plus de belles esperances,
on n'y a aucun égard. Les maîtres & les instructions ne
sont que pour les hommes: on prend un soin tout particulier
de les instruire de tout ce qu'on croit le plus propre [36] à
former l'esprit, pendant qu'on laisse languir les femmes, dans
l'oisiveté, dans la molesse [*sic*], & dans l'ignorance ou remper
dans les exercices les plus bas & les plus vils.

Mais aussi, il ne faut que des yeux pour reconnoître, qu'il
est en cela de deux Sexes, comme de deux freres dans une
famille, où le cadet fait voir souvent, nonobstant la negligence
avec laquelle on l'éleve, que son aîné n'a pardessus luy que
l'avantage d'étre venu le premier.

[Que l'étude est inutile à la pluspart des hommes.] A
quoy sert ordinairement aux hommes l'éducation qu'on leur
donne: elle est inutile à la pluspart pour la fin qu'on s'y
propose: & elle n'empêche pas que beaucoup ne tombent dans
le déreglement & dans le vice, & que d'autres ne demeurent
toûjours ignorans, & même ne devien-[37]-nent encore plus

woman is suited to all occupations. (No one pretends to this even among men). But I ask only that considering the two sexes in general, we recognize that one has as much aptitude as the other.

Let us contemplate what transpires in the little pastimes of children. Girls seem the gentlest, most talented, and cleverest. When fear or bashfulness does not bind their thoughts, they speak in a most intelligent and agreeable way. There is in their conversation the greatest vivacity, sprightliness, and freedom. They [35] more quickly comprehend what they are taught. When we pay them equal attention, girls are more diligent, and more patient at work, more obedient, more modest and more self-controlled. In a word: we see in them to the highest degree all the excellent qualities that are assumed, when they are found in young men, to make these boys more fit than their fellows for great things.

However, although the behavior of the two sexes when they are still in their cradles already suffices to convince us that the fairest sex also offers the most attractive potential, we pay no mind. Tutors and instruction are only for men. We take particular care to teach males everything that we believe is most suited [36] to shaping the mind, while we allow females to languish in idleness, softness, and ignorance—or to grovel in the lowest, most base activities.

But, likewise, it only takes eyes to see that the two sexes are in this like two brothers in a family—where the younger often shows (notwithstanding the negligence with which he is raised) that his elder [sibling] is superior to him only in being born first.

What end does the education given men ordinarily serve? It is mostly useless for the purpose for which it is proposed. It does not prevent many of them from falling into dissoluteness and vice and others of them from remaining permanently ignorant (even becoming [37] yet more foolish than they were). If they have some decency, playfulness, and civility, they lose it through education. Everything grates on them, and they grate on everything. One might say that they had spent their whole youths travelling in a country where they had associated solely with savages (so much rudeness and coarseness in manners do they take home with them). What

sots qu'ils n'étoient. S'ils avoient quelque chose d'honneste, d'enjoüé, & de civil, ils le perdent par l'étude. Tout les choque, & ils choquent tout; on diroit qu'ils ne se seroient occupez durant leur jeunesse, qu'à voyager dans un païs où ils n'auroient frequenté que des sauvages; tant ils raportent chez eux de rudesse & de grossiereté dans leurs manieres. Ce qu'ils ont appris est comme des marchandises de contrebande, qu'ils n'oseroient, ou ne sçauroient debiter: & s'ils veulent rentrer dans le monde, & y bien joüer leur personnage, ils sont obligez d'aller à l'école des Dames, pour y apprendre la politesse, la complaisance, & tout le dehors qui fait aujourd'huy l'essentiel des honnestes gens.

Si l'on consideroit cela de prés, [38] au lieu de mépriser les femmes, parce qu'elles n'ont pas de part aux sciences, on les en estimeroit heureuses: puis que si d'un costé, elles sont privées par là des moyens de faire valoir les talens, & les avantages qui leur sont propres; de l'autre costé, elles n'ont pas l'occasion de les gâter ou de les perdre: & nonobstant cette privation, elles croissent en vertu, en esprit & en bonne grace, à mesure qu'elles croissent en âge: & si l'on comparoit sans préjudice les jeunes hommes au sortir de leurs études, avec des femmes de leur âge, & d'un esprit proportionné, sans sçavoir comment les uns & les autres ont esté élevez, on croiroit qu'ils ont eu une éducation toute contraire.

L'exterieur seul, l'air du visage, les regards, le marcher, la contenance, les gestes, ont dans [39] les femmes quelque chose de posé, de sage, & d'honneste, qui les distingue assez des hommes. Elles observent en tout exactement la bien-seance: on ne peut estre plus retenu qu'elles le sont. On n'entend point sortir de leur bouche de paroles à double entente. Les moindres équivoques blessent leurs oreilles, & elles ne peuvent souffrir la veuë de tout ce qui choque la pudeur.

Le commun des hommes a une conduite toute opposée. Leur marcher est souvent precipité, leurs gestes bizarres, leurs yeux mal reglez: & ils ne se divertissent jamais davantage, que lors qu'ils s'entretiennent & se repaissent des choses qu'il faudroit taire ou cacher.

[Comparison des femmes avec les Sçavans.] Que l'on fasse conversation ensemble ou séparement avec les femmes, & avec ce qu'on appelle [40] sçavant dans le monde. On verra qu'elle

they have learned is like contraband merchandise that they do not dare or do not know how to sell. If they wish to enter the world and cut a good figure there, they are obliged to go to the "school of women" to learn courtesy, kindness and all the visible signs that make up the essence of a gentleman today.

If we consider this closely, [38] instead of despising women because they have no share of learning, we will esteem them fortunate. For if, on the one hand, they have been deprived of the means to cause their talents and unique aptitudes to be respected, on the other hand they have not had the occasion to spoil or lose these talents and aptitudes. And in spite of this deprivation, they grow in virtue, in intellect, and in good grace in proportion to their growth in years. If, without prejudice, we compare young men at the end of their schooling with women of their same age and equivalent intelligence (without knowing how both were raised), we would believe that they had had completely contrary educations.

The exterior alone (the appearance of the face, the looks, the carriage, the countenance, the gestures) has in [39] women some aspect of poise, discretion, and gentility that distinguishes them decisively from men. Women are exact in observing propriety in all things. No one could be more reserved than they are. Words with double meanings never pass their lips. The slightest equivocation wounds their ears, and they cannot suffer the sight of anything that offends modesty.

The majority of men display quite the opposite conduct. Their carriage is often precipitous, their gestures bizarre, their eyes poorly controlled, and they never amuse themselves so much as when they talk about and feed on things that should be kept quiet or hidden.

Have a conversation with women (in a group or individually) and with men [40] who have a reputation for being knowledgeable. You will see what a difference there is between them. You might say that men, while studying, put into their heads only those things that serve to suffocate their intellects and bring them to confusion. Only a few express themselves with clarity, and the struggle they have to get their words out spoils the flavor of whatever they can say [that is] of value.

difference il y a entre les uns & les autres. On diroit que
ce que les hommes se mettent dans la téte en étudiant ne
sert qu'à boucher leur esprit, & à y porter la confusion. Peu
s'énoncent avec netteté; & la peine qu'ils ont à arracher leurs
paroles, fait perdre le goust à ce qu'ils peuvent dire de bon; &
à moins qu'ils ne soient fort spirituels, & avec des gens de leur
sorte, ils ne peuvent soûtenir une heure de conversation.

Les femmes, au contraire, disent nettement & avec
ordre ce qu'elles sçavent: les paroles ne leur coûtent rien;
elles commencent & continüent comme il leur plaist; &
leur imagination fournit toûjours d'une maniere inépuisable,
lorsqu'elles sont en liberté. Elles ont le don de pro-[41]-poser
leurs sentimens avec une douceur & une complaisance, qui
servent autant que la raison à les insinûer: au lieu que les
hommes les proposent ordinairement d'une maniere seche &
dure,[.]

Si l'on met quelque question sur le tapis en presence des
femmes un peu éclairées; elles en découvrent bien plûtost le
point de veuë: Elles la regardent par plus de faces: ce que
l'on dit de vray trouve plus de prise dans leur esprit; & quand
on s'y connoist un peu, & qu'on ne leur est point suspect, on
remarque que les préjugez qu'elles ont, ne sont pas si forts
que ceux des hommes, & les mettent moins en garde contre
la verité qu'on avance. Elles sont éloignées de l'esprit de
contradiction & de dispute, auquel les sçavans sont si sujets:
elles ne pointillent point [42] vainement sur les mots, & ne
se servent point de ces termes scientifiques & mysterieux, si
propres à couvrir l'ignorance, & tout ce qu'elles disent est
intelligible & sensible.

J'ay pris plaisir à m'entretenir avec des femmes de toutes
les conditions differentes, que j'ay peu rencontrer à la ville
& aux champs, pour en découvrir le fort & le foible; & j'ay
trouvé dans celles que la necessité, ou le travail n'avoient
point rendu stupides, plus de bon sens que dans la pluspart
des ouvrages, qui sont beaucoup estimez parmy les sçavans
vulgaires.

En parlant de Dieu, pas une ne s'est avisée de me dire,
qu'elle se l'imaginoit, sous la forme d'un venerable vieillard
[opinion d'un grand Philosophe.] Elles disoient au contraire,
qu'elles ne pouvoient se l'imaginer, c'est à dire, [43] se le

Unless they are very bright or in the company of men of their own kind, they cannot sustain an hour's conversation.

Women, on the other hand, state what they know clearly and with order. Words cause them no trouble. They begin and continue as it pleases them. When they are at liberty, their imaginations are inexhaustible. They have the gift of [41] presenting their ideas with a gentleness and good nature that works as well as reason in winning assent—while men, in their turn, usually employ a dry, hard style.

If some topic is laid on the table in the presence of moderately bright women, they soon discover the point at issue. They consider it from many sides, and whatever truth is spoken takes strong hold on their minds. When we know a little about the matter at hand and, therefore, are not suspect to them, we find that they do not cling to prejudices as strongly as men and that they put themselves less on guard against truth[s] that we propose. The spirit of contradiction and disputatiousness to which educated men are so inclined is alien to women. They do not bicker [42] in vain about words and do not use mysterious, technical terms (which are so useful for concealing ignorance). Everything that they say is intelligible and sensible.

I have enjoyed talking with women from all different stations in life (whom I have been able to meet in the city and in the country) to discover their strengths and weaknesses. And I have found in those whom want and labor did not render stupid more common sense than in the majority of the works that are so highly esteemed by the ordinary literati.

In speaking of God not one woman was moved to tell me that she imagined Him in the guise of a venerable old man. On the contrary, they said that they could not picture Him, that is to say, [43] represent Him to themselves by some image resembling men. They imagined that there is a God, because they could not comprehend that either they or the things around them could be the works of chance or of some creature—and [because] the course of their affairs, not being a product of their prudent decisions (for success rarely came by the routes they had taken), it seemed that it had to be the action of a divine providence.

representer sous quelque idée semblable aux hommes: qu'elles
concevoient qu'il y a un Dieu; parce qu'elles ne comprenoient
pas que ni elles ni ce qui les environne soient les ouvrages du
hazard, ou de quelque creature: & que la conduite de leurs
affaires n'estant pas un effet de leur prudence, parce que le
succez en venoit rarement par les voyes qu'elles avoient prises,
il faloit que ce fût l'effet d'une providence divine.

Quand je leur ay demandé ce qu'elles pensoient de leur
ame; elles ne m'ont pas répondu que c'est une flamme fort
subtile, ou la disposition des organes de leur corps, ny
qu'elle soit capable de s'étendre ou de se resserver [ce sont
des opinions de Philosophes]: elles répondoient au contraire,
qu'elles sentoient bien qu'elle est distinguée de leurs corps, &
que [44] tout ce qu'elles en pouvoient dire de plus certain,
c'est qu'elles ne croyoient pas qu'elle fust rien de semblable à
aucune des choses qu'elles appercevoient par les sens; & que si
elles avoient étudié, elles sçauroient précisément ce que c'est.

Il n'y a pas une garde qui s'avise de dire comme les
medecins, que leurs malades se portent mieux, parce que la
Faculté Coctrice fait loüablement ses fonctions: & lors qu'elles
voyent sortir une si grande quantité de sang par une veine,
elles se raillent de ceux qui nient, qu'elle ait communication
avec les autres par la circulation.

Lorsque j'ay voulu sçavoir pourquoy elles croyoient que
les pierres exposées au Soleil & aux pluyes du midy, s'usent
plûtost que celles qui font au Septen-[45]-trion; nulle n'a esté
assez simple pour me répondre, que cela vient de ce que la
Lune les mord à belles dents, comme se l'imaginent assez
plaisamment quelques Philosophes; mais que c'est l'ardeur
du Soleil qui les desséche: & que les pluyes survenant les
détrempent plus facilement.

J'ay demandé tout exprés à plus de vingt, si elles
ne croyoient pas que Dieu puisse faire par une puissance
obedientielle ou extraordinaire, qu'une pierre soit élevée à la
vision beatifique [questions de Scholastique]: mais je n'en ay
pû tirer autre chose, sinon qu'elles croyoient que je me voulois
moquer d'elles par cette demande.

Le plus grand fruit que l'on puisse esperer des sciences;
c'est le discernement & la justesse pour distinguer ce qui
est vray & évident, d'avec ce qui est faux & [46] obscur, &

When I have asked them what they thought about their souls, they have not told me that the soul is a very subtle flame or the disposition of the organs of the body—nor that it is capable of extension or contraction. On the contrary, they report that they clearly sense that the soul is separate from the body and that **[44]** all that they could say about it for certain is that they did not believe that the soul had any resemblance to any thing that they perceived by the senses—and that if they had been educated they would have known precisely what it is!

No nurse thinks to say, like doctors, that her patients improve because the "concocting faculty" commendably performs its functions. And when nurses see a lot of blood run from a vein, they scoff at those who deny that a vein connects with others for the circulation of blood.

When I wanted to know how women explain the fact that stones exposed to the sun and to the rain in the South wear away sooner than stones in the North, **[45]** none has been so simple-minded as to tell me that it happens because the moon chews them to pieces—as some philosophers so amusingly imagine. But [women say] that it is the heat of the sun that dries the stones out, and, when rain follows, they dissolve more easily.

I have asked twenty or more women if they do not believe that God could (by a dispensation or extraordinary power) cause a stone to be elevated to the beatific vision. But I have not been able to get anything out of them—except that they think that I want to tease them with this question.

The greatest advantage that we can hope for from education is discernment and accuracy in distinguishing what is true and evident from what is false and **[46]** obscure (so that we can avoid falling into error or misunderstanding). We are strongly inclined to believe that men (at least those who pass for educated men) have this advantage over women. Nevertheless, if we have a little of this accuracy of which I speak, we will find that it is one of the qualities that men most lack. For not only are they obscure and confused in their speech (its quality of obscurity is often their only means for intimidating and winning the confidence of simple, credulous persons), but they even reject what is clear and evident

pour éviter ainsi de tomber dans l'erreur, & la méprise. On est assez porté à croire que les hommes, au moins ceux qui passent pour sçavans, ont cét avantage pardessus les femmes. Neantmoins si l'on a un peu de cette justesse dont je parle, on trouvera que c'est une des qualitez qui leur manque le plus. Car non seulement ils sont obscurs, & confus dans leur discours, & ce n'est souvent que par cette qualité qu'ils dominent & qu'ils attirent la creance des personnes simples & credules: mais même ils rejettent ce qui est clair & évident, & se raillent de ceux qui parlent d'une maniere claire & intelligible, comme estant trop facile & trop commune; & sont les premiers à donner dans ce qu'on leur propose d'obscur, comme estant plus [47] mysterieux. Pour s'en convaincre il ne faut que les écouter avec un peu d'attention, & les obliger de s'expliquer.

Les Femmes ont une disposition bien éloignée de celle-là. [Elles ont la iustesse d'esprit.] On observe que celles qui ont un peu veu le monde, ne peuvent souffrir que leurs enfans même parlent Latin en leur presence: Elles se défient des autres qui le font: & disent assez souvant qu'elles craignent, qu'il n'y ait quelque impertinence cachée sous ces habillemens étrangers. Non seulement on ne leur entend point prononcer ces termes de sciences, qu'on appelle consacrez: mais même elles ne sçauroient les retenir, quoy qu'on les repetât souvent, & qu'elles ayent bonne memoire: & lors qu'on leur parle obscurement, elles avoüent de bonne foy qu'el-[48]-les n'ont pas assez de lumiere ou d'esprit pour entendre ce que l'on dit, ou bien, elles reconnoissent que ceux qui leur parlent de la sorte, ne sont pas assez instruits.

Enfin si l'on considere de quelle façon les hommes & les femmes produisent ce qu'ils sçavent, on jugera que les uns sont comme ces ouvriers, qui travaillent aux Carrieres, & qui en tirent avec peine les pierres toutes brutes & toutes informes: & que les femmes sont comme des Architectes, ou des Lapidaires habiles, qui sçavent polir & mettre aisément en oeuvre, & dans leur jour ce qu'elles ont entre les mains.

Non seulement on trouve un tres-grand nombre de femmes qui jugent, aussi-bien des choses que si on leur avoit donné la meilleure éducation, sans avoir [49] ni les préjugez, ni les idées confuses, si ordinaires aux sçavans; mais même on en

and rail against people who speak in a clear, intelligible manner—[accusing them] of being too facile and too common. And they are the first to fall for whatever obscurity anyone proposes to them, simply because it is more [47] mysterious. To convince ourselves of this we need only to listen to them with a little attention and force them to explain themselves.

The female disposition is quite distant from this. We see that women who have some experience of the world do not even allow their children to speak Latin in their presence. They distrust others who do so and often say that they fear that there might be some impertinence hidden in this strange clothing. Not only do we not hear them use the technical terms that are held to be sacrosanct, but they would not even be able to remember them—although we repeat them frequently and women have good memories. When someone speaks to women obscurely, they frankly confess that they [48] do not have enough enlightenment or intelligence to understand what is said—or they recognize that those who speak to them in this way are not sufficiently well informed.

Finally, if we reflect on how men and women exhibit what they know, we will conclude that [men] are like laborers who work in quarries painfully extracting crude, unformed stones and that women are like architects or skilled masons who know how to polish and adroitly fit in place the things they hold between their hands.

Not only do we find a very large number of women who understand things as well as if they had been given the best educations (minus [49] the prejudices and the confused ideas so common to cultivated men); but we often see many women whose common sense is so accurate that they discuss the things that pertain to the most esoteric sciences as if they had always studied them.

They express themselves gracefully. They know the art of finding the most beautiful current expressions and of saying more with one word than men do with many. And if we discuss languages in general with them, they have thoughts on this topic that are found only among the most skillful grammarians. Finally, we notice that they acquire more [knowledge] of language from practice alone than most men do from practice combined with study.

voit-beaucoup qui ont le bon sens si juste, qu'elles parlent sur
les objets des plus belles sciences, comme si elles les avoient
toûjours étudiées.

Elles s'énoncent avec grace. [Elles sçavent l'art de parler.]
Elles ont l'art de trouver les plus beaux termes de l'usage &
de faire plus comprendre en un mot, que les hommes avec
plusieurs; & si l'on s'entretient des Langues en general, elles
ont là dessus des pensées qui ne se trouvent que dans les plus
habiles Grammairiens. Enfin on remarque qu'elles tirent plus
de l'usage seul pour le langage, que la pluspart des hommes
ne font de l'usage joint à l'étude.

[Elles sçavent l'éloquence.] L'eloquence est un talent qui
leur est si naturel & si particulier, qu'on ne peut le leur
dis-[50]-puter. Elles persuadent tout ce qu'elles veulent. Elles
sçavent accuser & defendre sans avoir étudié les loix; & il
n'y a gueres de Iuges qui n'ayent éprouvé qu'elles valent des
Avocats. Se peut-il rien de plus fort & de plus éloquent
que les lettres de plusieurs Dames, sur tous les sujets qui
entrent dans le commerce ordinaire, & principalement sur les
passions, dont le ressort fait toute la beauté & tout le secret
de l'éloquence. Elles les touchent d'une maniére si délicate, &
les expriment si naïvement, qu'on est obligé d'avoüer qu'on
ne les sent pas autrement, & que toutes les Rhetoriques
du monde ne peuvent donner aux hommes ce qui ne coûte
rien aux femmes. Les pieces d'éloquence & de poesie, les
harangues, les predications & les discours ne sont point de
[51] trop haut goust pour elles; & rien ne manque à leurs
critiques, que de les faire selon les termes & les regles de l'art.

Ie m'attens bien que ce traité ne leur échapera pas non
plus: que plusieurs y trouveront à redire: les unes qu'il n'est
pas proportionné à la grandeur ni à la dignité du sujet; que le
tour n'en est pas assez galant; les manieres assez nobles; les
expressions assez fortes, ni assez élevées; qu'il y a des endroits
peu touchez; qu'on pourroit y ajoûter d'autre remarques
importantes: mais, j'espere aussi que ma bonne volonté, & le
dessein que j'ay pris de ne rien dire que de vray, & d'éviter
les expressions trop fortes, pour ne point sentir le Roman,
m'excuseront auprès d'elles.

Elles ont encore cét avantage que l'éloquence de l'action
est [Elles ont l'éloquence de l'action.] **[52]** en elles bien

No one can dispute that eloquence is a natural talent peculiar to them. [50] They persuade everyone they want to persuade. Without having studied the law, they know how to prosecute and defend. And there are scarcely any judges who have not tested their worth as advocates. There could be nothing stronger and more eloquent than many women's letters on all the subjects that form part of ordinary experience—and principally on the topic of the passions, whose course constitutes the beauty and whole secret of eloquence. Women treat these things in such a delicate manner and express them so artlessly that we must confess that we do not perceive them otherwise—and that all the rhetoric in the world could not give men this [skill] that costs women nothing. Works of graceful writing and poetry, speeches, sermons, and lectures are not [51] too sophisticated dishes for them. And nothing is left to their critics but to have these prepared according to the terms and rules of art.

I am very aware that this treatise will not escape their attention either and that many will find something to criticize: some that it is not adequate to the grandeur or to the dignity of its subject, that its style is not gallant enough, its manner appropriately noble, its terms sufficiently strong or sublime, and that there are inadequately developed passages to which other important remarks could be added. But I also hope that my good will and the intent that I have stated (to speak nothing but the truth and to avoid overly dramatic expressions so as not to give [this essay] the feeling of a novel) will excuse me to them.

Women have the advantage that their eloquence with gestures [52] is more lively than men's. It is enough to see in their faces that they intend to touch [one] in order to yield to what they want. They have a grand, noble air; a majestic, free carriage; virtuous deportment; natural gestures; engaging manners; ease of speech; and sweet, supple voices. When the beauty and good grace that accompany women's discourse penetrate the mind, they open the door to the heart for them. When women speak of good or evil, we see an integrity in their faces that is most persuasive. And when they want to excite love for virtue, they put their hearts into it. And the ideas that they express on the subject (arrayed in the ornaments of

plus vive, que dans les hommes. C'est assez de voir à leur mine qu'elles ont dessein de toucher, pour se rendre à ce qu'elles veulent. Elles ont l'air noble & grand, le port libre & majestueux, le maintien honneste, les gestes naturels, les manieres engageantes, la parole facile, & la voix douce & flexible. La beauté & la bonne grace, qui accompagnent leurs discours, losqu'ils entrent dans l'esprit: leur ouvrent la porte du coeur. Quand elles parlent du bien & du mal, on voit sur leur visage ce caractere d'honnesteté, qui rend la persuasion plus forte. Et lorsque c'est pour la vertu qu'elles veulent donner de l'amour, leur coeur paroist sur leurs lèvres; & l'idée qu'elles en expriment, revétuë des ornemens du discours & des graces qui leur [53] sont si particulieres, en paroist cent fois plus belle.

C'est un plaisir d'entendre une femme qui se mêle de plaider [elles sçavent le droit & entendent la pratique.] Quelque embarras qu'il y ait dans ses affaires, elle les débroüille & les explique nettement. Elle expose précisément ses pretentions & celles de sa partie, elle montre ce qui a donné lieu au procez, par quelles voyes elle la conduit, les ressorts qu'elle a fait joüer, & toutes les procedures qu'elle a faites: & l'on découvre parmi tout cela une certaine capacité pour les affaires; que la pluspart des hommes n'ont point.

C'est ce qui me fait penser, que si elles étudioient le droit, elles y reüssiroient au moins comme nous. On voit qu'elles aiment plus la paix & la justice; elles souffrent avec peine les dif-[54]-ferens, & s'entremettent avec joye pour les terminer à l'amiable: leurs soins leur font trouver des biais & des expediens singuliers pour reconcilier les esprits: & elles font naturellement dans la conduite de leur maison, ou sur celle des autres, les principales reflexions d'équité, sur lesquelles toute la Jurisprudence est fondée.

Dans les recits que font celles qui ont un peu d'esprit, il y a toûjours avec l'ordre, je ne sçay quel agrément qui touche plus que dans les nôtres. Elles sçavent discerner ce qui est propre ou étranger au sujet; démêler les interests: designer les personnes par leur propre caractere: dénoüer les intrigues, & suivre les plus grandes comme les plus petites, quand elles en sont informées. Tout cela se voit enco-[55]-re mieux dans les

discourse and the graces that are so characteristically female) appear a hundred times more beautiful.

[53] It is enjoyable to hear a woman who exerts herself to plead a case. Whatever difficulties there are in her affairs, she disentangles them and explains them neatly. She precisely states her claims and those of her party. She shows what has caused the trial, through what paths she conducts it, the efforts that she has employed, and all the procedures that she has followed. There can be discovered amidst all this a certain capacity for business that most men lack.

This makes me think that if women studied law, they would succeed at it at least as well as we do. We see that they care more for peace and justice. They are pained by disputes [54] and happily serve as intermediaries to resolve them amiably. Their concern causes them to find subterfuges and unique expedients to reconcile minds, and in the management of their homes (or those of others) they naturally operate according to the principal considerations of justice on which all jurisprudence is founded.

In the speeches of those who have a little intelligence there is always (together with method) an indefinable charm that moves us more than [what we perceive] in our own. Women know how to distinguish between what is fitting or alien to a subject, [how] to separate themes, to sketch out personages each with its appropriate character, to unravel story lines, and to follow the greater plots as well as the lesser when they are made aware of them. All this is seen better [55] still in the stories and the novels of learned women who are still alive.

How many women are there who teach themselves as much from sermons, conversation, and some little books of piety as the doctors with St. Thomas in their studies and on their desks? The soundness and profundity with which women talk about the highest mysteries and all Christian morality would cause them often to be taken for great theologians if they had a cap and could cite some passages in Latin.

It seems that women are born to practice medicine and to restore health to the ill. Their neatness and good nature reduces pain by half. And not only are they fit to apply [56] remedies, but even to discover them. They invent an infinity [of cures], which are called "small" because they

histoires & dans les Romans des Dames sçavantes qui vivent
encore.

[Elles sçavent la Theologie.] Combien y en a-t-il qui
s'instruisent autant aux sermons, dans les entretiens & dans
quelques petits livres de pieté, que des Docteurs avec S.
Thomas dans leur cabinet, & sur les bancs. La solidité & la
profondeur avec laquelle elles parlent des plus hauts mysteres
& de toute la morale Chrêtienne, les feroient prendre souvent
pour de grands Theologiens, si elles avoient un chapeau, &
qu'elles pussent citer en Latin quelques passages.

[Elles entendent la Medecine.] Il semble que les femmes
soient nées pour exercer le Medecine, & pour rendre la santé
aux malades. Leur propreté & leur complaisance soulagent,
le mal de la moitié. Et non seulement elles sont propres à
appli-[56]-quer des remedes, mais mêmes à les trouver. Elles
en inventent une infinité qu'on appelle petits, parce qu'ils
coûtent moins que ceux d'Hypocrate, & qu'on ne les prescrit
pas par ordonnance: mais qui sont d'autant plus surs &
plus faciles, qu'ils sont plus naturels. Enfin elles font leurs
observations dans la pratique avec tant d'exactitude, & en
raisonnent si juste, qu'elles rendent souvent inutiles tous les
cahiers de l'Ecole.

[Elles sçavent le contraire des réveries Astrologiques.]
Entre les femmes de la campagne, celles qui vont travailler
aux champs, se connoissent admirablement aux bizarreries
des saisons; & leurs Almanacs sont bien plus certains que ceux
qu'on imprime de la main des Astrologues. Elles expliquent si
naïvement la fertilité, & la sterilité des années, par les vents,
par les [57] pluïes & par tout ce qui produit les changemens
de temps, qu'on ne peut les entendre là dessus, sans avoir
compassion des sçavans qui rapportent ces effets, aux Aspects,
aux Approches & aux Ascendans des Planettes. [D'où vient
la diversité des moeurs & des inclinations.] Ce qui me fait
juger que si on leur avoit appris, que les alterations ausquelles
le corps humain est sujet, luy peuvent arriver à cause de sa
constitution particuliere, par l'exercice, par le climas; par la
nourriture, par l'éducation & par les rencontres differentes
de la vie, elles ne s'aviseroient jamais d'en rapporter les
inclinations, ni les changemens aux Influences des Astres, qui
sont des corps éloignez de nous de plusieurs millions de lieuës.

cost less than those of Hippocrates and are not obtained by prescription—but which are all the more certain and easy for being more natural. Finally, in practice they make their observations with such exactitude and so accurate an analysis that they often render all the school manuscripts useless.

Among country women, those who go to work in the fields are admirable experts on the subject of the caprices of the seasons. Their almanacs are more dependable than those that are published by astrologers. Women explain the fertility and the sterility of years so simply—by winds and by [57] rains and by everything that changes the seasons—that one cannot understand this subject without feeling compassion for the educated men who tie these developments to aspects, approaches and ascents of planets. This brings me to conclude that if women had been taught that the changes to which the human body is subject might take place in it because of its characteristic structure (through exercise, climate, nutrition, education and the different things that influence life), they would never have thought to link its tendencies nor its changes to the influences of stars, which are bodies many millions of leagues away from us.

It is true that there are sciences about which women are not heard to speak, for they are [58] not sciences in common use nor [relating to] social life. Algebra, geometry, optics—they almost never leave the studies nor learned academies to come into the midst of the world. And as their greatest use is to give precision to thought, they should only figure secretly in ordinary activities (like hidden springs that drive great machines). That is, we should apply them to topics of conversation and think and speak accurately and geometrically without making it appear that we are geometricians.

All these observations on the quality of the mind can be made without difficulty in the company of women of modest standing. But if you go to court and partake of the conversation of [59] ladies, you will notice quite another thing. It appears that their genius is naturally proportional to their class. With regard to exactness, discernment, and politeness—they have a turn of mind [that is] fine, delicate [and] easy—an indefinable grandeur and nobility that is

[Pourquoy on ne les entend pas parler de certaines sciences.] Il est vray qu'il y a des sciences dont on n'entend point parler les femmes, parceque ce ne sont [58] point de sciences de mise ni de societé. L'Algebre, la Geometrie, l'Optique, ne sortent presque jamais des cabinets ni des Academies sçavantes, pour venir au milieu du monde. Et comme leur plus grand usage est de donner la justesse dans les pensées, elles ne doivent paroître dans le commerce ordinaire, que secretement & comme des ressorts cachez, qui font joüer de grandes machines. C'est à dire, qu'il en faut faire l'application sur les sujets d'entretien, & penser & parler juste & geometriquement; sans faire paroître qu'on est Geometre.

[Que tout cela est plus visible dans les Dames.] Toutes ces observations sur les qualitez de l'esprit, se peuvent faire sans peine avec les femmes de mediocre condition: mais si on va jusques à la Cour, & qu'on ait part aux entretiens des [59] Dames, on y pourra remarquer toute autre chose. Il semble que leur genie soit proportionné naturellement à leur état. Avec la justesse, le discernement, & la politesse, elles ont un tour d'esprit, fin, delicat, aisé; & je ne sçay quoy de grand & de noble, qui leur est particulier. On diroit que les objets comme les hommes, ne s'approchent d'elles, qu'avec respect. Elles les voyent toûjours par le bel endroit, & leur donnent en parlant tout un autre air que le commun. En un mot, que l'on montre à ceux qui ont du goust deux lettres de Dames de conditions differentes, on reconnoîtra aisément laquelle est de plus haute qualité.

[Que les sçavantes, qui sont en grand nombre, sont plus estimables que les sçavans.] Combien y a-t-il eu de Dames, & combien y en a-t-il encore, qu'on doit mettre au nombre des sçavans, si on ne veut pas les [60] mettre au dessus. Le siecle où nous vivons en porte plus que tous les siecles passez: & comme elles ont égalé les hommes, elles sont plus estimables qu'eux, pour des raisons particulieres. Il leur a falu surmonter la molesse où on éleve leur sexe, renoncer aux plaisirs & à l'oisiveté où on les reduit, vaincre certains obstacles publics, qui les éloignent de l'étude, & se mettre au dessus des idées desavantageuses que le vulgaire a des sçavantes, outre celles qu'il a de leur Sexe en general. Elles ont fait tout cela: & soit que les difficultez ayent rendu leur esprit plus-vif & plus

particularly theirs. We might say that objects, like men, approach them only with respect. Women always view them from the best side and, when speaking [of them], give them quite another appearance than the ordinary. In a word, if we show those who have taste two letters from ladies of different standing, they will easily recognize which is of the higher rank.

How many ladies have there been (and how many are there still) who should be counted among the number of the learned—if we did not wish **[60]** to place them higher? The century in which we live contains more of them than all previous centuries. And, as they have equaled men, they are more admirable than men for some specific reasons. They have had to surmount the indolence in which members of their sex are raised, to renounce the pleasures and the idleness to which they are reduced, to conquer certain public obstacles that impede their pursuit of education, and to rise above the prejudicial ideas that ordinary people have about learned ladies (in addition to prejudices that generally prevail about their sex). They have done all this. And whether the struggle has rendered their minds more lively and penetrating or whether these qualities of intellect are natural to them, they have made themselves (in proportion) more adept than men.

It could be said, nevertheless, (without diminishing the reputations **[61]** that these illustrious ladies deserve) that opportunity and outside help have brought them their position—as these things have many educated men among us—and that there are an infinite number of other women who would not have done less if they had had equal advantages. And since we are unjust enough to believe that all women are indiscrete when we know five or six who are, we must also be fair enough to conclude that their sex is capable of education since we see many who have mastered it.

It is commonly imagined that the Turks, the barbarians, and the savages are not as gifted as the people of Europe. However, it is certain that if we were to see five or six of them here who had the capacity or the title **[62]** of a "doctor" (which is not impossible), we would correct our opinion. We would confess that these people, being men like us, are capable of the same things and that if they were taught, they

pénétrant, soit que ces qualitez leur soient naturelles, elles se sont renduës à proportion plus habiles que les hommes.

On peut dire neantmoins, sans diminuer les sentimens que **[61]** [Qu'il font reconnoistre que les femmes en general sont capables de sciences.] ces illustres Dames meritent, que c'est l'occasion & les moyens exterieurs, qui les ont mises en cét état, aussi-bien que les plus sçavans parmy nous, & qu'il y en a une infinité d'autres qui n'en auroient pas moins fait, si elles eussent eu de pareils avantages. Et puisque l'on est assez injuste pour croire que toutes les femmes sont indiscretes, lorsqu'on en connoist cinq ou six qui le sont; on devroit aussi estre assez équitable, pour juger que leur sexe est capable des sciences, puisque l'on en voit quantité, qui ont pû s'y élever.

On s'imagine vulgairement que les Turcs, les Barbares, & les Sauvages n'y sont pas si propres que les peuples de l'Europe. Cependant, il est certain, que si l'on en voyoit icy, cinq ou six qui eussent la capacité ou le titre **[62]** de Docteur, ce qui n'est pas impossible, on corrigeroit son jugement, & l'on avoüeroit que ces peuples estant hommes comme nous, sont capables des mêmes choses, & que s'ils estoient instruits, ils ne nous cederoient en rien. Les femmes avec lesquelles nous vivons, valent bien les Barbares & les Sauvages, pour nous obliger d'avoir pour elles des pensées qui ne soient pas moins avantageuses, ny moins raisonnables.

Si le vulgaire s'opiniâstre, nonobstant ces observations, à ne vouloir pas que des femmes soient aussi propres aux sciences que nous, il doit au moins reconnoistre qu'elles leur sont moins necessaires. L'on s'y applique à deux fins, l'une de bien connoître les choses qui en sont l'objet, & l'autre de devenir vertueux **[63]** par le moyen de ces connaissances. Ainsi dans cette vie qui est si courte, la science se doit uniquement rapporter à la vertu; & les femmes possedant celle-cy, on peut dire qu'elles ont par un bonheur singulier, le principal avantage des sciences sans les avoir étudiées.

[Que les femmes ont autant de vertu que nous.] Ce que nous voyons tous les jours, nous doit convaincre qu'elles ne sont pas moins Chrétiennes, que les hommes. Elles reçoivent l'Evangile avec soumission & avec simplicité. Elles en pratiquent les maximes d'une façon exemplaire. Leur respect pour tout ce qui concerne la religion a toûjours paru

would yield to us in nothing. The women with whom we live deserve as much as the barbarians and savages: [i.e.,] that we require ourselves to think of them in ways that are no less favorable nor reasonable.

If the common man is still determined to believe— notwithstanding these observations—that women are not as fit for education as we are, he must at least recognize that educations are less necessary for women. We apply ourselves to education to achieve two goals: the one—to better understand the things which are its object; the other—to become virtuous **[63]** by means of learning. Thus in this life which is so short learning should especially be linked with virtue. Women possess this [quality]. One might say that women have, by a singular good fortune, the principal advantage of study without having studied.

What we see every day must convince us that women are not less Christian than men. They receive the Gospel humbly and with simplicity. They practice its maxims in an exemplary fashion. Their respect for everything that concerns religion has always appeared so great that they pass without contradiction for having more devotion and piety than we [have]. It is true that their religious practices sometimes go to excess, but I do not **[64]** find this extremism so culpable. It is the inevitable result of the ignorance in which they are raised. If their zeal is immoderate, at least their conviction is true. And it might be that if they understood virtue perfectly, they would adopt it completely—since even in the midst of obscurity they bind themselves to it so strongly.

Compassion, which is the virtue of the Gospel, seems to have a predilection for their sex. The misfortune of their neighbor no sooner prods their brains than it touches their hearts and makes tears come to their eyes. Is it not women's hands that always offer the greatest gifts during public calamities? Do not women still today have particular care of the poor or **[65]** of the sick in the parishes? [Is it not women] who go to visit those who are in prisons and serve those who are in hospitals? Are not pious sisters (to whom we have given the name of the charity that they exercise so worthily) prevalent in the wards [of the city]—relied upon to

si grand qu'elles passent sans contredit, pour avoir plus de devotion & de pieté que nous. Il est vray que leur culte va quelquefois jusques à l'excez: mais je ne [64] trouve pas que cét excez soit si blâmable. L'ignorance où on les éleve en est la cause necessaire. Si leur zele est indiscret, au moins leur persuasion est veritable: & l'on peut dire, que si elles connoissoient parfaitement la vertu, elles l'embrasseroient bien autrement; puisqu'elles s'y attachent si fort au travers des tenebres même.

[Elles sont charîtables.] Il semble que la compassion qui est la vertue de l'Evangile soit affectée à leur Sexe. Le mal du prochain ne leur a pas plûtost frappé l'esprit, qu'il touche leur coeur, & leur fait venir les larmes aux yeux. N'est-ce pas par leurs mains que se sont toûjours faites les plus grandes distributions, dans les calamitez publiques; Ne sont-ce pas encore auhourd'huy les Dames qui ont particulierement soin des pauvres ou [65] des malades dans les Parroisses, qui les vont visiter dans les prisons, & servir dans les hôpitaux? Ne sont-ce pas de pieuses filles [Les filles de la Charité] répanduës dans les quartiers, qui ont charge de leur aller porter à certaines heures du jour, la nourriture & les remedes necessaires, & à qui l'on a donné le nom de la charité qu'elles exercent si dignement?

[Celles de l'Hostel Dieu] Enfin, quand il n'y auroit au monde de femmes qui pratiquassent cette vertu envers le prochain, que celles qui servent les malades dans l'Hôtel-Dieu, je ne crois pas que les hommes pussent sans injustice prétendre en cela l'avantage pardessus leur Sexe. Ce sont proprement ces filles là desquelles il faloit enrichir la galerie des femmes fortes: C'est de leur vie qu'il faudroit faire les plus grands éloges, & [66] honnorer [*sic*] leur mort des plus excellens Panegyriques: puisque c'est-là qu'on voit la religion Chrestienne, c'est à dire la vertu vraymently heroïque se pratiquer à la rigueur dans ses commandemens & dans ses conseils: de jeunes filles renoncer au monde; & à elles mêmes, resoluës à une chasteté & à une pauvreté perpetuelle, prendre leur croix, & la Croix du monde la plus rude, pour se mettre le reste de leurs jours sous le joug de Iesus Christ, se consacrer dans un Hôpital, où l'on reçoit indifferemment toutes sortes de malades de quelque païs ou Religion que ce soit, pour

go to the poor and the sick to carry nourishment and essential medicines at certain hours of the day?

Finally, if there were in the world no women who practiced this virtue toward their neighbor but those who serve the sick in the Hotel Dieu[3], I do not believe that men could without injustice pretend to superiority over the female sex in this. Rightly these are young women with whom the gallery of outstanding women must be enriched. The most fulsome eulogies should be composed about their lives **[66]** and the greatest panegyrics to honor their deaths. For it is there that we see the Christian religion (i.e., truly heroic virtue) practiced with rigor in its commandments and counsels—by young women renouncing the world and themselves, committed to perpetual chastity and poverty, to take up their crosses (and the roughest Cross in the world) to place themselves for the rest of their days under the yoke of Jesus Christ. [They] consecrate themselves in a hospital where all kinds of sick people (from any country and of any religion) are received without discrimination. [They] serve all without distinction and burden themselves (in imitation of their Husband) with all the infirmities of humanity. [They] are not discouraged to have their eyes ceaselessly assaulted by the sight of the **[67]** most frightening spectacles, their ears by the curses and cries of the sick, and [their noses] by the odor of all the infections of the human body. And as a sign of the spirit that motivates them, [they] carry the sick in their arms from bed to bed and encourage the wretches not with empty words, but by the effective, personal example of an invincible patience and charity.

Can anything be conceived that is greater among Christians? Other women are no less inclined to comfort their neighbor. They lack only the opportunity—or have other work that deters them. I find that it is as unworthy to assume from this (as common persons do) that women are naturally men's servants as to pretend that people who have received particular talents **[68]** from God should be the servants and slaves of those for the good of whom they employ [their gifts].

---

[3] A hospital near the university of Paris under the sponsorship of the cathedral. It was founded in the 9th century and expanded in the 17th.

les servir tous sans distinction, & se charger à l'exemple
de leur Epoux de toutes les infirmitez des hommes, sans se
rebuter d'avoir sans cesse les yeux frappez des spectables les
[67] plus affreux: Les oreilles des injures, & des cris des
malades, & l'odorat de toutes les infections du corps humain:
& pour marque de l'esprit qui anime, porter de lit en lit
entre leurs bras, & encourager les miserables, non pas par de
vaines paroles, mais par l'example effectif & personnel d'une
patience, & d'une charité invincible.

    Se peut-il rien concevoir de plus grand parmy les
Chrétiens: Les autres femmes ne sont pas moins portées à
soulager le prochain. Il n'y a que l'occasion qui leur manque,
ou d'autres occupations qui les en détournent & je trouve qu'il
est aussi indigne de s'imaginer de là comme fait le vulgaire,
que les femmes soient naturellement servantes des hommes;
que de prétendre que ceux qui ont receu de Dieu des talens
[68] particuliers, soient les serviteurs & les esclaves de ceux
pour le bien desquels ils les employent.

    [Comment elles vivent dans le celibat.] Quelque genre de
vie qu'embrassent les femmes, leur conduit a toûjours quelque
chose de remarquable. Il semble que celles qui vivent hors
de mariage, & qui demeurent dans le monde, n'y restent que
pour servir d'exemple aux autres. La modestie Chrestienne
paroist sur leur visage & dans leurs habits. La vertu fait leur
principal ornement. Elles s'eloignent des compagnies, & des
divertissemens mondains; & leur application aux exercices de
pieté, fait bien voir qu'elles ne se sont point engagées dans les
soins ny dans les embarras du mariare [*sic*], pour jouir d'une
plus grande liberté d'esprit, & n'estre obligées que de plaire à
Dieu.

    [69][Comment elles vivent dans les monasteres.] Il y a
autant de Monasteres sous la conduite des femmes que des
hommes: & leur vie n'y est pas moins exemplaire. La retraite
y est plus grande: la penitence aussi austere; & les Abesses
y valent bien les Abbez. Elles font des reglemens avec une
sagesse admirable, & gouvernent leurs filles avec tant de
prudence, qu'il n'y arrive point de desordre. Enfin l'éclat
des maisons Religieuses, les grands biens qu'elles possedent,
& leurs solides établissemens sont l'effet du bon ordre qu'y
apportent les Superieures.

Whatever kind of life women embrace, their conduct is always somewhat remarkable. It seems that those who live outside of marriage and who remain in the world stay there only to serve as an example to others. Christian modesty appears on their faces and in their dress. Virtue is their principal ornament. They keep themselves apart from company and secular amusements, and their application to pious exercises shows that they have not assumed the cares or the burdens of marriage so that they might enjoy a greater freedom of mind and be obligated only to please God.

[69] There are as many monasteries under the management of women as of men, and their way of life is no less exemplary. Their seclusion is greater, their penitential life is as austere, and their abbesses are as worthy as abbots. With admirable wisdom abbesses establish regulations and govern their nuns with such prudence that there is no disorder. Indeed, the fame of the female religious houses, the great property that they possess, and their solid foundations are the result of the good order that their superiors have maintained in them.

Marriage is the most natural and ordinary state for human beings. When they enter into it, it is for the remainder of their lives. In it, they spend the years of their lives during which people should by guided only by reason. And the different vicissitudes of nature and of fortune to which this condition [70] is subject, exercising further those who are in it, give them an opportunity to improve their intellects. It does not take a great deal of experience to understand that women are better suited for marriage than we are. Young women are able to run a house at an age when males still need a tutor. And the most common expedient to set a young man on the right road is to give him a wife who restrains him by her example, who moderates his passions, and who retrieves him from debauchery.

What patience do women not resort to in order to live at peace with their husbands? They submit to their orders. They do nothing without their advice. They refrain from many things in order to avoid their husbands' displeasure. And they often deprive [71] themselves of the most respectable entertainments so as to keep themselves free from suspicion.

[Comment elles vivent dans le mariage.] Le mariage est l'état le plus naturel, & le plus ordinaire aux hommes. Quand ils y sont engagez c'est pour le reste de leur vie. Ils y passent les âges où on ne doit agir que par raison. Et les differens accidens de la nature & de la fortune ausquels cette condi-[70]-tion est sujette, exerçant davantage ceux qui y sont, leur donne occasion d'y faire paroistre plus d'esprit. Il ne faut pas grande experience pour sçavoir que les femmes y sont plus propres que nous. Les filles sont capables de conduire une maison à l'âge où les hommes ont encore besoin de maistre & l'expedient le plus commun, pour remettre un jeune homme dans le bon chemin, c'est de luy donner une femme qui le retient par son exemple qui modere ses emportemens & le retire de la débauche.

Qu'elle [*sic*] complaisance n'employent point les femmes pour vivre en paix avec leurs maris. Elles se soûmettent à leurs ordres, elles ne font rien sans leur avis, elles se contraignent en beaucoup de choses pour éviter de leur déplaire; & elles se privent sou-[71]-vent des divertissemens les plus honnestes, pour les exempter de soupçon. L'on sçait lequel des deux Sexes est le plus fidelle à l'autre, & support plus patiemment les malheurs qui surviennent dans le mariage, & y fait paroistre plus de sagesse.

Presque toutes les maisons ne sont reglées que par les femmes, à qui leurs maris en abandonnent le gouvernement: & le soin qu'elles prennens de l'éducation des enfans; est bien plus considerable aux familles & plus important à l'Etat, que celuy qu'elles ont des biens. [Comment elles élevent leurs enfans.] Elles se donnent toutes entieres à leur conservation. La crainte qu'il ne leur arrive du mal est si grande, qu'elles en perdent souvent le repos. Elles se privent avec joye, des choses les plus necessaires, afin qu'il ne leur manque rien. Elles ne sçauroient les [72] voir souffrir le moins du monde, qu'elles ne souffrent elles-mêmes jusques au fond de l'ame: & on peut dire que la plus grande de leur peine est de ne les pouvoir soulager, en se chargeant de leurs douleurs.

[Le soin qu'elles prennent de leur instruction.] Qui ignore avec quelle application elles travaillent à les instruire de la vertu, autant que leur petit âge en est capable. Elles tâchent de leur faire connoitre & craindre Dieu, & leurs [*sic*] enseignent

We know which of the two sexes is the more faithful to the other and more patiently endures the misfortunes that marriage entails—and which, thereby, demonstrates more wisdom.

Almost all homes are run entirely by wives to whom husbands have completely abandoned their management. And the care that women take with the education of children is more extensive in families and more important to the state than the care they take of property. Mothers devote themselves entirely to the protection of their children. The fear that their children will become ill is so great that they often lose sleep [worrying about it]. They happily deprive themselves of necessities so that their children will lack nothing. They would not know how **[72]** to watch their children suffer the least little bit without suffering themselves to the depth of their souls. We may say that the greatest of their pains is their inability to relieve the discomforts of their children by taking their children's pains on themselves.

Who is unaware of the diligence with which mothers apply themselves to the instruction of their children in virtue—in so far as their children's youth permits? They try to bring their children to the knowledge and fear of God and to teach them to adore Him in a manner appropriate for them. Women take care to put their children into the hands of tutors as soon as the children are ready, and they take every possible precaution in choosing tutors so as to provide their children with the best education. And what is even more praiseworthy: they back up instruction by setting good examples.

[73] If we wanted to go in complete detail into all the situations of life and all the virtues that women practice in them—and to examine the most important circumstances among them, we would need to construct a very large panegyric. We could describe how far women's moderation in drinking and eating goes, their patience in adversity, their strength and courage in supporting troubles, their fatigues, their vigils and their fasts, their moderation in pleasure and in passion, their inclination to do good, their prudence in business, their integrity in every deed. In a word, we could demonstrate that there is no virtue that is not common to

à l'adorer d'une maniere qui leur soit proportionnée. Elles
ont soin de les mettre entre les mains des maistres, aussi-tost
qu'ils y sont proprés, & choisissent ceux-cy avec toute la
precaution possible, pour rendre leur éducation meilleure. Et
ce qui est encore plus estimable, c'est qu'elles joignent le bon
exemple à l'instruction.

[73][Qu'un plus ample détail seroit avantageux aux
femmes.] Si l'on vouloit descendre dans un détail entier
de toutes les rencontres de la vie, & de toutes les vertus
que les femmes y pratiquent, & en examiner les plus
importantes circonstances, il y auroit dequoy faire un tres
ample Panegyrique. On pourroit representer jusques où va
leur sobrieté dans le boire & dans le manger; la patience dans
les incommoditez; la force & le courage à supporter les maux,
les fatigues, les veilles, & les jeûnes; La moderation dans les
plaisirs & dans les passions: l'inclination à faire du bien la
prudence dans les affaires, l'honnesteté en toutes les actions:
en un mot on pourroit faire voir qu'il n'y a point de vertu
qui ne leur soit commune avec nous, & qu'il y a au contraire
quantité de défauts considerables qui sont particuliers aux
hommes.

[74]Voila les observations generales & ordinaires sur ce qui
concerne les femmes, par raport aux qualitez de l'esprit, dont
l'usage est la seule chose qui doive mettre de la distinction
entre les hommes.

Comme il n'y a guères de rencontres où l'on ne puisse
découvrir l'inclination, le genie, le vice, & la vertu, & la
capacité des personnes, ceux qui se voudront détromper
eux-mêmes sur le sujet des femmes, ont toûjours occasion de
le faire, en public ou en particulier, à la Cour, & à la grille,
dans les divertissemens, & dans les exercices, avec les pauvres
comme avec les riches, en quelque état & de quelque condition
qu'elles soient. Et si l'on considere avec sincerité & sans
interest ce qu'on pourra remarquer à leur égard, on trouvera
[75] que s'il y a quelques apparences peu favorables aux
femmes, il y en a encore plus qui leur sont tres-avantageuses;
que ce n'est point faute de merite; mais de bonheur ou de
force, que leur condition n'est pas égale à la nôtre; & enfin
que l'opinion commune est un préjugé populaire & mal fondé.

them and us—and that, on the other hand, there are many serious shortcomings that are peculiar to men.

[74] These are general, ordinary observations about what concerns women with regard to the quality of their minds—the use of which is the only thing that ought to create distinctions between people.

As there is scarcely a situation in which we cannot discover the propensity, genius, vice, virtue, and capacity of people, those who would undeceive themselves on the topic of women always have an opportunity to do so in public or in private, at court and at the barred window [of the convent], in entertainments and at work, with the poor as with the rich—in whatsoever state and whatsoever condition women be. And if we ponder sincerely and without self-interest the things that we can discover to woman's credit, we will find [75] (1) that if there are some appearances that do not reflect well on women, there are yet more that are very much to their advantage; (2) that it is not for want of merit, but of luck or power, that women's condition is not equal to ours; and, indeed, (3) that the commonplace opinion [about women] is a popular and poorly founded prejudice.

[76] [blank]

[77]   De L'Egalité des Deux Sexes

Seconde Partie

Où l'on fait voir pourquoy les témoignages qu'on peut
apporter contre le sentiment de l'égalité des deux
Sexes, tirez des Poëtes, des Orateurs, des Historiens,
des Iurisconsultes, & des Philosophes, sont tous vains
& inutiles.

Ce qui confirme le vulgaire dans la pensée qu'il a des
femmes, c'est qu'il s'y voit appuyé par le sentiment [78]
des sçavans. Ainsi la voix publique de ceux qui domminent
par la creance, s'accordant au desavantage des femmes, avec
certaines apparences generales, il ne faut pas s'étonner de les
voir si mal dans l'esprit des personnes simples & sans lumiere.
Et il arrive en cela, comme en une infinité d'autres choses,
que l'on se fortifie dans un préjugé par un autre.
     L'idée de la verité estant attachée naturellement à celle
de la science, l'on ne manque pas de prendre pour vray ce que
proposent ceux qui ont la reputation d'étre sçavans: & comme
le nombre de ceux qui ne le sont que de nom, est beaucoup
plus grand, que de ceux qui le sont en effet, le commun des
hommes qui compte seulement les voix, se range du costé
des [79] premiers, & embrasse d'autant plus volontiers leurs
opinions qu'elles se trouvent plus conformes à celles dont il
est déja imbu.
     C'est pourquoy voyant que les Poëtes, les Orateurs, les
Historiens, & les Philosophes, publient aussi que les femmes
sont inferieures aux hommes, moins nobles & moins parfaites,
il se le persuade davantage, parce qu'il ignore que leur science
est le même préjugé que le sien, sinon qu'il est plus étendu &
plus specieux; & qu'ils ne font que joindre à l'impression de
la coûtume, le sentiment des Anciens sur l'authorité desquels
toute leur certitude est fondée: & je trouve qu'a l'égard du
Sexe, ceux qui ont de l'étude, & ceux qui n'en ont point,
tombent dans une erreur pareille, qui est de juger que [80]
ce qu'en disent ceux qu'ils estiment est veritable, parce qu'ils
sont déja prévenus, qu'ils disent bien, au lieu de ne se porter

[77]   The Equality of the Two Sexes

Part Two

In which it is demonstrated that the evidence against the equality of the sexes taken from the works of poets, orators, historians, lawyers, and philosophers is completely futile and useless.

Ordinary people are confirmed in the ideas they have about women because they see them supported by the opinions [78] of experts. Since the public pronouncements of those men who are deferred to as authorities accord in disparaging women with certain general appearances, it is not surprising to see that women are held in such low esteem by simple, unenlightened people. And it happens in this, as in an infinity of other things, that we strengthen ourselves in one prejudice by another.

Since the concept of truth is naturally linked with that of knowledge, we do not hesitate to accept as true whatever is proposed by persons who have the reputation of being experts. And since the number of those who are experts in name is much greater than those who are so in fact, the ordinary man (who only counts voices) ranges himself on the side of the [79] former and accepts their opinions all the more willingly as these opinions are found to conform to ideas with which he is already imbued.

The ordinary man is further reinforced in his opinion because he sees poets, orators, historians, and philosophers also saying that women are inferior to men (less noble and less perfect). He is not aware that academic thought—apart from being more extensive and more specious—is as prejudiced as his own. Experts have only combined their impressions with tradition (the opinions of the ancient authors on whose authority experts base their convictions). I have found that with regard to gender those who have studied and those who have not fall into a comparable error. [They] conclude that [80] what is said by those whom they esteem is true because they are already disposed to believe that these people know what they are talking about. [They should], instead, hold in

à croire qu'ils disent bien qu'aprés avoir reconnu qu'ils ne
disent rien que de veritable.

[Contre les authoritez des Poëtes & des Orateurs.] Les
Poëtes & les Orateurs n'ayant pour but que de plaire & de
persuader, la vrai semblance leur suffit, à l'égard du commun
des hommes. Ainsi l'exageration & l'hyperbole estant tres-
propres à ce dessein, en grossissant les idées, selon qu'on en a
besoin ils font le bien & le mal petit & grand comme il leur
plaît, & par un tour trop ordinaire, ils attribuënt à toutes les
femmes en general, ce qu'ils ne connoissent qu'en quelques
particulieres. Ce leur est assez d'en avoir veu quelques-unes
hypocrites, pour leur faire dire que tout le [81] sexe est sujet à
ce défaut. Les ornemens dont ils accompagnent leurs discours,
contribuënt merveilleusement à leur attirer la creance de ceux
qui ne sont point sur leurs gardes. Ils parlent avec facilité &
avec grace, & employent certaines manieres, lesquelles estant
belles, agreables, & peu communes, ébloüissent l'esprit &
l'empéchent de discerner la verité. On voit contre les femmes
quantité de pieces assez fortes en apparence; & l'on s'y rend,
faute de sçavoir que ce qui en fait la force & la verité, ce sont
les figures de l'éloquence, les Methaphores, les Proverbes, les
Descriptions, les Similitudes, les Emblêmes: & parce qu'il y
a d'ordinaire beaucoup de genie, & d'adresse dans ces sortes
d'ouvrages; l'on s'imagine aussi qu'il n'y a pas moins de
verité.

[82]Tel se persuade que les femmes aiment qu'on leur en
conte, parce qu'il aura lû le sonnet de Sarazin sur la chûte
de la premiere, qu'il feint n'étre tombée que pour avoir prêté
l'oreille aux fleurettes du Demon. Il est vray que l'imagination
est plaisante, le tour joli, l'application assez juste dans son
dessein, & la chûte tres-agreable; mais si l'on examine la piece
au fond, & qu'on la reduise en Prose, l'on trouvera qu'il n'y a
rien de plus faux ni de plus fade.

Il y a des gens assez simples, pour s'imaginer que les
femmes sont plus portées à la furie que les hommes, pour
avoir lû que les Poëtes ont representé les Furies sous la figure
des femmes; sans considerer que cela n'est qu'une imagination
Poëtique: & que les peintres qui dépeignent les Har-[83]-pies
avec un visage de femme, dépeignent aussi le Demon sous
l'apparence d'un homme.

reserve their confidence that these persons offer good advice until they have discovered that these people speak nothing but the truth.

Poets and orators, who have no objective but to please and persuade, are, with regard to their publics, content with the appearance of truth. Since exaggeration and hyperbole are very useful to their scheme, they enlarge ideas. When they have need, they make the good and the evil of as little and as much importance as it pleases them. And employing a very common maneuver, they attribute to all women in general what they know to be true of only a few individuals. It is enough for them to have seen a few female hypocrites for them to claim that all the [members of the] **[81]** sex are subject to this fault. The decorations that ornament their speech contribute marvelously to persuading people who are not on their guard. These artists speak with facility and grace, and they employ a certain manner which, being beautiful, agreeable, and out of the ordinary, dazzles the mind and prevents it from discerning the truth. We see a mass of work directed against women that seems to make a strong case. We are persuaded by it because we do not know what gives it its appearance of power and truth (e.g., eloquence, metaphors, proverbs, descriptions, analogies, symbols). Because there is ordinarily much genius and cleverness in this kind of work, we assume that there is, as well, no less truth.

[82] One, for example, might persuade himself that women love to hear flatteries, because he has read Sarazin's[1] sonnet on the fall of the first woman (in which he pretends that she fell only because she listened to the flattery of the devil). It is true that his conception is amusing, his style pretty, his execution appropriate enough to his intent, and the outcome most agreeable. But if we examine the piece thoroughly and turn it into prose we find that nothing is more false nor more insipid than it is.

Some people are simple-minded enough to imagine that women fly into rages more quickly than men, for they have read that poets have represented the Furies with the figures

---

[1] Jean François Sarazin (1615?–1654) was secretary to the Prince de Conti and the author of a number of historical and poetical works.

I'en ay veu entreprendre de prouver que les femmes sont inconstantes, sur ce qu'un Poëte Latin celebre a dit qu'elles sont sujettes à un changement continuël, & qu'un François les a plaisamment comparées à une giroüette qui se meut au gré du vent; faute de prendre garde que toutes ces manieres de parler des choses, ne sont propres qu'à égayer l'ésprit & non pas à l'instruire.

L'eloquence vulgaire est une optique parlante, qui fait voir les objets sous telle figure & telle couleur que l'on veut; & il n'y a point de vertu qu'on ne puisse representer comme un vice, par les moyens qu'elle fournit.

Il n'y a rien de plus ordinai-[84]-re, que de trouver dans les Auteurs que les femmes sont moins parfaites & moins nobles que les hommes: mais pour des raisons on n'y en voit point. Et il y a grande apparence qu'ils en ont esté persuadez comme le vulgaire. Les femmes n'ont point de part avec nous aux avantages exterieurs, comme les sciences, & l'authorité, en quoy l'on met communément la perfection: donc elles ne sont pas si parfaites que nous. Pour en estre convaincu serieusement, il faudroit montrez qu'elles n'y sont pas admises, parce qu'elles n'y sont pas propres. Mais cela n'est pas si aisê, qu'on s'imagine: & il ne sera pas difficile de faire voir le contraire dans la suite: & que cette erreur vient de ce qu'on n'a qu'une idée confuse de la perfection & de la noblesse.

[85]Tous les raisonnemens, de ceux qui soutiennient que le beau Sexe n'est pas si noble, ny si excellent que le nostre, sont fondez sur ce que les hommes estant les maistres, on croit que tout est pour eux; & je suis assuré qu'on croiroit tout le contraire, encore plus fortement; c'est à dire, que les hommes ne sont que pour les femmes, si elles avoient toute l'authorité, comme dans l'Empire des Amazones.

Il est vray qu'elles n'ont icy que les emplois qu'on regarde comme les plus bas. Et il est vray aussi qu'elles n'en sont pas moins à estimer: selon la religion & la raison. Il n'y a rien de bas que le vice, ny de grand que la vertu, & les femmes faisans paroistre plus de vertu que les hommes, dans leurs petites occupations, meritent plus d'estre estimées. Ie [86] ne scay même si à regarder simplement leur employ ordinaire, qui est

of women. [They] have not considered that this is only a poetic image—and that painters who depict Harpies **[83]** with female faces also depict the devil in the guise of a man.

I have seen some men undertake to prove that women are fickle because a famous Latin poet[2] has said that they are subject to constant change—and a French [poet] has humorously compared them to a weather vane that moves at the whim of the wind. We must be careful, for all such ways of speaking about things are fit only to amuse the mind and not to instruct it.

Mere eloquence is spoken imagery that makes objects appear in whatever shape and color one wants. There is no virtue that cannot be represented as a vice using the techniques that eloquence provides.

Nothing is more common **[84]** than to find authors claiming that women are less perfect and less noble than men—but for reasons that are never stated. There is a great likelihood that literary men have formed this conviction in the same way as ordinary people. Women have no share with us in the public honors (like academic fields and positions of authority) that usually indicate the pinnacle of human achievement. Therefore, they are not as perfect as we are. Seriously to persuade someone of this, it has to be proven that women are not admitted [to these posts] because they are not fit for them. But this is not so easy to do as is imagined, and in what follows it will not be difficult demonstrate the contrary—and the fact that this error derives from a confused idea of perfection and nobility.

[85] All the arguments of those who maintain that the fair sex is not as noble or as excellent as ours are based on the fact that men, being the masters, believe that everything belongs to them. I am convinced that we would draw the opposite conclusion even more strongly (i.e., that men only exist for women) if women were to possess total authority as they do in the empire of the Amazons.

It is true that women in our society only have the jobs that are held in lowest esteem. And it is also true that they are not less to be respected because of this—according

---

[2]Virgil, *Aeneid* iv, 569: *varium et mutabile semper femina*

de nourrir & d'élever les hommes dans leur enfance, elles ne
sont pas dignes du premier rang dans la societé civile.
[Que les femmes sont plus estimables que les hommes
par rapport à leur employ.] Si nous estions libres & sans
Republique, nous ne nous assemblerions que pour mieux
conserver nostre vie, en joüissant paisiblement des choses qui
y seroient necessaires, & nous estimerions davantage ceux
qui y contribuëroi[e]nt le plus. C'est pourquoy nous avons
accoûtumé de regarder les Princes comme les premiers de
l'Etat, parce que leurs soins & leur prévoyance est la plus
generale, & la plus étenduë, & nous estimons à proportion
ceux qui sont audessous d'eux. La pluspart preferent les
soldats aux Iuges, parce qu'ils s'opposent directement à ceux
[87] qui attaquent la vie d'une maniere plus terrible, &
chacun estime les personnes à proportion qu'il les juge utiles.
Ainsi les femmes semblent estre les plus estimables, puisque
le service qu'elles rendent est incomparablement plus grand,
que celuy de tous les autres.

L'on pourroit absolument se passer de Princes, de soldats,
& de marchands, comme l'on faisoit au commencement du
monde, & comme le font encore aujourd'huy les Sauvages.
Mais on ne se peut passer de femmes dans son enfance. Les
Etats estans bien pacifiez, la pluspart des personnes qui ont
l'authorité, sont comme mortes & inutiles. Les femmes ne
cessent jamais de nous estre necessaires. Les Ministres de la
Iustice ne sont gueres que pour conserver les biens à ceux [88]
qui les possédent. & les femmes sont pour nous conserver
la vie: les soldats s'employent pour des hommes faits, &
capables de se deffendre, & les femmes s'employent pour les
hommes, lorsqu'il ne sçavent pas encore ce qu'ils sont, s'ils
ont des ennemis ou des amis, & lorsqu'ils n'ont point d'autres
armes que des pleurs contre ceux qui les attaquent. Les
Maistres, les Magistrats, & les Princes, n'agissent souvent
que pour leur gloire, & leur interest particulier, & les femmes
n'agissent que pour le bien des enfans qu'elles élevent. Enfin
les peines & les soins, les fatigues & les assiduites, ausquelles
elles s'assujettissent, n'ont rien de pareil en aucun état de la
societé civile.

Il n'y a donc que la fantaisie qui les fasse moins estimer.
[89] On recompenseroit largement un homme qui auroit

to religion and reason. There is nothing low but vice, nor grand but virtue. And in their humble occupations women, demonstrating more virtue than men, deserve more to be honored. I [86] am not at all certain but that with respect to their ordinary employment (which is to nourish and raise men in their infancy) women may not be worthy of the first rank in society.

If we were free and without a government, we would associate with each other only so that we might better preserve our lives while peacefully enjoying the things that are necessary to life. And we would value most those people who contribute the most [to the quality of life]. This is why we have become accustomed to thinking of princes as the men who rank first in the state. Their responsibility and foresight is the most comprehensive and extensive. We honor those who are beneath them to a proportional degree. Most people prefer soldiers to judges, because soldiers directly confront those [87] who assault life in the most terrible way (and each of us values persons to the degree that he considers them to be useful). Thus women seem to be the most valuable members of society, for the service they render is incomparably greater than the contributions of all others.

We could entirely do without princes, soldiers, and merchants (as people did at the beginning of the world, and as savages do today). But in our infancies we cannot do without women. If states are at peace, most of the persons who hold positions of authority in them are like the dead and the useless. [But] women never cease to be necessary to us. The only function of ministers of justice is to protect the property of people [88] who have some. And women exist to preserve life for us. Soldiers are employed by adult men [who are] capable of defending themselves. And women exert themselves for men [at a time] when men do not yet know what they are, whether they have enemies or friends, and [at an age] when they have no other weapons against those who attack them than tears. Masters, magistrates, and princes often act only for their own glory and particular interests. And women act only for the good of the children they raise. Indeed, the pains and the cares, the fatigues and vigils to

apprivoisé un Tigre: l'on considere ceux qui sçavent dresser des chevaux, des Singes, & des Elephans: on parle avec éloge d'un homme, qui aura composé un petit ouvrage qui luy aura coûté un peu de temps & de peine; & l'on neglige les femmes qui mettent, plusieurs années à nourrir & à former des enfans: & si l'on recherche bien la raison, l'on trouvera que c'est parce que l'un est plus ordinaire que l'autre.

[Contre les témoignages qu'on peut tirer de l'histoire.] Ce que les Historiens disent au desavantage des femmes, fait plus d'impression sur l'esprit que les discours des Orateurs. Comme ils semblent ne rien avancer d'eux-mêmes, leur témoignage est moins suspect; outre qu'il est conforme à ce dont on est déja persuadé; rapportant que [90] les femmes estoient autrefois ce qu'on croit qu'elles sont à present. Mais toute l'authorité qu'ils ont sur les esprits, n'est que l'effet d'un préjugé assez commun à l'égard de l'antiquité, qu'on se represente sous l'image d'un venerable vieillard, qui ayant beaucoup de sagesse, & d'experience; n'est pas capable d'estre trompe, ny de rien dire que de vray.

Cependant, les Anciens n'étoi[e]nt pas moins hommes que nous, ny moins sujets à l'erreur, & l'on ne doit pas plûtost se rendre à present à leurs opinions, qu'on auroit fait de leur temps. On consideroit autrefois les femmes, comme l'on fait aujourd'huy, & avec aussi peu de raison. Ainsi tout ce qu'en ont dit les hommes doit estre suspect, parce qu'il sont iuges & parties: & lorsque quelqu'un rapporte [91] contr'elles le sentiment de mille Autheurs, cette histoire ne doit estre considerée que comme une tradition de préjugez, & d'érreurs. Il y a aussi-peu de fidelité & d'exactitude dans les histoires anciennes, que dans les recits familiers, où l'on reconnoist assez, qu'il n'y en a presque point. Ceux qui les ont écrites y ont mélé leurs passions, & leur interest: & la pluspart n'ayant eu que des idées fort confuses du vice & de la vertu, ont souvent pris l'un pour l'autre: & ceux qui les lisent avec la préoccupation ordinaire, ne manquent pas de tomber dans le même défaut. Et dans le préjugé où ils estoient, ils ont eu soin d'exagerer les vertues & les avantages de leur Sexe; & de rabaisser & d'affoiblir, le merite des femmes par un interest contraire. Cela est si facile à re-[92]-connoistre qu'il n'en faut point apporter d'exemple.

which women subject themselves have nothing to equal them in any of society's stations.

Nothing but a fantasy has led to women being unappreciated. **[89]** A man who can tame a tiger will be generously compensated. People who know how to train horses, apes, and elephants are respected. We rave about a man who has composed a small treatise that cost him little time or effort. And we neglect women who devote many years to nourishing and training their children. If we look for a reason, it is to be found in the fact that what the one does is more ordinary than what the other does.

What historians have to say in disparaging women makes a stronger impression on the mind than the speeches of orators. Since historians seem to have nothing of their own to put forward, their testimony is less suspect (besides, it conforms to what we are already persuaded of—reporting that **[90]** women were formerly what we believe them to be now). But all the authority historians have over the minds of people is only the effect of a very common prejudice with respect to antiquity (which we imagine in the guise of a venerable elder who, having much wisdom and experience, cannot be deceived or speak anything but the truth).

However, the ancients were no less men than ourselves (i.e., no less subject to error), and we need no sooner surrender now to their opinions than we would have in their own day. Women were looked on formerly as they are today—with as little reason. Thus everything that men have said about women must be suspect, for men are both judges and defendants in this case. When someone cites **[91]** against women the opinions of a thousand authors, this history must be understood as nothing but a tradition of prejudice and error. There is as little trustworthiness or accuracy in the ancient histories as in commonplace accounts that are well known to contain almost none at all. The men who wrote them mixed their passions and their self-interest into them, and most [ancient authors], having had only very confused ideas about vice and virtue, have often mistaken the one for the other. People who read these texts with the ordinary prejudice [against women], invariably fall into the same fault. And in the prejudice where they were they have taken care

[Ce que l'on trouve dans l'histoire à l'avantage des femmes.] Neanmoins, si l'on sçait débroüiller un peu le passé, l'on trouve de quoy faire voir que les femmes n'en ont point cedé aux hommes, & que la vertu qu'elles ont fait paroistre est plus excellente, si on la considere sincerement dans toutes ses circonstances. L'on peut remarquer qu'elles ont donné d'aussi grandes marques d'esprit & de capacité dans toutes sortes de rencontres. Il y en a eu qui ont gouverné de grands Etats & des Empires avec une sagesse & une moderation qui n'a point eu d'exemple: d'autres ont rendu la justice avec une integrité pareille à celle de l'Areopage; plusieurs ont rétably par leur prudence & par leurs conseils les Royaumes dans le calme, & leurs maris sur le Thrô-[93]-ne. On en a veu conduire des armées, ou se dessendre [*sic*] sur des murailles avec un courage plus qu'Heroïque. Combien y en a t'il eu dont la chasteté n'a pû recevoir aucune atteinte, ny par les menaces épouvantables, ny par les promesses magnifiques qu'on leur faisoit, & qui ont souffert avec une generosité surprenante, les plus horribles tourmens pour la cause de la Religion? Combien y en a-t'il eu, qui se sont renduës aussi habiles que les hommes dans toutes les sciences, qui ont penetré ce qu'il y a de plus curieux dans la nature, de plus fin dans la Politique, & de plus solide dans la Morale, & qui se font elevées à ce qu'il y a de plus haut dans la Theologie Chrétienne. Ainsi l'histoire dont ceux qui sont prévenus contre le Sexe, abusent pour l'abaisser [94] peut servir à ceux qui le regardent avec des yeux d'équité pour montrer qu'il n'est pas moins noble que le nostre.

[Contre les iurisconsultos.] L'autorité des Iurisconsultes a un grand poids, à l'égard de beaucoup de gens, sur ce qui concerne les femmes, parce qu'ils font une profession particuliere de rendre à un châcun ce qui luy appartient. Ils mettent les femmes sous la puissance de leurs maris, comme les enfans sous celle de leurs peres, & disent que c'est la nature qui leur a assigné les moindres fonctions de la societé; & qui les a éloignées de l'authorité publique.

L'on croit étre bien fondé de le dire aussi aprés eux. Mais il est permis, sans blesser le respect qu'ils meritent de n'étre pas en cèla de leur sentiment. On les embarasseroit fort, si on les obli-[95]-geoit de s'expliquer intelligiblement sur ce qu'ils

to exaggerate the virtues and the superior traits of their [own] sex and (from a contrary interest) to play down and to undercut the deserts of women. That is so easy to **[92]** see that it is not necessary to give another example.

Nevertheless, if we know how to root about a little bit in the past, we find things that make us realize that women have not yielded to men—and that the virtue women have demonstrated has been more perfect (if we sincerely consider it in all its circumstances). We can see that women have shown great signs of spirit and capacity in all kinds of situations. Some have governed large states and empires with a wisdom and moderation that has no parallel. Others have rendered justice with an integrity equal to that of the Council of the Areopagus. Many have by their wisdom and their counsels restored kingdoms to peace and husbands to thrones. **[93]** They have been seen to lead armies or defend themselves on fortifications with more than heroic courage. How many have there been whose chastity has remained inviolate—neither from the frightening threats nor the magnificent promises that have been made them? [How many] have (with an astonishing magnanimity) suffered the most horrible torments for the sake of religion? How many have made themselves as adept as men in all the fields of learning? [How many] have penetrated the most curious things in nature, the most subtle in politics, the most profound in ethics—and who have raised themselves to the highest levels of Christian theology? Thus the history that is abused by those who are prejudiced against the female sex in order to abase women **[94]** can serve people who study it in a spirit of fairness to demonstrate that the female gender is not less noble than our own.

In the opinion of many men, the authority of legal experts bears great weight in matters concerning women, for legal experts make a particular profession of assigning to each person what pertains to him. They subject women to the power of their husbands—like children to their fathers. And they claim that nature has assigned women the minor roles in society and excluded them from public authority.

We believe ourselves to be on firm ground when we repeat their words. But we may, without failing to show them the respect that they deserve, not share their opinion. We would

appellent Nature en cét endroit, & de faire entendre comment
elle a distingué les deux Sexes, comme ils prétendent.
    Il faut considerer que ceux qui ont fait ou compilé les
Loix estant des hommes, ont favorisé leur Sexe, comme les
femmes auroient peut-estre fait si elles avoient esté à leur
place: & les Loix ayant esté faites dépuis l'établissement
des societez, en la maniere qu'elles sont à present à l'égard
des femmes, les Iurisconsultes qui avoient aussi leur préjugé,
ont attribué à la nature une distinction, qui ne vient que
de la coûtume. Outre qu'il n'étoit pas necessaire de changer
l'ordre qu'ils trouvoient étably, pour obtenir la fin qu'ils
se proposoient, qui estoit de bien gouver-[96]-ner un État,
en exerçant la justice. Enfin s'ils s'opiniâtroient à soûtenir
que les femmes sont naturellement dépendantes des hommes,
on les combattroit par leurs propres principes, puisqu'ils
reconnoissent eux-mêmes, que la dépendance & la servitude
sont contraires à l'ordre de la nature, qui rend tous les
hommes égaux.
    La dépendance estant un rapport purement corporel &
civil, elle ne doit estre considerée que comme un effet de
hazard, de la violence, ou de la coûtume: si ce n'est celle où
sont les enfans à l'égard de ceux qui leur ont donné la vie.
Encore ne passe-t'elle point un certain âge; où les hommes
estant supposez avoir assez de raison & d'experience pour se
pouvoir gouverner eux-mêmes, sont affranchis par les Loix:
de l'authorité d'autruy.
    [97] Mais entre les personnes d'un âge égal ou approchant,
il ne devroit y avoir qu'une subordination raisonnable, selon
laquelle ceux qui ont moins de lumiere se soûmettent
volontairement à ceux qui en ont davantage. Et si l'on oste
les Actions civiles que les Loix ont données aux hommes, &
qui les rendent les Chefs de la famille, on ne peut trouver
entr'eux & leurs femmes, qu'une soûmission d'experience
& de lumieres. Les uns & les autres s'engagent ensemble
librement en un temps où les femmes ont autant de raison, &
souvent plus que leur maris. Les promesses & les conventions
du mariage sont réciproques: & le pouvoir égal sur le corps:
et si les Loix donnent au mary plus d'authorité sur les bien
la nature donne à la femme plus de [98] puissance & de droit
sur les enfans. Et comme la volonté de l'un n'est pas la regle

embarrass them a great deal if we were to oblige [95] them
to define intelligibly what in this instance they mean by
"nature"—and to explain to us how nature has distinguished
between the two sexes (as they pretend).

We must take into account that those who have made
or compiled the laws, being men, have favored their sex
(as women would perhaps have done if they had been in
their place). And the laws, having been laid down from
the beginning of society as they are now with respect to
women, legal scholars, who also have their prejudice, have
attributed to nature a distinction that derives from custom
alone. Besides, it was not necessary for them to change the
order that they found established [in society] to achieve the
end that they proposed (i.e., the good governance [96] of
the state through the exercise of justice). If, indeed, they
were to be obstinate in maintaining that women are naturally
subservient to men, we should fight them using their own
principles—for they themselves recognize that dependence
and servitude are contrary to the order of nature (which
makes all people equal).

Subservience, being a purely physical and civil relationship, must be understood simply as an effect of chance,
violence, or custom—unless it is the kind that children
experience with regard to those who have given them life.
Even this [kind of subservience] does not continue past a
certain age when people, being supposed to have sufficient
reason and experience to be able to govern themselves, are
liberated by law from the authority of others.

[97] But between persons of an equal or approximate age
there should only be a reasonable degree of subordination—
according to which those who have least understanding submit
themselves voluntarily to those who have more. If we remove
the civil statutes that the laws have provided for men (which
make men the heads of their families), we can find between
men and their wives no [grounds for] subordination but those
[dictated by differences] of experience and intelligence. Both
marry freely at the same age—when women have as much
(often more) capacity for reason as their husbands. The
promises and conventions of marriage are reciprocal, and the
power over the body is equal. If the laws give a husband more

de l'autre, si une femme est obligée de faire les choses dont
son mary l'avertit celui-cy ne l'est pas moins de suivre ce
que sa femme luy fait entendre estre de son devoir: & hors
les choses raisonnables, on ne peut contraindre une femme de
se soumettre à son mary, que parce qu'elle à moins de force.
Ce qu'on appelle agir de Turc à Maure, et non pas en gens
d'esprit.
   [Comme les Philosophes.] L'on n'aura pas beaucoup de
peine à se départir de l'opinion des sçavans, dont je viens
de parler parce qu'on pourra aisément reconnaitre que leur
profession ne les engage pas à s'informir [*sic*] si exactement
de ce que les choses sont en elles-mêmes & que l'apparence &
la vray semblan-[99]-ce suffisent aux Poëtes & aux Orateurs:
le témoignage de l'antiquité aux Historiens, & la Coûtume
aux Iurisconsultes pour arriver à leur but: mais pour ce qui
est du sentiment des Philosophes, on ne le quittera pas si
facilement: parce qu'il semble qu'ils sont au dessus de toutes
les considerations précedentes, comme en effet ils doivent
estre, & qu'ils passent pour examiner les choses de plus
prés: ce qui leur attire la creance commune, & fait tenir
pour indubitable ce qu'ils proposent sur tout lorsqu'ils ne
détruisent point les sentiments où l'on est.
   Ainsi le vulgaire se fortifie dans l'opinion qu'il a de
l'inégalité des deux Sexes & parce qu'il y voit aussi ceux
desquels il regarde les iugements, comme la regle des siens,
faute de sçavoir, [100] que presque tous les Philosophes n'ont
point d'autre regle que luy, & que ce n'est pas par science
qu'ils prononcent, principalement sur la matiere dont il s'agit.
[Ce que c'est que les Philosophes de l'Ecole.] Ils ont porté
leurs préjugez dans les Ecoles, & ils n'y ont rien appris qui
servist à les en tirer: au contraire, toute leur science est
fondée sur les jugemens qu'ils ont fait dés le berceau; & c'est
parmi eux un crime ou une erreur de revoquer en doute ce
qu'on a crû avant l'âge de discretion. On ne leur apprend
point á connoitre l'homme par le corps, ni par l'esprit: Et
ce qu'ils en enseignent communement peut tres bien servir à
prouver qu'il n'y a entre nous & les bêtes que le plus & le
moins. On ne leur dit pas un mot des Sexes: on suppose
qu'ils les connoissent assez; bien loin [101] d'en examiner la
capacité & la difference veritable & naturelle, ce qui est un

authority over property, nature gives a wife more [98] power and right over children. Since the will of the one is not the rule of the other—if a wife is obligated to do the things that her husband insists on, he is not less [bound] to follow what his wife shows him to be his duty. And apart from reasonable things, the only way a woman can be constrained to submit to her husband is through her having less strength [than he]. That is how Turks are said to behave with Moors—not the way of people of intelligence.

We will not have much difficulty ridding ourselves of the opinions of the experts of whom I have been speaking, for we can easily see that their profession does not require them to inform themselves (with accuracy) of what things are in themselves. To achieve their goal, appearance and verisimilitude [99] suffice poets and orators; the testimony of antiquity, historians; and tradition, legal experts. But we will not free ourself of the opinions of philosophers so easily, for it seems that they are above all the aforementioned considerations. Indeed, they should be, for philosophers have a reputation for examining things most closely. This earns them the trust of the masses and makes what they propose appear indubitable—especially when what they say does not contradict opinions we already hold.

Thus ordinary people confirm themselves in the opinion they hold about the inequality of the two sexes, and because they see that this opinion is held by those whose judgments they accept as setting the standard for their own, they fail to realize [100] that almost all philosophers have no other standard of judgment than they [do]—and that it is not principally from knowledge that philosophers pronounce on the matter that is at hand. Philosophers have carried their prejudices into the schools, and there they have learned nothing that would serve to free them from those prejudices. On the contrary: their whole science is based on opinions that they have held since the cradle, and among them it is a crime or an error to call into doubt what one has believed before the age of discretion. They are not taught to understand man in the flesh or the spirit. And what they commonly teach about him can very well serve to prove that there is between us and the beasts no difference but a matter of degree. They

point des plus curieux, & peut-estre aussi des plus-importans
de la Physique & de la Morale. Ils passent des années entieres,
& quelques uns toute leur vie, à des bagatelles, & à des Estres
de raison, & à ruminer s'il y a au delà du monde des espaces
imaginaires, & si les atomes ou la petite poussiere, qui paroît
dans les rayons du Soleil, est divisible á d'infini. Quel fond
peut-on faire sur ce que des sçavans de cette sorte disent,
quand il s'agit de choses serieuses & importantes?

On pourroit penser neanmoins qu'encore qu'ils s'instruisent
si mals, leurs principes suffisent peut-estre pour découvrir
lequel des deux Sexes a naturellement quelque avantage sur
l'autre; [102] mais cette pensée ne peut venir qu'à ceux ou
qui ne les connoissent pas, ou qui en sont prévenus. La connoissance de nous-mêmes est absolument necessaire pour bien
traiter cette question, & particulierement la connoissance du
corps, qui est l'organe des sciences; de même que pour sçavoir
comment les lunettes d'approche grossissent les objects, il
faut en connoître la fabrique. Ils n'en parlent qu'en passant,
non plus que de la verité & de la science, c'est à dire, de la
methode d'acquerir des connoissances certaines & veritables,
sans quoy il est impossible de bien examiner si les femmes en
sont aussi capables que nous & sans m'amuser à rapporter les
idées qu'ils en donnent, je diray icy en general, ce que j'en
crois.

Tous les hommes estant faits [103] [En quoy consiste la
science.] les uns comme les autres ont les mêmes sentiments,
& les mêmes idées des choses naturelles; par exemple de la
lumiere de la chaleur, & de la dureté, & toute la science que
l'on tâche d'en avoir, se réduit à connoître au vray quelle est
la disposition particuliere, interieure & exterieure de chaque
objet pour produire en nous les pensées & les sentimans
que nous en avons. Tout ce que les Maîtres peuvent faire
pour nous conduire à cette connoissance, c'est d'appliquer
nôtre esprit à ce que nous remarquons, pour en examiner les
apparences, & les effets, sans précipitation ni préjugé, & de
nous montrer l'ordre qu'il faut tenir dans la disposition de
nos pensées, pour trouver ce que nous cherchons.

Par exemple, si une personne sans étude me prioit de
luy [104] [En quoy consiste la liquidité.] expliquer, en quoy
consiste la liquidité de l'eau; je ne luy en affirmerois rien,

are not told the first word about the sexes. **[101]** Far from examining the capacities and the true and natural differences between the sexes (which is a most intriguing subject and perhaps also the most important topic in natural and moral philosophy), they suppose that they already understand these things adequately. They pass entire years (some of them all their lives) at trifles: meditating on "entia rationis," speculating about the existence of imaginary spaces beyond the universe, and wondering if an atom or the tiny dust speck that appears in the rays of the sun is infinitely divisible. What foundation can one lay using the things that experts of this kind teach when the matter at hand is about something serious and important?

One might think, nevertheless, that although philosophers teach themselves so poorly, their principles could suffice perhaps to reveal which of the two sexes naturally has some advantage over the other; **[102]** but this idea can only occur to those who either do not know philosophers or who are prejudiced in their favor. Knowledge of ourselves is absolutely necessary in order to deal with this question—and particularly the knowledge of the body, which is the organ of learning (just as in order to know how small telescopes enlarge objects, we have to know their construction). Philosophers speak of this only in passing—no more than of truth and knowledge (i.e., of the method of acquiring true and certain knowledge, without which it is impossible properly to examine whether women are as capable of it as we [are]). Without amusing myself by reciting the ideas they have put forth, I will state here in general what I believe.

All people, being made **[103]** one like another, have the same sensations and the same ideas about natural things (e.g., about light, heat, solidity). All the knowledge that we work to acquire comes down to comprehending truly what the particular disposition (interior and exterior) of each object is that produces in us the thoughts and impressions that we have of it. All that teachers can do to lead us to this knowledge is to [urge us to] apply our minds to what we see to examine its appearances and effects without haste or prejudice and to show us the order that must be preserved in the disposition of our thoughts to find what we seek.

mais je luy demanderois ce qu'elle en a observé, comme, que si l'eau n'est renfermée dans un vase, elle se repand; c'est à dire, que toutes ses parties se separent & se desunissent d'elles-mêmes, sans que l'on introduise de corps étranger; que l'on y fait entrer ses doigts sans peine, & sans y trouver la resistance des corps durs, & qu'en y mettant du sucre ou du sel, on s'apperçoit que ces deux sortes de corps se dimînuent peu à peu, & que leurs parcelles sont emportées dans tous les endroits de la liqueur.

Iusques-la je ne luy apprendrois rien de nouveau; & si je luy avois fait entendre de la même façon, ce que c'est qu'estre en repos, ou en mouvement, je **[105]** la porterois à reconnoître que la nature des liqueurs consiste en ce que leurs parties insensibles sont dans un mouvement perpetuel, ce qui oblige de les enfermer dans un vase, & les dispose à donner aisément entrée aux corps durs; & que les parcelles de l'eau estant petites, lisses, pointues, venant à s'insinuer dans les pores du sucre, en ébranlent & en divisent les parties par leur rencontre, & se mouvant en tout sens, emportent en tous les endroits du vase, ce qu'elles ont separé.

Cette idée des liqueurs, qui est une partie détachée du corps de la Physique paroîtroit bien plus claire, si on la voyoit dans son rang: & elle n'a rien que le commun des femmes ne soit capable d'entendre. Le reste de toutes nos connoissances estant proposé avec ordre, n'a pas plus **[106]** de difficulté, & si l'on y fait attention, l'on trouvera que chaque science de raisonnement demande moins d'esprit, & moins de temps qu'il n'en faut pour bien apprendre le Point ou la Tapisserie.

[Il ne faut pas moins d'esprit pour apprendre le Point & la Tapisserie, que pour apprendre la Physique.] En effet les idées des choses naturelles sont necessaires, & se forment toûjours en nous de la même façon. Adam les avoit comme nous les avons & les enfans les ont comme les vieillards, & les femmes comme les hommes: & ces idées se renouvellent, se fortifient, & s'entretiennent par l'usage continuel des sens. L'esprit agit toûjours , & qui sçait bien comment il agit en une chose découvre sans peine comment il agit en toutes les autres. Il n'y a que le plus & le moins entre l'impression du Soleil ou celle d'une étincelle. Pour **[107]** bien penser la-dessus, l'on n'a besoin ni d'adresse, ni d'exercice de corps.

For example, if an uneducated person were to ask me to explain to him [104] what the liquidity of water consists of, I would tell him nothing. But I would ask him what he has observed: how if water is not confined in a vessel, it scatters (i.e., all its parts separate and disunite themselves without a foreign body being interposed); how we can stick our fingers into it without difficulty and without finding in it the resistance of a hard body; and how, if we put sugar or salt in it, we see that these two kinds of substances shrink little by little and their particles are carried off to every part of the liquid.

Up to this point I will have taught him nothing new. If by the same means I had made him understand what it is to be at rest or in motion, I [105] would bring him to acknowledge that the nature of liquids consists in this: that their insensible particles are in perpetual movement (which requires that they be enclosed in a vessel and disposes them to give easy entry to hard bodies) and that the particles of water (being small, smooth, and pointed)—happening to insinuate themselves into the pores of the sugar, shaking it, and dividing its parts by their encounter and moving in every way—carry the bits of sugar that they have separated throughout the vessel.

This concept of liquids, which is a part detached from the body of physics, would appear even clearer, if we saw it in its context. And it contains nothing that the ordinary woman would not be able to understand. The remainder of our knowledge (if professed in an orderly fashion) is no more [106] difficult. If we think about it, we will find that each field of rational inquiry requires less intelligence and less time than is necessary to master embroidery and tapestry work.

Indeed, our ideas about natural phenomena are necessary to us, and they always take shape in us in the same way. Adam got them like we get them. Children get them like old people—and women, like men. These ideas are renewed, strengthened, and maintained by the continued functioning of the senses. The mind is always active, and whoever understands how it deals with one thing can easily discover how it functions in connection with all others. There is only "more" or "less" between the impression made by the sun

Il n'en est pas de même des ouvrages dont j'ay parlé. Il y faut encore plus appliquer son esprit: Les idées en estant arbitraires, sont plus difficiles à prendre, & à retenir, ce qui est cause qu'il faut tant de temps pour bien sçavoir un métier, c'est qu'il dépend d'un long exercice, il faut de l'adresse pour bien garder les proportions sur un cannevas, pour distribuer également la soye ou la laine, pour mélanger avec justesse les couleurs; pour ne pas trop serrer ni trop relâcher les points, pour n'en mettre pas plus en un rang qu'en l'autre, pour faire les Nuances imperceptibles: En un mot, il faut sçavoir faire & varier en mille manieres differentes les ouvrages de l'art [108] pour y estre habile, au lieu que dans les sciences il ne faut que regarder avec ordre des ouvrages tous faits, & toûjours uniformes: & toute la difficulté d'y reüssir vient moins des objets & de la disposition du corps, que du peu de capacité dans les Maîtres.

Il ne faut donc plus tant s'étonner de voir des hommes & des femmes sans étude s'entretenir des choses qui regardent les sciences, puisque la Methode de les apprendre ne sert qu'à rectifier le bon sens, qui s'est confondu par la précipitation, par la coûtume, & par l'usage.

L'idée qu'on vient de donner de la science en general pourroit suffire pour persuader les personnes depréoccupées, que les hommes & les femmes en sont également capables; Mais parceque l'opinion contraire est [109] des plus enracinées, il faut pour l'arracher entiérement; la combattre par principes afin que joignant les apparences favorables au beau Sexe, qu'on a presentées dans la premiere partie, avec les raisons physiques, qu'on va apporter, l'on puisse absolument étre convaincu en sa faveur.

and that by a spark. To **[107]** think clearly on that, there is no need of skill or bodily exertion.

It is not the same with the kinds of works of which I have spoken. The mind must be applied to them even more. Their ideas, being arbitrary, are more difficult to learn and to retain. This is why much time is needed to learn a trade (it is because it depends on long practice). Skill is essential for maintaining the proportions on an [embroidery] canvas—for distributing silk or wool equally, for accurately blending colors, for making stitches that are not too tight or too loose, for not putting more stitches in one row than in another, and for making imperceptible nuances. In a word: to be accounted skilled a person must know how to do and to vary handiwork in a thousand different ways–**[108]**–while in academic fields one needs only to observe in an orderly way totally completed and always uniform works. And all the obstacles to success derive less from objects and the disposition of the body than from the limited capacity of masters.

It is not too surprising, therefore, to see uneducated men and women discussing things that relate to academics—since the method of learning these things serves only to correct common sense (which is confused by haste, custom, and habit).

The explanation that we have just given of knowledge in general might suffice to persuade unbiased people that men and women are equally competent. But because the contrary opinion is **[109]** very deeply rooted, it is necessary (in order to rip it up completely) to combat it with principles, so that, joining the appearances favorable to the fair sex that we presented in the first part [of this treatise] with the arguments from nature that we are going to produce, we could absolutely be convinced in women's favor.

Que les femmes considerées selon les principes de
la saine Philosophie, sont autant capables que les
hommes de toutes sortes de Connoissances.

[L'esprit n'a point de Sexe.] Il est aisé de remarquer que
la difference des Sexes ne regarde que le Corps: n'y ayant
proprement que cette partie qui serve à la production des
hommes; & l'Esprit ne faisant qu'y préter son consentement,
& le faisant en tous de la mesme ma-[110]-niere, on peut
conclure qu'il n'a point de Sexe.

[Il est égal dans sous les hommes.] Si on le considere en
luy-méme, l'on trouve qu'il est égal & de même nature en
tous les hommes, & capable de toutes sortes de pensées: les
plus petites l'occupent comme les plus grandes; il n'en faut
pas moins pour bien connoistre un Ciron, qu'un Elephant:
quiconque sçait en quoy consiste la lumiere & le feu d'une
étincelle, sçait aussi ce que c'est que la lumiere du Soleil.
Quand on s'est accoûtumé à penser aux choses qui ne
regardent que l'Esprit, l'on y voit tout au moins aussi clair
que dans ce qu'il y a de plus materiel, qui se connoît par les
sens. Ie ne découvre pas plus de difference entre l'esprit d'un
homme grossier & ignorant, & celuy d'un homme délicat &
éclairé, qu'entre l'esprit d'un mê-[111]-me homme consideré
à l'âge de dix ans, & à l'âge de quarante, & comme il n'en
paroît pas davantage entre celuy des deux Sexes, on peut dire
que leur difference n'est pas de ce costé là. La constitution
du Corps, mais particulierement l'éducation, l'exercice, & les
impressions de tout ce qui nous environne estant partout les
causes naturelles & sensibles de tant de diversitez qui s'y
remarquent. [Doù [sic] vient la difference qui est entre les
hommes.]

[L'Esprit agit dans les femmes comme dans les hommes.]
C'est Dieu qui unit l'Esprit au Corps de la femme, comme
à celuy de l'homme, & qui l'y unit par les mêmes Loix. Ce
sont les sentimens, les passions, & les volontez qui font &
entretiennent cette union, et l'esprit n'agissant pas autrement
dans un Sexe, que dans l'autre, il y est également capable
des mêmes choses. [112] [Il s'aperçoit des choses de la même
façon dans les deux Sexes.] Cela est encore plus clair à
considerer seulement la teste, qui est l'unique organe des

That women, considered according to the principles
of sound philosophy, are as capable as men of all kinds
of knowledge.

It is easy to realize that the difference between the sexes
concerns only the body—being, correctly, only [in] this part
that serves for the production of men. Since the mind
participates [in this activity] only by giving its assent (and
giving it in all people in the same manner), **[110]** we can
conclude that it is sexless.

If we consider the mind in itself, we find that it is equal
and of the same nature in all people—and capable of all
kinds of thoughts. The smallest [ideas] engage it just like the
greatest. No less [intellect] is needed to know a gnat than
an elephant. Whosoever understands the light and the fire
of a spark comprehends what the light of the sun is. When
we have become accustomed to thinking about things that
relate to the mind alone, we see them all at least as clearly as
the more substantial things that we perceive by the senses. I
do not discern any greater difference between the mind of a
coarse, ignorant man and that of a refined, enlightened one
than between the mind of the same **[111]** man considered at
the age of ten and at the age of forty. As no greater [difference]
appears between the minds of the two sexes, we can say
that the difference between them is not in that aspect [of
their being]. The constitution of the body—but particularly
education, exercise, and the influence of everything that
surrounds us—[these things] are everywhere the natural,
evident causes of much of the diversity that is seen [between
the sexes].

God joins the mind to the flesh of a woman as to that
of a man, and He unites them by the same laws. Feelings,
passions, and will make and maintain this union. And the
mind, not functioning differently in one sex than in the other,
is equally capable of the same things [in both]. **[112]** That
is even clearer when the head (which is the sole organ of
knowledge and the place where the mind performs all its
functions) alone is considered. The most precise [study of]
anatomy does not show us any difference between men and
women in this part [of the body]. The brains of women

sciences, et où l'Esprit fait toutes ses fonctions. L'Anatomie la plus exacte ne nous fait remarquer aucune difference dans cette partie entre les hommes & les femmes: le cerveau de celles-cy est entièrement semblable au nôtre: les impressions des sens, s'y reçoivent, & s'y ressemblent de même façon & ne s'y conservent point autrement pour l'imagination & pour la Memoire. Les femmes entendent comme nous, par les oreilles, elles voyent par les yeux, & elles goustent avec la langue; & il n'y a rien de particulier dans la disposition de ces organes, sinon que d'ordinaire elles les ont plus delicats, ce qui est un avantage. De sorte que les objets exterieurs les touchent de la [113] même façon; la lumiere par les yeux, & le son par les oreilles. [Les femmes sont capables de la Metaphysique.] Qui les empêchera donc de s'appliquer à la consideration d'elles-mêmes; d'examiner en quoy consiste la nature de l'Esprit; combien il a de sortes de pensées, & comment elles s'excitent à l'occasion de certains mouvemens corporels; de consulter ensuite les idées naturelles qu'elles ont de Dieu, & de commencer par les choses spirituelles à disposer avec ordre leurs pensées, & à se faire la science qu'on appelle Methaphysique.

[Elles sont capables de la Physique & de la Medecine.] Puisqu'elles ont aussi des yeux & des mains, ne pourroient-elles pas faire elles-mêmes, ou voir faire à d'autres la dissection d'un Corps humain en considerer la Symmetrie & la structure, remarquer la diversité, la difference & le rapport de ses parties, [114] leurs figures, leurs mouvemens, & leurs fonctions, les alterations, dont elles sont susceptibles, & conclure de là le moyen de les conserver dans une bonne disposition, & de les y rétablir, quand elle est une fois changée.

Il ne leur faudroit plus pour cela, que connoistre la nature des Corps exterieurs, qui ont rapport avec le leur, en découvrir les proprietez, & tout ce qui les rend capables d'y faire quelque impression bonne ou mauvaise: cela se connoît par le ministere des sens, & par les diverses experiences qu'on en fait: & les femmes estant également capables de l'un & de l'autre, peuvent apprendre aussi bien que nous, la Physique & la Medecine.

Faut-il tant d'ésprit, pour connoître, que la respiration est [115] absolument necessaire à la conservation de la vie: &

are just like ours. Sense impressions are received there and arranged in the same way and not retained differently for the imagination and memory. Women hear as we do—through the ears. They see through the eyes, and they taste with the tongue. And there is nothing unique in the arrangement of these organs—except that they are ordinarily more delicate in women (which is an advantage). Consequently, exterior objects affect women in the [113] same way [that they do us]: light through the eyes and sound through the ears. Who, therefore, will prevent women from applying themselves to the study of themselves: to the investigation of the nature of the mind (i.e., how many kinds of thoughts it has, and how they are excited by certain corporeal movements)? And, subsequently, [who will prevent women] from reflecting on the innate ideas that they have about God and from beginning through spiritual things to dispose their thoughts in order and to practice the science called metaphysics?

Since women too have eyes and hands, would they not be able to perform for themselves (or watch others perform) the dissection of a human body? [Could they not] consider its symmetry and structure—notice the diversity, the difference and the relationship of its parts, [114] their shapes, their movements, and their functions, and the changes to which they are susceptible—and learn from that how to keep bodies healthy and how to restore them to health once it has failed?

Nothing more is required for women to do that than to understand the nature of external bodies that have a bearing on their own—to discover their properties, and to identify all that enables these things to make an impression (good or bad) on their own persons. This is understood through the agency of the senses and by means of various experiments that can be conducted. And women, being equally capable of both, can learn physics and medicine as well as we.

Does it take much intelligence to understand that respiration is [115] absolutely necessary for the preservation of life? —and that it consists of the movement of air, which, entering by the channel of the nose and the mouth, insinuates itself into the lungs to cool the blood that circulates through them, and [that it] there causes different changes depending on how it is thickened (more or less) by the mixture of

qu'elle se fait par le moyen de l'air, qui entrant par le Canal du nez & de la bouche, s'insinuë dans les poulmons pour y rafraichir le sang qui y passe en circulant, & y cause des alterations differentes, selon qu'il est plus ou moins grossier par le mélange des vapeurs & des exhalaisons, dont on le voit quelquefois mélé.

[En quoy consiste le goust.] Est-ce une chose si difficile, que de découvrir que le goust des alimens consiste de la part du Corps, dans la differente maniere dont ils sont delayez sur la langue par la salive. Il n'y a personne qui ne sente aprés le repas que les viandes qu'on met alors dans la bouche, s'y divisant tout autrement que celles dont on s'est nourry y causent un sentiment moins agréable. Ce qui [116] reste à connoître des fonctions du corps humain, considerés avec ordre, n'a pas plus de difficulté.

[Elles peuvent connoistre les Passions.] Les Passions sont assurément ce qu'il y a de plus curieux en cette matiere. On y peut remarquer deux choses, les mouvemens du corps, avec les pensées & les émotions de l'ame qui y sont jointes. Les femmes peuvent connoître cela aussi aisément que nous. Quant aux causes qui excitent les Passions, on sçâit comment elles le font, quand on a une fois bien compris par l'étude de la Physique la maniere dont les choses qui nous environnent, nous importent, & nous touchent; & par l'experience & l'usage, comment nous y joignons & en separons nos volontez.

[Elles peuvent apprendre la Logique.] En faisant des Meditations regulieres sur les objets des trois [117] sciences dont on vient de parler, une femme peut observer que l'ordre de ses pensées doit suivre celuy de la nature, qu'elles sont justes lorsqu'elles sont conformes, qu'il n'y a que la précipitation dans nos iugemens, qui empêche cette justesse, & remarquant ensuite l'Economie qu'elle auroit gardée pour y arriver, elle pouroit faire des reflexions, qui luy seviroient de règle pour l'avenir & s'en former une Logique.

Si l'on disoit nonobstant cela, que les femmes ne peuvent pas acquerir par elles-mêmes ces connoisances ce qui se diroit gratis; au moins ne pourroit on nier qu'elles le puissent avec le secours des Maistres & des livres, comme l'ont fait les plus habiles gens, dans tous les siecles.

the vapors and exhalations with which we sometimes see it mixed?

Is it so difficult a thing to discover that the taste of foods derives, as far as the body is concerned, from the different ways in which foods are diluted on the tongue by the saliva? Everyone senses that after a meal the food that we then put in our mouths (which break down in a totally different fashion than that with which we were nourished) causes a less agreeable feeling. What **[116]** remains to be understood about the functions of the human body (being considered in an orderly way) is not more difficult [to comprehend].

The passions are surely the most curious aspects of this subject. We can notice two things about them: the movements of the body, and the thoughts and the emotions of the soul that are joined to them. Women can understand that as easily as we [can]. Once we have figured out from the study of physiology how the things that surround us affect us and stimulate us, we learn how the things that excite the passions operate—and, by experience and practice, how we let our wills become involved (or not) in these passions.

While meditating regularly on the topics of the three **[117]** sciences of which we have just spoken, a woman might observe that the order of her thoughts has to follow that of nature: that her thoughts are accurate when they conform [to nature, and] that only haste in our judgments impedes this precision. Then noticing the economy [of steps] that she should have observed in arriving at her goal, she could make some reflections that would serve her as a rule for the future and could form a [system of] logic for herself.

If it were said, notwithstanding, that women cannot acquire this knowledge by themselves (which would be unfounded), at least it could not be denied that women could learn it with the help of teachers and of books (as have the most clever men in all ages).

It is enough to note that order is a **[118]** recognized attribute of the [female] sex to convince ourselves that [women are] capable of understanding the formulae of mathematics. And since we attribute to women more inventiveness and artifice than men have, we would contradict ourselves even to

[Le Mathematiques.] Il suffit d'alléguer la propre-**[118]**-té reconnuë du Sexe pour faire croire qu'il est capable d'entendre les proportions de Mathematique: & nous nous contredirions nous-mesmes de douter, que s'il s'appliquoit à la construction des Machines il n'y reüssist aussi bien que le nôtre puisque nous luy attribüons plus de genie, & plus d'artifice.

[Elles sont capables de l'Astronomie.] Il ne faut que des yeux & un peu d'attention pour observer les Phenomenes de la nature, pour remarquer que le Soleil, & tous les corps lumineux, qui sont au Ciel, sont des feux veritables, puis qu'il nous frappent & nous éclairent de même que les feux d'cy [*sic*] bas, qu'ils paroissent successivement répondre à divers endroits de la terre, & pour pouvoir ainsi juger de leurs mouvements & de leurs cours: & quiconque peut rouler dans sa teste **[119]** de grands desseins, & en faire joüer les ressorts, y peut aussi faire rouler avec justesse toute la machine du monde, s'il en a une fois bien observé les diverses apparences.

[Distinction entre les sciences.] Nous avons déja trouvé dans les femmes toutes les dispositions qui rendent les hommes propres aux sciences, qui les regardent en eux-mêmes: & si nous continüons d'y regarder d'aussi prés, nous y trouverons encore celles qu'il faut pour les sciences, qui les concernent comme liez avec leurs semblables dans la societé civile.

C'est un défaut de la Philosophie vulgaire de mettre entre les sciences une si grande distinction, qu'on ne peut gueres suivant la Methode qui luy est particuliere, reconnoître aucune liaison entr'elles. Ce qui est **[120]** cause que l'on restreint si fort l'étenduë de l'esprit humain, en s'imaginant, qu'un même homme n'est presque jamais capable de plusieurs sciences; que pour estre propre à la Physique & à la Medecine, on ne l'est pas pour cela à l'Eloquence, ny à la Theologie; & qu'il faut autant de genies differens, qu'il y a de sciences differentes.

Cette pensée vient d'une part, de ce que l'on confond ordinairement la nature avec la coûtume, en prenant la disposition de certaines personnes, à une science plûtost qu'à l'autre, pour un effet de leur constitution naturelle, au lieu que ce n'est souvent qu'une inclination casuelle, qui vient de la necessité, de l'éducation ou de l'habitude; & de l'autre part, faute d'avoir remarqué qu'il n'y a pro-**[121]**-prement qu'une

doubt that if women applied themselves to the construction of machines, they would succeed as well as our [sex does].

Only eyes and a little awareness are needed to observe the phenomena of nature: to notice that the sun and all the luminous bodies in the sky are really fires (since they impress us and provide light for us just like fires here below), and to be able thus to understand their movements and their course (since they appear to respond in succession to different places on the earth). And whoever can turn over [119] great designs in his head and set their internal works in play can also accurately revolve the whole mechanism of the universe—if he has once carefully observed its various attributes.

We have already found in women all the dispositions that render men fit for the sciences that deal with people in themselves. And if we continue to examine them closely, we will find in them further dispositions needed for [the study of] the sciences that concern them as they are bound with their fellows in society.

It is a weakness of ordinary philosophy to make sharp distinctions between sciences so that we can scarcely (following the method that is characteristic of it) recognize any links among them. [120] We have thereby so strictly limited the range of the human mind—imagining that one and the same person is almost never capable of learning many sciences (that to be suited to physical science and medicine one is not [fit] for rhetoric or theology—and that there must be as many different kinds of minds as there are different sciences).

This thought derives, on the one hand, from the fact that people ordinarily confound nature with custom by taking the disposition of certain persons to one science rather than another for an effect of their natural constitutions. Instead, this is often only a casual inclination that springs from necessity, education, or habit. And people, on the other hand, fail to notice that there is, [121] properly, only one science in the world: the science of ourselves. All the other sciences are mere special applications of it.

Indeed, the problem we have today in learning languages, ethics, and the rest [of the fields of knowledge] derives from the fact that we do not know their relationship to this universal science. This may be the reason why all those

science au monde, qui est celle de nous-mêmes, & que toutes les autres n'en sont que des applications particulieres.

En effet, la difficulté que l'on trouve aujourd'huy à apprendre les Langues, la Morale, & le reste consiste en ce qu'on ne sçait pas les rapporter à cette science generale: d'où il pourroit arriver, que tous ceux qui croiroient les femmes capables de la Physique, & de la Medecine, n'estimeroient pas pour cela qu'elles le fussent de celles dont on va parler. Cependant, la difficulté est égale des deux côtez: il s'agit par tout de bien penser. On le fait en appliquant serieusement son esprit aux objets qui se presentent, pour s'en former des idées claires & distinctes, pour les envisager par toutes leurs fa-[122]-ces, & tous les rapports differens, & pour n'en juger, que sur ce qui paroît manifestement veritable. Il ne faut avec cela que disposer ses pensées dans un ordre naturel, pour avoir une science parfaite. Il n'y a rien en cela qui soit au dessus des femmes; & celles qui seroient instruites par cette voye, de la Physique & de la Medecine, seroient capables d'avancer de même dans toutes les autres.

[Elles sont capables de la Grammaire.] Pourquoy ne pourroient-elles pas reconnoître que la necessité de vivre en societé nous obligeant de communiquer nos pensées par quelques signes exterieurs, le plus commode de tous est la parole, qui consiste dans l'usage des mots, dont les hommes sont convenus. Qu'il doit y en avoir autant de sortes qu'il y a d'idées; qu'il faut qu'ils ayent [123] entr'eux quelque rapport de son & de signification pour les pouvoir apprendre & retenir plus aisément, & pour n'estre pas obligé de les multiplier à l'infini, qu'il les faut arranger dans l'ordre le plus naturel, & le plus conforme à celuy de nos pensées, & n'en employer dans le discours, qu'autant qu'on en a besoin pour se faire entendre.

Ces refléxions mettroient une femme en état de travailler en Academicienne à la perfection de sa langue natûrelle, reformant où retranchant les mauvais mots, en introduisant de nouveaux, reglant l'usage sur la raison, & sur les idées justes qu'on a des Langues: Et la methode avec laquelle elle auroit appris celle de son païs, luy serviroit merveilleusement à apprendre celles des étrangers, à en découvrir les délica-[124]-tesses, à en lire les autheurs, & à devenir ainsi tres-habile dans la Grammaire, & dans ce qu'on appelle Humanitez.

who believe that women are capable of physical science and medicine might not have judged them fit for those [sciences] of which we are about to speak. However, the difficulty is equal on both sides: it is a question above all of thinking correctly. This is done by seriously applying the mind to objects that present themselves—to form clear and distinct ideas of them, to view them in all their facets [122] and in all their different relations, and to predicate of them only what appears manifestly true. Then, in order to have a perfect science, it is necessary only to dispose one's thoughts in a natural order. There is nothing in this that is beyond women, and those who would be instructed in physical science and medicine by this method would be able to advance by the same route in all other [fields].

Why could women not recognize that the necessity of living in society obligates us to communicate our thoughts by some external sign—the most convenient of which is speech (which consists of the use of words on which people agree)? [Why could women not recognize] that there must be as many kinds [of words] as there are ideas, that they must have [123] among them some relationship of sound and meaning to make it possible to learn and to retain [them] most easily (and so that it is not necessary to multiply them infinitely), that they must be arranged in the most natural order that conforms best to that of our thoughts and not be employed in discourse beyond what is needed to make sense?.

These reflections would position a woman to work like an academician in perfecting her natural language: improving or cutting out inadequate words, introducing new ones, and governing usage by reason and by the accurate ideas that we have of languages. And the means by which she would have learned the language of her country would serve her marvelously to acquire the languages of strangers—to discover the nuances thereof, [124] to read their authors, and thus to become highly skilled in grammar and in what are called the "humanities."

Women as well as men speak only to make things understood as they understand them—and to dispose their fellows to do what they want them to do (this is called "persuasion"). Women naturally succeed at this better than

[L'Eloquence.] Les femmes, aussi bien que les hommes, ne parlent que pour faire entendre les choses comme elles les connoissent, & pour disposer leurs semblables à agir comme elles souhaittent, ce qu'on appelle persuader. Elles y reüssissent naturellement mieux que nous. Et pour le faire encore avec art, elles n'auroient qu'à s'étudier à presenter les choses, comme elles se presentent à elles, ou qu'elles s'y presenteroient, si elles estoient à la place de ceux qu'elles voudroient toucher. Tous les hommes estans faits de même maniere, sont presque toûjours émûs de même par les objets; & s'il y a quelque difference, elle vient de leurs inclinations, [125] de leurs habitudes, ou de leur état: ce qu'une femme connoîtroit avec un peu de refléxion & d'usage; & sçachant disposer ses pensées, en la façon la plus convenable, les exprimer avec politesse & avec grace, & y ajuster les gestes, l'air du visage, & la voix, elle possederoit la veritable Eloquence.

[La Morale.] Il n'est pas croyable que les femmes puissent pratiquer si hautement la vertu, sans estre capables d'en penétrer les maximes fondamentales. En effet, une femme déja instruite, comme on l'a representée, découvriroit elle-même les regles de sa conduite; en découvrant les trois sortes de devoirs qui comprennent toute la Morale; dont les premiers regardent Dieu, les seconds nous regardent nous-mêmes, & les troisiémes nôtre prochain. Les idées [126] claires & distinctes qu'elle auroit formées de son esprit, & de l'union de l'ésprit avec le corps, la porteroient infailliblement à reconnoître qu'il y a un autre esprit infini, Autheur de toute la nature, & à concevoir pour luy les sentimens sur lesquels la Religion est fondée. Et aprés avoir appris par la Physique en quoy consiste le plaisir des sens, & de quelle façon les choses exterieures contribuënt à la perfection de l'esprit & à la conservation du corps, elle ne manqueroit pas de juger qu'il faut estre ennemi de soi-même pour n'en pas user avec beaucoup de moderation. Si elle venoit ensuite à se considerer comme engagée dans la societé civile avec d'autres personnes semblables à elle, & sujettes aux mêmes passions, & à des besoins qu'on ne peut satis-[127]-faire sans une assistance mutuelle; elle entreroit sans peine dans cette pensée de laquelle dépend toute nostre justice, qu'il faut traiter les autres, comme on veut estre

we [do]. Moreover, to do it artfully, they would only have to learn to present things as they appear to them—or as these things would present themselves if women were in the position of the people they want to influence. Since all people are constructed in the same way, they are almost always affected the same by objects. And if there is some difference, it derives from their inclinations, **[125]** their habits, or their state. With a little reflection and practice a woman could come to understand this and, knowing how to dispose her thoughts in the most convenient fashion (expressing them with politeness and with grace) and how to adapt her gestures, the expression on her face, and her voice to her thoughts, she could possess true eloquence.

It is not to be believed that women could practice virtue as loftily [as they do] without being capable of delving into its fundamental principles. Indeed, a woman (already instructed as we have represented her) would discover the rules of her conduct for herself. [She would] discover [that there are] three kinds of duties that encompass all of morality: the first concern God, the second ourselves, and the third our neighbor. The clear and distinct ideas **[126]** that she would have formed of her mind and of the union of the spirit with the body would bring her unfailingly to recognize that there is another Spirit—infinite, the author of all nature—and to conceive for Him the feelings on which religion is based. And after having learned from physical science in what the pleasure of the senses consists and how external things contribute to the perfecting of the mind and to the preservation of the body, she would not fail to conclude that a person has to be an enemy to himself not to use these things with great moderation. If she came next to consider herself as [a person] involved in society with other persons like her (and subject to the same passions and to needs that cannot be satisfied **[127]** without mutual assistance), she would have no difficulty arriving at the thought on which our whole [sense of] justice depends: that we must treat others as we wish to be treated—and that we must for that [reason] curb our desires (the disorder of which—that is called "cupidity"—causes all the trouble and all the unhappiness of life).

traité; & qu'on doit pour cela reprimer ses desirs, dont le
déreglement qu'on appelle Cupidité, cause tout le trouble &
tout le malheur de la vie.

[Le droit & la Politique.] Elle se confirmeroit davantage
dans la persuasion du dernier de ces devoirs, si elle poussoit
plus loin sa pointe, en découvrant le fond de la Politique,
& de la Jurisprudence. Comme l'une & l'autre ne regarde
que les devoirs des hommes entr'eux, elle jugeroit que pour
comprendre à quoy ils sont obligez dans la societé civile, il faut
sçavoir ce qui les a portez à la former. Elle les considereroit
donc comme hors de cette societé, & elle les [128] trouveroit
tous entierement libres & egaux, & avec la seule inclination de
se conserver, & un droit égal sur tout ce qui y seroit necessaire.
Mais elle remarqueroit que cette égalité les engageant dans
une guerre, ou une défiance continuelle, ce qui seroit contraire
à leur fin, la lumiere naturelle dicteroit, qu'ils ne pourroient
vivre en paix, sans relâcher chacun de son droit, & sans faire
des conventions, & des contracts: que pour rendre ces actions
valides & se tirer d'inquietude, ce seroit une necessité d'avoir
recours à un Tiers, lequel prenant l'authorité contraindroit
chacun de garder ce qu'il auroit promis aux autres; que
celui-cy n'ayant esté choisi que pour l'avantage de ses sujets,
il ne devroit point avoir d'autre but; & que pour arriver à la
fin de son éta-[129]-blissement, il faudroit qu'il fût maître des
biens & des personnes, de la paix, & de la guerre.

En examinant à fond cette matiere, qui empecheroit
qu'une femme ne trouvast ce que c'est que l'Equité naturelle;
ce que c'est que Contract, authorité, & obeissance; quelle est
la nature de la Loy, quel usage on doit faire des peines, en
quoy consiste le droit Civil & celuy des gens, quels sont les
devoirs des Princes, & des sujets: En un mot, elle apprendroit
par ses propres refléxions & par les Livres, ce qu'il faut pour
estre Iurisconsulte, & Politique.

[La Géographie.] Aprés qu'elle auroit acquis une parfaite
connoissance d'elle-même, & qu'elle se seroit solidement
instruite des regles generales de la conduite des hommes, elle
seroit peut-étre bien-aise de [130] s'informer aussi de quelle
maniere on vit dans le païs étrangers. Comme elle auroit
remarqué que les changemens de temps, de saisons, de lieu,
d'âge, de nourriture, de compagnie, d'exercice luy auroient

She might all the more convince herself of the necessity of the least of these moral obligations if she were to push further to the point of discovering the grounds for politics and law. As both these things concern nothing but the duties people have to each other, she would decide that to understand what people are obligated to in society, she must comprehend their motives in forming it. She would then picture human beings without a social context—and she would **[128]** find them all [to be] completely free and equal, [each] with the sole inclination to preserve himself and an equal right to all that is necessary to this [end]. But she would observe that since this equality would lead them into a war or a continual state of strife that was contrary to their end, the natural light [of reason] would dictate that they could not live in peace without each of them easing up on his right[s] and without making some pacts and contracts. To render these [legal] actions valid and to extricate themselves from disturbance[s] recourse to a third party would be necessary. [This third party], assuming authority, would constrain each to keep the promises he had made to the others. Having been chosen only for the advantage of his subjects, he should have no other goal. And, to fulfill **[129]** the purpose for which he is appointed, it would be necessary that he be master of property and persons, peace and war.

While examining this matter in depth, what would prevent a woman from discovering what constitutes natural justice: i.e., contract, authority, and obedience, the nature of the law, the use to be made of the penalties which make up civil codes and the laws of nations, and the duties of princes and their subjects? In a word, she could learn from her own reflections and from books all that is required to be a lawyer or a politician.

Once she had acquired a perfect knowledge of herself and been solidly instructed in the general rules of human conduct, she might easily (perhaps) **[130]** inquire as to how people live in foreign lands. Since she would have noticed that changes in time, season, place, age, diet, companions, [and] exercise have caused alterations and different emotions in her, she would have no trouble discovering that those various things produce the same effects on whole communities of people. They have

causé des alterations & des passions differentes, elle n'auroit
pas de peine à reconnoître que ces diversitez-là produisent le
même effet, à l'égard des peuples entiers: [D'où la diversité
des moeurs qui se voit entre les peuples.] qu'ils ont des
inclinations, des coûtumes, des moeurs, & des loix differentes,
selon qu'ils sont plus prés ou plus loin des Mers, du Midy, ou
du Septentrion, selon qu'il y a des plaines, des montagnes,
des rivieres, & des bois chez-eux, que le terroin est plus
ou moins fertile, & porte des nourritures particulieres; &
selon le commerce, & les affaires qu'ils ont avec d'autres
peuples voisins, ou éloi-[131]-gnez; Elle pourroit étudier
toutes ces choses, & apprendre ainsi quelles sont les moeurs,
les richesses, la religion, le governement, & les interests
de vingt ou trente Nations differentes, aussi facilement que
d'autant de familles particulieres. Car pour ce qui est de la
situation des Royaumes, du rapport des Mers & des Terres,
des Isles & du Continent; il n'y a pas plus de difficulté à
l'apprendre dans une Carte, qu'à sçavoir les quartiers & les
ruës de sa Ville, & les routes de la Province où l'on demeure.
   [L'histoire prophane.] La connoissance du present pourroit luy faire naître l'envie de connoître aussi le passé; &
ce qu'elle auroit retenu de Geographie luy seroit d'un grand
secours dans ce dessein, luy donnant moyen d'entendre mieux
les affaires, comme les guerres; les **[132]** voyages, & les
negotiations, luy marquant les lieux où elles seront faites; les
passages, les chemins, & la liaison des Etats. Mais ce qu'elle
sçauroit de la maniere d'agir des hommes en general, par les
refléxions qu'elle auroit faites sur elle-même, la feroit entrer
dans le fin de la Politique, des interests, & des passions; &
l'aideroit à découvrir, le mobile & le ressort des entreprises,
la source des revolutions, & à suppléer dans les grands
desseins, les petites choses qui les ont fait reüssir, & qui sont
échapées aux Historiens: & suivant les idées justes qu'elle
auroit du vice & de la vertu, elle remarqueroit la flaterie, la
passion, & l'ignorance des Autheurs, & se garantiroit ainsi de
la corruption, que l'on prend dans la lecture des Histoires,
où ces défauts sont mé-[133]-lez ordinairement. Comme la
Politique ancienne n'estoit pas si rafinée que la moderne, &
que les interests des Princes estoient moins liez autrefois qu'à
present, & le commerce moins étendu, il faut plus d'esprit,

different inclinations, customs, manners, and laws according to whether they are nearer to or farther from seas or from the south or the north; whether there are plains, mountains, rivers, and forests around them; whether their soil is more or less fertile and yields special foods; whether they have trade and conduct business with other peoples—either neighboring or distant. **[131]** A woman could study all these things and thus become familiar with the customs, the resources, the religion, the government, and the interests of twenty or thirty different nations as easily as so many individual families. It is no more difficult to find out from a map how kingdoms are situated (the relationships of seas and lands, of islands and continents) than to become acquainted with the districts and the streets of the town and the roads of the province where one lives.

Knowledge of the present would cause a desire to be born in a woman to know the past. The information that she had acquired from geography would be of great help to her in this project—giving her a way to better understand affairs like wars, **[132]** voyages, and treaties (showing her where they took place—paths, roads, and the connections between states). But what she had learned of the way men generally behave (through her own observations) would equip her to penetrate the plot[s] of politics, interests, and passions. And it would help her to discover the motive power and the springs of enterprises [and] the source of revolutions. [And it would enable her] to fill in the little things that have made great strategies succeed—[details] that have escaped [the notice of] historians. And by means of her sound ideas of vice and virtue, she would spot flattery, passion, and the ignorance of authors and guard herself thus from the corruption that we encounter in reading histories (which are commonly shot through with these defects). **[133]** Since ancient politics were not as subtle as [are] modern [politics] (the selfishness of princes being less restrained formerly than now and commerce less extensive), more intelligence is needed to understand and

pour entendre & démêler les Gazettes, que Titelive & Quinte curse.

[L'histoire Ecclesiastique & la Theologie.] Il y a quantité de personnes qui trouvent l'histoire Ecclesiastique plus agreable & plus solide, que l'histoire prophane ou civile: parce qu'on y remarque, que la raison & la vertu sont poussées plus loin; & que les passions & les préjugez couverts du prétexte de la religion, font prendre à l'esprit un tour tout particulier dans sa conduite. Vne femme s'y appliqueroit avec d'autant plus d'affection, qu'elle la jugeroit, plus importante: elle se convaincroit que les Livres de L'Ecritu-[134]-re ne sont pas moins authentiques que tous les autres que nous avons; qu'ils contiennent la veritable Religion, & toutes les maximes sur lesquelles elle est fondée; que le nouveau Testament où commence proprement l'histoire du Christianisme, n'est pas plus difficile à entendre que les Autheurs Grecs & Latins; que ceux qui le lisent dans la simplicité des enfans, ne cherchant que le Royaume de Dieu, en découvrent la verité & le sens avec plus de facilité & de plaisir que celuy des Enigmes, des Emblêmes, & des Fables. Et aprés s'estre reglé l'esprit par la morale de Iesus Christ, elle se trouveroit en état de diriger ses semblables, de lever leurs scrupules, & de resoudre les cas de conscience avec plus de solidité, que si elle s'étoit remply la téte de tous [135] les Casuistes du monde.

Ie ne vois rien qui empéchast que dans la suite de son étude, elle n'observat aussi facilement que seroit un homme comment l'Evangile est passé de main en main, de Royaume en Royaume, de siecle en siecle, jusqu'au sien; qu'elle ne prît par la lecture des Peres l'idée de la vraye Theologie, & ne trouvât qu'elle ne consiste qu'à sçavoir l'histoire des Chrétiens & les sentimens particuliers, de ceux qui en ont écrit. Ainsi elle se rendroit aisez habile pour faire des ouvrages sur la Religion, pour annoncer la verité, & pour combattre les nouveautez, en montrant ce qui a toûjours esté crû, & dans toute l'Eglise, sur les matieres contestées.

[Le droit Civil.] Si une femme est capable de s'instruire par l'histoire de ce que sont toutes les societés publiques, [136] comment-elles se sont formées, & comment-elles se maintiennent en vertu d'une authorité fixe & constante, exercée par des Magistrats & des Officiers subordonnez

unravel the newspapers than [the works of] Titus Livy³ and Quintus Curtius.⁴

There are many people who find ecclesiastical history more enjoyable and more sound than secular or civil history, for they perceive that reason and virtue are thrust more to the fore in it (and that [the sight of] passions and prejudices covered with a pretext of religion makes the mind take a particular turn in its behavior). A woman would apply herself to this study with so much the more affection, for she would judge it [to be] more important. She might convince herself: that the books of the Scriptures **[134]** are no less authentic than all the others that we have; that they contain the true religion and all the principles on which it is based; that the New Testament (where the history of Christianity properly begins) is not more difficult to understand than the Greek and Latin authors; that those who read it with the simplicity of children (seeking only the kingdom of God) will discover truth and sense in it with more facility and delight than those [who look for] enigmas, symbols and fables. And, having patterned her mind on the ethical system of Jesus Christ, she would find herself prepared to guide her fellows, to lighten their burdens, and to resolve cases of conscience with more dependability than if she had filled her head with all **[135]** the casuistries in the world.

I see nothing that would prevent her, in the pursuit of her studies, from observing (as easily as would a man) how the Gospel has been passed from hand to hand, from kingdom to kingdom, from century to century, unto our own time. [There is nothing to prevent] her from acquiring the concept of true theology by reading the fathers—and finding that it consists only in knowing the history of Christianity and the unique thoughts of those who have written about it. In this way she might render herself sufficiently skilled to write books on religion, to proclaim the truth, and to combat novelties (demonstrating what has always been believed in the whole church about disputed matters).

---

³Titus Livius (59 B.C.–A.D. 17), Roman historian.
⁴Roman who wrote a history of Alexander the Great; the date of his life is uncertain.

les uns aux autres, elle ne l'est pas moins de s'informer de l'application de cette authorité, dans les Loix, les Ordonnances, & les Reglemens, pour la conduite de ceux qui y sont soûmis, tant pour le rapport des personnes, selon les diverses conditions, que pour la possession & pour l'usage des biens. Est-ce une chose si difficile à sçavoir, quel rapport il y a entre un mary & sa femme, entre le pere & les enfans, entre le maistre & les domestiques, entre un Seigneur, & ses vasseaux, entre ceux qui sont alliez, entre un Tuteur & un Pupille? Y a-t'il tant de mystère à entendre ce que c'est que de pos-[137]-seder par achat, par échange, par donation, par legs, par testament, par prescription, par usufruit, & quelles sont les conditions necessaires pour rendre ces usages valides?

[Le Droit Canon.] Il ne paroist pas qu'il falle [*sic*] plus d'intelligence pour bien prendre l'esprit de la societé Chrétienne, que celuy de la societé Civile; pour former une idée juste de l'authorité, qui luy est particuliere, & sur laquelle est fondée toute sa conduite, & pour distinguer précisément celle que Iesus Christ a laissée à son Eglise, d'avec la domination qui n'appartient qu'aux Puissances temporelles. Aprés avoir fait cette distinction absolument necessaire pour bien entendre le Droit Canon une femme le pourroit étudier, & remarquer comment l'Eglise s'est reglée sur le [138] Civil, & comment l'on a mêlé la jurisdiction seculiere avec la spirituelle; en quoy consiste la Hierarchie; quelles sont les fonctions des Prélats, ce que peuvent les Conciles, les Papes, les Evéques, & les Pasteurs: ce que c'est que Discipline, quelles en sont les regles, & les changemens: Ce que c'est que Canons, privileges, & exemptions: Comment se sont établis les benefices, quel en est l'usage & la possession: En un mot, qu'elles [*sic*] sont les Coûtumes & les Ordonnances de l'Eglise, & les devoirs de tous ceux qui la composent. Il n'y a rien là dequoy une femme ne soit tres-capable, & ainsi elle pourroit devenir tres-sçavante dans le Droit Canon.

Voila quelques idées generales des plus hautes connoissances dont les hommes se sont [139] servis pour signaler leur esprit & pour faire fortune, & dont ils sont depuis si long-temps en possession au préjudice des femmes. Et quoy qu'elles n'y ayent pas moins de droit qu'eux, ils ont neantmoins à leur égard des pensées & une conduite qui

If a woman is capable of using history to teach herself what all public societies are like **[136]** (i.e., how they are formed, and how they preserve themselves by means of fixed, constant authority exercised by magistrates and officers subordinated one to another), she is not less [able] to inquire into the application of this authority in laws, ordinances, and rules for the direction of those subject to these things (as much for the relationship of persons according to their diverse conditions as for the possession and the use of goods). Is it so difficult to understand the relationship of a husband and his wife, a father and children, a master and servants, a lord and his vassals, [ties] among those who are allied, between a tutor and a pupil? Is there such a mystery in understanding possession **[137]** of goods by purchase, exchange, donation, bequest, inheritance, prescription, [and] usufruct—and the conditions necessary to render these arrangements valid?

It would not seem that more intelligence would be needed to comprehend the spirit of Christian than civil society—to form an accurate idea of the authority that is particular to the church and on which all its conduct is based and to distinguish precisely what Jesus Christ has bequeathed to his church from the dominion that belongs only to temporal powers. After having made this distinction, which is absolutely necessary for a good understanding of canon law, a woman could study this law and discover how the church has patterned itself on the **[138]** civil code and how secular and spiritual jurisdictions are combined. [She could find out] what the hierarchy consists of, what the functions of prelates are, what councils, popes, bishops, and pastors can do; what discipline is; what [its] rules and amendments are; what canons, privileges, and exemptions are; how benefices are established; what the use and possession of them is. In a word—what the customs and ordinances of the church and the duties of all those who compose it are. There is nothing here that a woman is not very capable of understanding, and, consequently, she could become deeply learned in canon law.

These are some general ideas about the fields of advanced learning that men used **[139]** to earn a reputation for intelligence and to make their fortunes and of which, for so long a time, they have been in possession to the detriment

sont d'autant plus injustes, qu'on ne voit rien de pareil dans l'usage des biens du corps.

L'on a jugé à propos que la prescription eust lieu pour la paix & la seureté des familles: c'est à dire, qu'un homme qui auroit joüy du bien d'autruy sans trouble & de bonne foy, durant un certain espace de temps, en demeureroit possesseur, sans qu'on y peust rien prétendre aprés. Mais on ne s'est jamais avisé de croire que ceux qui en estoient décheus par negligence, ou autrement, fussent incapables d'y [140] rentrer par quelque voye, & l'on n'a jamais regardé leur inhabilité que comme civile.

Au contraire, l'on ne s'est pas contenté de ne point rappeller les femmes au partage des sciences & des emplois, aprés une longue prescription contr'elles; on a passé plus loin, & l'on s'est figuré que leur exclusion est fondée sur une impuissance naturelle de leur part.

[Ce n'est point à cause d'une indisposition naturelle que les femmes sont excluës des sciences.] Cependant il n'y a rien de plus chimerique que cette imagination. Car soit que l'on considere les sciences en elles-mêmes, soit qu'on regarde l'organe qui sert à les acquerir, on trouvera que les deux Sexes y sont également disposez. Il n'y a qu'une seule methode, & une seule voye pour insinuër la verité dans l'esprit, dont elle est la nourriture, comme il n'y en a qu'une pour [141] faire entrer les alimens, dans toutes sortes d'éstomacs pour la subsistance du corps. Pour ce qui est des differentes dispositions de cét organe, qui rendent plus ou moins propres aux sciences, si l'on veut reconnoistre de bonne foy ce qui en est, on avoüera que le plus est pour les femmes.

[Qui sont ceux qui sont les plus propres aux sciences.] L'on ne peut disconvenir, que ceux d'entre les hommes qui sont si grossiers & si materiels, ne soient ordinairement stupides, & qu'au contraire les plus délicats sont toûjours les plus spirituels. Ie trouve là-dessus l'experience trop generale & trop constante, pour avoir besoin de l'appuyer icy de raisons: ainsi le beau Sexe estant d'un temperamment plus délicat que le nostre, ne manqueroit pas de l'égaler au moins, s'il s'appliquoit à l'étude.

Ie prévois bien que cette pen-[142]-sée ne sera pas goûtée de beaucoup de gens qui la trouveront un peu forte. Ie n'y

of women. And although women have no less right to these fields than men, men have nevertheless in respect to women thoughts and behavior that are so much the more unjust that nothing has been seen to equal it in the use of the goods of the body.

It has been judged appropriate that a regulation be in place for the peace and the security of families: that a man who shall have enjoyed the possessions of another without trouble and in good faith during a certain period of time should remain in possession of them without any further claim being able to be laid against him. But it has never occurred to anyone to believe that people who have forfeited possessions through negligence or otherwise are unable to [140] recover them by any means. We have never regarded the incapacity of these people as other than a legal matter.

However, we have not been content—after a long prescription against them—to just not admit women to a share in education and the professions. We have gone further and have imagined that women's exclusion is based on a natural helplessness on their part.

There is nothing, however, more fanciful than this invention. For whether we consider learning in itself or the organ that serves to acquire it, we will find that the two sexes are equally equipped. There is but one method and one route for introducing into the mind the truth that is the mind's nourishment (as there is but one by which [141] to introduce food into all kinds of stomachs for the sustenance of the body). As to the different dispositions of this organ that render [one] more or less fit for education—if we are willing honestly to recognize it for what it is, we will admit that women possess most of them.

We cannot deny that among men those who are especially crude and rough are ordinarily stupid, and that, on the other hand, the most refined men are always the most intelligent. I find the experience of this to be too general and too consistent to need the support of arguments here. The members of the fair sex, therefore, being of a more delicate temperament than [persons of] our [gender], will not fail at least to equal our [sex] if they apply themselves to study.

sçaurois que faire; l'on s'imagine qu'il y va de l'honneur de nostre Sexe de le faire exprimer par tout: & moy je crois qu'il est de la justice de rendre à un chacun ce qui luy appartient.

[Les deux Sexes ont un droit égal sur les Sciences.] En effet nous avons tous hommes & femmes, le même droit sur la verité, puisque l'esprit est en tous également capable de la connoistre, & que nous sommes tous frappez de la même façon, par les objets qui font impression sur le corps. Ce droit que la nature nous donne à tous sur les mêmes connoissances, naist de ce que nous en avons tous autant de besoin les uns que les autres. Il n'y a personne qui ne cherche à estre heureux, & c'est à quoy tendent toutes nos actions; & [143] pas un ne le peut estre solidement que par des connoissances claires, & distinctes; & c'est en cela que Iesus Christ même, [Le bonheur consiste dans la connoissance.] & saint Paul nous font esperer, que consistera le bonheur de l'autre vie. Un avare s'estime heureux, lorsqu'il connoît; qu'il possede de grandes richesses; un ambitieux lorsqu'il s'apperçoit qu'il est au dessus de ses semblables. En un mot, tout le bonheur des hommes, vray ou imaginaire, n'est que dans la connoissance, c'est à dire dans la pensée qu'ils ont de posseder le bien qu'ils recherchent.

C'est ce qui me fait croire qu'il n'y a que les idées de la verité qu'on se procure par l'étude, & qui sont fixes & independentes de la possession, ou du manquement des choses, qui puissent faire la vraye felicité de [144] cette vie. Car ce qui fait qu'un avare ne peut estre heureux, dans la simple connoissance qu'il a des richesses; C'est que cette connoissance pour faire son bonheur, doit estre liée avec le desir ou l'imagination de les posseder pour le present: Et lors que son Imagination les luy represente comme éloignées de luy, & hors de sa puissance, il ne peut y penser sans s'affliger. Il en va tout autrement de la science qu'on a de soy-même, & de toutes celles qui en dépendent: mais particulierement de celles qui entrent dans le commerce de la vie. Puis donc que les deux Sexes sont capables de la même felicité; Ils ont le même droit sur tout ce qui sert à l'acquerir.

[Que la vertu consiste dans la connoissance.] Lorsque l'on dit que le bonheur consiste principalement dans la connoissance de la verité; on [145] n'en exclut pas la vertu: on

I foresee that this thought **[142]** will not be appreciated by many men who will find it a bit extreme. I do not know what to do about that. They imagine that it adds to the honor of our sex to have it represented in everything, and me, I believe that it is justice to render to each [gender] what pertains to it.

Indeed, we all—men and women—have the same right to the truth, for the mind in each of us is equally capable of knowing it and we are all stimulated in the same way by the objects that make an impression on the body. The right that nature gives us all to the same knowledge is born of the fact that we all have the same need of it—one as another. There is no one who does not seek to be happy. (That is what all our actions tend toward.) And **[143]** no one could be thoroughly happy but by clear and distinct knowledge. (It is in this that Jesus Christ himself and St. Paul made us hope that the happiness of the other life will consist.) An avaricious man believes himself happy when he knows that he possesses great riches; an ambitious man, when he perceives that he is above his fellows. In a word, all the happiness of men, true or imaginary, is only in the knowledge—that is to say, in the thought—that they possess the good that they seek.

This convinces me that only the ideas of truth (which we obtain through study and which are firm and independent of the possession or the lack of things) can make for true happiness in **[144]** this life. For what causes an avaricious man not to be able to be happy in the simple knowledge he has of riches is that to make him happy, this knowledge must be linked with the hope or the fantasy of possessing them now. And when his imagination depicts them to him as distant from him and beyond his power, he cannot think of them without making himself miserable. It is completely otherwise with the knowledge that we have of ourselves and with all the things that depend on it (but particularly of those things that enter into the business of life). Since the two sexes then are capable of the same happiness, they have the same right to everything that serves to acquire it.

When we say that happiness consists principally in the knowledge of truth, we **[145]** do not exclude virtue. On the contrary we judge virtue to be most essential to happiness.

estime au contraire que celle-cy en fait le plus essentiel. Mais un homme n'est heureux par la vertu qu'autant qu'il connoît qu'il en a, ou qu'il tache d'en avoir. Cela veut dire, qu'encore qu'il suffise pour estimer un homme heureux, de voir qu'il pratique la vertu, quoy qu'il ne la connoisse pas parfaitement, & même que cette pratique avec une connoissance confuse & imparfaite puisse contribuer à acquerir le bonheur de l'autre vie, il est certain qu'il ne peut lui même s'estimer solidement heureux, sans s'appercevoir qu'il fait le bien: comme il ne se croiroit point riche, s'il ne sçavoit, qu'il possede des richesses.

[Pourquoy si peu de gens aiment la vertu.] Ce qui est cause qu'il y a si peu de gens qui ayent du goust & de l'amour pour la veritable ver-[146]-tu, c'est qu'ils ne la connoissent pas, & n'y faisant point d'attention, lors qu'ils la pratiquent, ils ne sentent point la satisfaction qu'elle produit, & qui fait le bonheur dont nous parlons. Cela vient de ce que la vertu n'est pas une simple speculation du bien auquel on est obligé, mais un desir effectif, qui naît de la persuasion qu'on en a: & on ne la peut pratiquer avec plaisir sans ressentir de l'émotion[.] Parce qu'il en est comme des liqueurs les plus excellentes qui semblent quelquefois ameres ou sans douceur, si lors qu'elles sont sur la langue, l'esprit est occupé ailleurs, & ne s'applique point au mouvement qu'elles y causent.

[Qu'il faut estre sçavant pour estre solidement vertueux.] Non seulement les deux Sexes ont besoin de lumiere pour trouver leur bonheur dans la pratique de la vertu, ils en ont enco-[147]-re besoin pour la bien pratiquer. C'est la persuasion qui fait agir, & l'on est d'autant plus persuadé de son devoir, qu'on le connoît plus parfaitement. Le peu qu'on a dit icy sur la Morale, suffit pour insinuer que la science de nous-mêmes est tres-importante pour rendre plus forte la persuasion des devoirs ausquels on est obligé: & il ne seroit pas difficile de montrer comment toutes les autres y contribuent, ni de faire voir que la raison pourquoy tant de personnes pratiquent si mal la vertu, ou tombent dans le dereglement, c'est uniquement l'ignorance de ce qu'ils sont.

[D'où vient-que quelques Sçavants son[t] vicieux.] Ce qui fait croire communément, qu'il n'est pas besoin d'étre sçavant pour estre vertueux, c'est que l'on voit dans le vice quantité de gens, qui passent d'ailleurs pour habiles, d'où l'on [148] se

But a person is made happy by virtue only so far as he knows that he practices it (or tries to). It could be said that although it suffices to deem a person happy to see that he practices virtue (although he does not have perfect knowledge of it) and even though this practice (with a confused and imperfect knowledge) can contribute to acquiring happiness in the other life, it is certain that he cannot judge himself to be thoroughly happy without himself perceiving that he lives righteously (as he would not believe himself rich if he did not know that he possessed riches).

The reason why there are so few people who have a taste and a love for true virtue **[146]** is because they do not know it. And not paying attention to it when they practice it, they do not feel the satisfaction that it produces (and which constitutes the happiness of which we are speaking). This occurs because virtue is not a simple speculation about the good that we ought to do, but an effective desire that is born from the conviction that we have about the good. And we cannot take pleasure in practicing virtue without experiencing emotion—for the situation is like that with the best liqueurs (that sometimes seem bitter or without sweetness if, when they are on the tongue, the mind is occupied elsewhere and does not apply itself to the sensation they cause).

Not only do the two sexes have need of enlightenment to find their happiness in the practice of virtue, they have further **[147]** need of it to practice virtue well. Persuasion causes action, and we are all the more persuaded of our duty as we know it more perfectly. The little that we have said here about morality suffices to suggest that knowledge of ourselves is very important for strengthening our commitment to the duties to which we are obligated. And it would not be difficult to show how all the other [fields of knowledge] contribute to morality—nor to demonstrate that the reason why so many people practice virtue so badly or fall into misrule is especially their ignorance of what they are.

What commonly causes the belief that a man does not need to be a scholar in order to be virtuous is the fact that we see a horde of people [steeped] in vice who still pass for being clever. From this we **[148]** conclude that not only is knowledge useless for virtue, it is often injurious to

figure que non seulement la science est inutile pour la vertu: mais même qu'elle y est souvent pernicieuse. Et cette erreur rend suspect aux esprits foibles & peu instruits, la pluspart de ceux qui sont en reputation d'estre plus éclairez que les autres, & donne en même temps du mépris & de l'aversion pour les plus hautes connoissances.

L'on ne prend pas garde qu'il n'y a que les fausses lumieres qui laissent ou jettent les hommes dans le desordre: parceque les idées confuses que la fausse Philosophie donne de nous-mêmes, & de ce qui entre dans le corps de nos actions, broüillent tellement l'esprit, que ne sçachant ce qu'il est, ni ce que sont les choses qui l'environnent, ni le rapport qu'elles ont avec luy, & ne pouvant soûtenir le poids des dif-[149]-ficultez qui se presentent dans cette obscurité, il faut necessairement qu'il succombe & qu'il s'abandonne à ses passions, la raison estant trop foible pour l'arréter.

[Que l'étude ne donneroit point d'orgueil aux femmes.] Ce n'est donc que sur une terreur Panique qu'est fondée l'imagination bizarre qu'a le vulgaire, que l'étude rendroit les femmes plus méchantes & plus superbes. Il n'y a que la fausse science capable de produire un effet si mauvais. On ne peut apprendre la veritable, sans en devenir plus humble, & plus vertueux, & rien n'est plus propre à rabaisser la fumée, & à se convaincre de sa foiblesse, que de considerer tous les ressorts de sa machine; la délicatesse de ses organes, le nombre presque infini d'alterations, & de déreglemens penibles ausquels elle est si sujette. Il n'y a [150] point de meditation plus capable d'inspirer de l'humilité, de la moderation, & de la douceur à un homme tel qu'il puisse estre, que de faire attention par l'étude de la Physique, à la liaison de son esprit avec le corps, & de remarquer qu'il est assujetty à tant de besoins; que la dépendence où il est dans ses fonctions des plus delicates parties du corps, le tient sans cesse exposé à mille sortes de troubles & d'agitations fâcheuses; que quelques lumieres qu'il ait acquises, il ne faut presque rien pour les confondre entierement; qu'un peu de bile ou de sang plus chaud ou plus froid qu'à l'ordinaire, le jettera peut-etre dans l'extravagance, dans la folie, & dans la fureur, & luy fera souffrir des convulsions épouvantables.

it. And this error causes weak and poorly instructed minds to be suspicious of most people who have a reputation for being brighter than others and, at the same time, produces contempt and aversion for the most sublime knowledge.

We do not notice that only false enlightenment abandons people to disorder or shoves them into it, because the confused ideas that false philosophy gives [us] of ourselves (and of what enters into the substance of our actions) so confound the mind, that, not knowing what it is nor what the things that surround it are, nor the relationship that they have with it, and not being able to sustain the weight of the **[149]** difficulties that confront it in this obscurity, the mind must necessarily succumb and surrender itself to its passions—reason being too weak to stop it.

Only a panicky terror, therefore, supports the bizarre fantasy of common people that education would make women more wicked and arrogant. Only false knowledge can produce so bad an effect. We cannot learn truth without growing humbler and more virtuous. And nothing is better able to beat down the fumes of pride and convince us of our weakness than the contemplation of all the springs of our "machine" (the delicateness of its organs, the almost infinite number of impairments and painful dislocations to which it is subject). There is no **[150]** subject for meditation [that is] more capable of inspiring humility, moderation, and gentleness in a person (whatever sort he might be) than to ponder (through the study of physical science) the connection of his mind with the body: to notice that it is subjected to so many needs; that the dependence which it has in its functions on the most delicate parts of the body holds it exposed unceasingly to a thousand kinds of trouble and vexatious agitations; that whatever insights it has acquired, the slightest thing is able completely to confound it; that a little bile or blood (warmer or cooler than usual) will perhaps launch it into excess, folly, and fury and make it suffer horrible convulsions.

As these reflections should meet with **[151]** acceptance in the mind of a woman as easily as in that of a man, very far from inspiring pride in her, they would dispel it. And if after her mind were filled with the most excellent understanding she would recall in her memory all her past

Comme ces refléxions trou-[151]-veroient prise dans
l'esprit d'une femme, aussi-bien que dans celuy d'un homme,
elles en chasseroient l'orgueil, bien loin de l'y faire venir. Et
si apres s'estre rempli l'esprit des plus belles connoissances,
elle r'appeloit dans sa memoire toute sa conduite passée, pour
voir comment elle seroit arrivée à l'état heureux où elle se
trouveroit, [Avis tres-important pour tous les sçavans.] bien
loin de s'en élever au dessus des autres, elle verroit de quoy
s'humilier davantage; puisqu'elle observeroit necessairement
dans cette reveue, qu'elle avoit auparavant une infinité de
préjugez dont elle n'a pû se défaire qu'en combattant avec
peine les impressions de la coûtume, de l'exemple, & des
passions qui l'y retenoient malgré elle; que tous les efforts
qu'elle a faits pour découvrir la verité, luy ont esté presque
inutiles, [152] que ç'a esté comme par hazard qu'elle s'est
presentée à elle, & lors qu'elle y pensoit le moins, & en des
rencontres qui n'arrivent gueres qu'une seule fois en la vie, &
à tres-peu de personnes; d'où elle concluroit infailliblement
qu'il est injuste & ridicule d'avoir des ressentimens ou du
mépris pour ceux qui ne sont pas éclairez comme nous, ou
qui sont dans un sentiment contraire, & qu'il faut avoir pour
eux encore plus de complaisance, & de compassion; parce que
s'ils ne voyent pas la verité comme nous, ce n'est pas leur
faute: mais c'est qu'elle ne s'est pas presentée à eux, quand
ils l'ont recherchée, & qu'il y a encore quelque voile de leur
part ou de la nôtre, qui l'empéche de paroître à leur esprit
dans tout son iour: & considerant qu'elle tiendroit pour vray
[153] ce qu'elle auroit crû faux auparavant, elle jugeroit sans
doute qu'il pourroit encore arriver dans la suite, qu'elle fist
de nouvelles découvertes par lesquelles elle trouveroit faux ou
erronée [*sic*], ce qui luy auroit semblé tres-veritable.

Si il y a eu des femmes qui soient devenuës méprisantes,
se sentant plus de lumiere; il y a aussi quantité d'hommes qui
tombent tous les jours dans ce vice; & cela ne doit pas estre
regardé comme un effet des sciences qu'elles possedoient; mais
de ce que l'on en faisoit mystere à leur Sexe; & comme d'un
costé ces connoissances sont d'ordinaire fort confuses, & que
de l'autre, celles qui les ont se voyent un avantage qui leur
est particulier, il ne faut pas s'étonner qu'elles en prennent
un sujet d'éleve-[154]-ment: & c'est une necessité presque

conduct to see how she had come to the happy state in which she finds herself, far from exalting herself over others, she would see reason to humble herself more. Since she would necessarily notice in this review that she formerly had an infinite number of prejudices of which she was able to rid herself only by fighting hard against the impressions [springing] from custom, example, and the passions that held her back despite herself—that all the efforts that she has made to discover the truth have been almost useless to her, [152] that it has been as if by chance that truth has presented itself to her (and when she was thinking least about it and in encounters that happen scarcely but once in a lifetime and to very few people)—from this she would infallibly conclude that it is unjust and ridiculous to harbor resentments or scorn for those who are not enlightened as we [are] or who are of a contrary opinion. [She would find that] it is necessary to show them even more kindness and compassion. For if they do not see the truth as we [see it], it is not their fault. But it is because the truth has not presented itself to them when they sought it, and there is some veil on their side or ours that prevents it from appearing in their minds in all its light. And considering that she would have taken for true [153] what she would previously have believed [to be] false, she would doubtless conclude that it could yet happen in the future that she might make new discoveries by means of which she would find [to be] false and erroneous what had seemed very true to her.

If there have been some women who, sensing a superior degree of enlightenment in themselves, have become contemptuous [of others], there are also a great many men who fall into this vice every day. And that should not be regarded as an effect of the knowledge that women possess, but of the fact that we have made it a mystery to their sex. And since, on one hand, such knowledge is ordinarily very confused and, on the other, those who have it see an advantage for themselves that is uniquely theirs, it should not be surprising that women make it an excuse for haughtiness. [154] And it is almost an infallible necessity that in this condition the same thing happens to them that happens to people who, being of low birth and little wealth, have (with difficulty) made a dazzling

infaillible, que dans cét état, le même leur arrive, qu'à ceux
qui ayant peu de naissance & de bien, ont fait avec peine une
fortune éclatante lesquels se voyant élevez à un poste où ceux
de leur sorte n'ont point accoûtumé de monter, l'esprit de
vertige les prend, & leur presente les objets tout autrement
qu'ils ne sont. Au moins est-il tres-vraisemblable que l'orgueil
prétendu des sçavantes, n'étant rien en comparaison de celuy
de ces sçavans qui prennent le tître de Maîtres & de Sages: les
femmes y seroient moins sujettes, si leur Sexe entroit avec le
nôtre en partage égal des avantages qui le produisent.

[Que les sciences sont necessaires à autre chose qu'aux
emplois.] C'est donc une erreur populaire que de s'imaginer
que l'étude est inutile aux femmes, parce [155] dit-on, qu'elles
n'on[t] point de part aux emplois, pour lesquels on s'y
applique. Elle leur est aussi necessaire que le bonheur & la
vertu, puisque sans cela on ne peut posseder parfaitement ni
l'un ni l'autre. Elle l'est pour acquerir la justesse dans les
pensées & la justice dans les actions: elle l'est pour nous
bien connoître nous-mêmes & les choses qui nous environnent,
pour en faire un usage legitime, & pour regler nos passions,
en moderant nos desirs. Se rendre habile pour entrer dans
les charges & les dignitez, c'est un des usages de la science:
& il en faut acquerir le plus qu'on peut pour estre Iuge,
ou Evêque, parce qu'on ne peut autrement se bien acquiter
des fonctions de ces Etats, mais non pas precisément pour y
arriver & pour devenir plus heureux par la posses-[156]-sion
des honneurs & des avantages qu'ils produisent, ce seroit faire
de la science un usage bas & sordide.

Ainsi il n'y a que le peu de lumiere, ou un interest secret &
aveugle, qui puisse faire dire que les femmes doivent demeurer
excluës des sciences par la raison qu'elle n'y ont jamais eu de
part publiquement. [Il n'y a point de prescription en matiere
de science.] Il n'est pas des biens de l'esprit comme de ceux
du corps, il n'y a point de prescription contre: & quelque
temps que l'on en ait esté privé, il y a toûjours droit de
retour. Les mêmes biens du corps ne pouvant estre possedez
en même temps par plusieurs personnes, sans diminution de
part & d'autre, l'on a eu raison pour le salut des familles,
d'y maintenir les possesseurs de bonne foy au préjudice des
anciens proprietaires.

fortune. Seeing themselves elevated to a position to which those of their kind are not accustomed to rise, their heads are turned and objects are represented to them completely other than as they are. At least it is very likely that the alleged pride of educated women, being nothing in comparison to that of educated men who assume the titles of "masters" and "sages," women would be less subject to it if their sex would enter with ours into an equal share of the advantages that it generates.

It is, therefore, a popular error to imagine that study is useless for women because, [155] as is said, women have no share in the jobs for which we apply ourselves to education. Education is as necessary to them as happiness and virtue, since without it we could not perfectly possess either the one or the other. It is [needed] for acquiring precision in thought and justice in action. It is [needed] for knowing ourselves well and the things that surround us, for making a legitimate use of them and for regulating our passions while moderating our desires. To equip oneself to enter into offices and honors is one of the uses of education. It is necessary to acquire as much education as we can in order to be a judge or bishop (for otherwise we cannot discharge the duties of these estates well)—but not just to obtain these offices and to become happy through the possession [156] of the honors and the advantages that they entail. This would make a base and sordid use of education.

Thus only dim-wittedness or a hidden, blind self-interest can lead us to assert that women should continue to be excluded from education for the reason that they have never had a public place in it. The goods of the mind are not dealt with like those of the body. There is no statute of limitations concerning them. And however long we have been deprived of them, there is always a right to reclaim them. Since the same corporeal goods cannot be possessed at the same time by many people without diminishing one or another shares, upholding (to the prejudice of former proprietors) the [rights of] people who have held property in good faith has been justified for the well-being of families.

[157] But for the advantages of the mind it is totally otherwise. Each person has a right to everything that makes

[157] Mais pour les avantages de l'esprit, il en est tout autrement. chacun [*sic*] a droit sur tout ce qui est du bon sens: le ressort de la raison n'a point de borne; elle a dans tous les hommes une égale jurisdiction. Nous naissons tous juges des choses qui nous touchent; & si nous ne pouvons pas tous en disposer avec un pouvoir égal, nous pouvons au moins les connoistre tous également. Et comme tous les hommes joüissent de l'usage de la lumiere & de l'air, sans que cette communication soit préjudiciable à personne, tous peuvent aussi posseder la verité sans se nuire les uns aux autres. Et même plus elle est connuë, plus elle paroist belle & lumineuse: plus il y a de personnes qui la cherchent, & plûtost on la découvre: & si les deux Sexes y avoient travaillé également, on **[158]** l'auroit plûtost trouvée. De sorte que la verité & la science sont des biens imprescriptibles: & ceux qui en ont esté privez y peuvent rentrer sans faire tort à ceux qui en sont déja les maîtres. Il ne peut donc y avoir que ceux qui veulent dominer sur les esprits par la creance, qui ayent sujet d'apprehender ce retour, dans la crainte que si les sciences devenoient si communes, la gloire ne le devint aussi: & que celle où ils aspirent, ne se diminuast par le partage.

good sense. The domain of reason has no boundary; it has an equal jurisdiction over all people. We are all born to be judges of the things that affect us. And if we are not all able to dispose of them with an equal power, we can at least all know them equally. And as all people enjoy the use of light and air without this intercourse being prejudicial to anyone, all can also possess the truth without one injuring others. And it is even the case that the more the truth is known, the more it appears beautiful and luminous. The more people there are who seek it, the sooner we discover it. And if the two sexes had worked equally at it, we **[158]** would sooner have found it. Consequently, truth and knowledge are inalienable property. And those who have been dispossessed of them can regain them without doing harm to those who are already their masters. Only those then who want to dominate minds through [blind] faith can have grounds to apprehend this change—for fear that if learning should become very common, glory would also—and that the glory to which they aspire would be diminished by sharing.

Que les femmes ne sont pas moins capables que les
hommes des Emplois de la societé.

C'est pourquoy il n'y a aucun inconvenient que les femmes
s'appliquent à l'étude comme nous. Elles sont capables
d'en **[159]** faire aussi un tres-bon usage, & d'en tirer
les deux avantages que l'on en peut esperer, l'un d'avoir
les connoissances claires & distinctes, que nous desirons
naturellement, & dont le desir est souvent étouffé & aneanty
par la confusion des pensées & par les besoins & les agitations
de la vie; & l'autre d'employer ces connoissances pour leur
conduite particuliere & pour celle des autres dans les differens
états de la societé, dont on fait partie. Cela ne s'accorde pas
avec l'opinion commune. Il y en a beaucoup que croiront
bien que les femmes peuvent apprendre ce que l'on comprend
sous les sciences Physiques ou naturelles; mais non pas
qu'elles soient aussi propres que les hommes, à celles qu'on
peut appeller Civiles, comme la Morale, la Iurisprudence,
& la Poli-**[160]**-tique, & que si elles peuvent se conduire
elles-mêmes par l'application des maximes de ces dernieres,
elles ne pourront pas pour cela conduire les autres.

L'on a cette pensée faute de prendre garde que l'esprit
n'a bésoin dans toutes ses actions que de discernement & de
justesse, & que quiconque a une fois ces deux qualitez en une
chose, peut les avoir aussi aisément & par la même voye dans
tout le reste. La Morale ou le Civil ne change point la nature
de nos actions: elles demeurent toûjours Physiques: parce que
la Morale n'est autre chose, que de sçavoir la maniere dont les
hommes regardent les actions de leurs semblables par rapport
aux idées qu'ils ont du bien ou du mal, du vice & de la vertu,
de la justice & de l'injustice: & de même qu'ayant **[161]** une
fois bien compris les regles du mouvement dans la Physique,
on peut les appliquer à tous les changemens & à toutes les
varietez qu'on remarque dans la nature: aussi sçachant une
fois les veritables maximes des sciences Civiles, l'on a pas plus
de difficulté à en faire l'application aux incidens nouveaux qui
surviennent.

Ceux qui sont dans les Emplois, n'ont pas toûjours plus
d'esprit que les autres pour avoir eu plus de bon-heur; &
même il n'est pas necessaire qu'ils en ayent plus que le

That women are not less fit than men for posts in society.

That is why there is no harm in women applying themselves to study like we [do]. Women, too, can **[159]** make very good use of education and derive from it the two advantages that we can hope for from it: the one, to get the clear and distinct knowledge that we naturally desire (which desire is often stifled and destroyed by the confusion of [our] thoughts and by the needs and upheavals of life); and the other, to employ this knowledge [to direct] their [own] conduct and that of others in the different stations in society in which we participate. This [idea] is not in accord with the common opinion. There are many people who will readily believe that women can learn whatever is contained in the physical or natural sciences, but not that they are as fit as men for the sciences that can be called "civil" (i.e., morality, law, and **[160]** politics)—and that even if women could govern themselves using the principles of the latter, they could not, for that [reason alone], govern others.

We think this because we fail to attend to the fact that the mind needs nothing (in all its actions) but discernment and precision—and that whosoever once employs these two qualities in one situation can employ them as easily and by the same process in all the rest. [The labels] "moral" or "civil" do not change the nature of our actions. Actions always remain physical, for morality is nothing but knowing how men view the deeds of their fellows with respect to the ideas they have of good or evil, vice and virtue, justice and injustice. And likewise, having **[161]** once comprehended the laws of movement in physics we can apply them to all the mutations and to all the diversity that we see in nature. Also, once we know the true principles of the civil sciences, we do not have much difficulty making application of them to new incidents as they occur.

Those who are in the professions—having had more good fortune—do not always have greater intelligence than others. They need not even have more [wit] than the common [run of humankind] (although it is to be hoped that we only admit to professions those people who are most fit for them). We

commun; quoy qu'il soit à souhaiter qu'on n'y admît que ceux qui y seroient les plus propres. Nous agissons toûjours de la même façon & par les mêmes regles en quelque état que nous nous trouvions; sinon que plus les états sont relevez, plus [162] nos soins & nos veuës sont étenduës, parce qu'il y faut plus agir. [*sic*] & tout le changement qui arrive aux hommes; que l'on met au dessus des autres, & [*sic*] [est] comme celuy d'une personne qui estant montée au haut d'une Tour porte sa veuë plus loin; & découvre plus de differens objets que ceux qui demeurent en bas: c'est pourquoy si les femmes sont autant capables que nous de se bien conduire elles-mêmes, elles le sont aussi de conduire les autres, & d'avoir part aux emplois & aux dignitez de la societé Civile.

[Elles sant [*sic*] capables d'enseigner.] Le plus simple & le plus naturel usage que l'on puisse faire en public des sciences qu'on a bien apprises, c'est de les enseigner aux autres: & si les femmes avoient étudié dans les Universitez, avec les hommes, ou dans celles qu'on auroit établies pour elles en par-[163]-ticulier, elles pourroient entrer dans les degrez, & prendre le tiltre de Docteur & de Maître en Theologie & en Medecine, en l'un & en l'autre Droit, & leur genie qui les dispose si avantageusement à apprendre les disposeroit aussi à enseigner avec succez. Elles trouveroient des methodes & des biais insinuans pour inspirer leur doctrine; elles découvriroient adroitement le fort & le foible de leurs disciples, pour se proportionner à leur portée, & la facilité qu'elles ont à s'énoncer, & qui est un des plus excellens talens des bons Maîtres, acheveroit de les rendre des Maîtresses admirables.

[Elles sont capables des dignitez Ecclesiastiques.] L'employ le plus approchant de celuy de Maître, c'est d'estre Pasteur ou Ministre dans l'Eglise, & l'on ne peut montrer qu'il y ait autre chose que la Coûtume [164] qui en éloigne les femmes. Elles ont un esprit comme le nostre, capable de connoistre & d'aimer Dieu, & ainsi de porter les autres à le connoistre & à l'aimer. La foy leur est commune avec nous: l'Evangile & ses promesses ne s'adressent pas moins à elles. La charité les comprend aussi dans ses devoirs, & si elles sçavent en pratiquer les actions, ne pourroient-elles pas aussi en enseigner publiquement les maximes. Quiconque peut prêcher par les exemples, le peut encore à plus forte raison par

always act in the same way and according to the same rules in whatever state we find ourselves—except that the more elevated our posts are, the more **[162]** our responsibilities and our perceptions are expanded (because there is more necessity [for us] to act). The only change that occurs in people who are placed over others is like that in a person who, being set on top of a tower, sees farther and discovers more different objects than those who stay below. This is why, if women are as able as we [are] by themselves to conduct themselves well, they are also [fit] to govern others and to share in the professions and in the offices of civil society.

The simplest and most natural public use that we can make of the educations that we have well acquired is to pass them on to others. If women had studied in the universities with men (or in schools that we might have established especially for women) **[163]** they could have taken degrees, assumed the titles of "doctor" and "master" (both in theology and medicine, [and] in one and the other [kinds] of law). And their nature, which so readily inclines them to learn, would dispose them also to teach with success. They would find methods and indirect strategies to instill their doctrine. To adjust themselves to students' capacities, they would adroitly discover the strength[s] and weakness[es] of their disciples. And the facility they have in expressing themselves (which is one of the best talents of good masters) would put the finishing touch to making them admirable teachers.

The profession most closely approaching teaching is that of pastor or minister in the church, and we can show that there is no other thing than custom **[164]** that keeps women from it. They have a mind like ours (capable of knowing and loving God and, thus, able to bring others to know and to love Him). Their faith is the same as ours. The Gospel and its promises are no less addressed to them. Charity includes them, too, in its duties—and if they know how to practice its deeds, could they not also publicly teach its principles? Whoever can preach by examples can also [preach] (with all the more reason) with his words. And a woman who would join [her] natural eloquence to the moral law of Jesus Christ would be as competent as [any] other person to exhort, to direct, to correct—to admit into Christian society those who

ses paroles: Et une femme qui joindroit l'éloquence naturelle
à la morale de Iesus-Christ, seroit aussi capable qu'un autre,
d'exhorter, de diriger, de corriger, d'admettre dans la societé
Chrétienne ceux qui en seroient dignes, & d'en retrancher
ceux qui refuseroient [165] d'en observer les reglemens, aprés
s'y estre soûmis. Et si les hommes estoient accoûtumez à voir
les femmes dans une chaire, ils n'en seroient pas plus touchez
que les femmes le sont des hommes.

[Elles peuvent avoir l'authorité.] Nous ne nous sommes
assemblez en societé, que pour vivre en paix, & pour trouver
dans une assistance mutuelle tout ce qui est necessaire pour
le corps & pour l'esprit. On ne pourroit en joüir sans trouble,
s'il n'y avoit point d'Authorité; c'est à dire, qu'il faut pour
cela que quelques personnes ayent le pouvoir de faire des
loix, & d'imposer des peines à ceux qui les violent. Pour
bien user de cette authorité, il faut sçavoir à quoy elle oblige,
& estre persuadé, que ceux qui la possedent, ne doivent
avoir pour but en l'employant que de [166] procurer le salut
& l'avantage de ceux qui leur sont inferieurs. Les femmes
n'estant pas moins susceptibles de cette persuasion que les
hommes, ceux-ci ne pourroient-ils pas se soûmettre à elles. Et
consentir non seulement de ne pas resister à leurs ordres; mais
même de contribuër autant qn'ils [*sic*] pourroient pour obliger
à leur obeïr, ceux qui en feroient difficulté.

[Elles peuvent estre Reines.] Ainsi rien n'empécheroit
qu'une femme ne fût sur un Trône, & que pour gouverner
ses peuples, elle n'étudiast leur naturel, leurs interests, leurs
loix, leurs coûtumes, & leurs usages, qu'elle n'eust égard
qu'au merite dans la distribution des charges. qu'elle ne
mist dans les Emplois de la robe & l'épée que des personnes
équitables: & dans les dignitez de l'Eglise que des gens [167]
de lumiere & d'exemple. Est-ce une chose si difficile, qu'une
femme ne le puisse faire, que de s'instruire du fort & du
foible d'un Etat, & de ceux qui l'environnent, d'entretenir
chez les étrangers des Intelligences secrettes pour découvrir
leurs desseins, & pour rompre leurs mesures, & d'avoir des
Espions & des Emissaires fidels dans tous les lieux suspects,
pour estre informé exactement de tout ce qui s'y passe, à quoy
l'on auroit interest: Faut-il pour la conduite d'un Royaume,
plus d'application, & plus de vigilance que les femmes en ont

are worthy of it, and to cut out those who would refuse [165] to observe its rules after having submitted themselves to it. And if men were accustomed to see women in a pulpit, they would not be more affected by the sight than women are [to see] men [there].

We congregate in society only for the purpose of living in peace and finding in mutual assistance all the body's and the mind's necessities. We would not (without difficulty) be able to enjoy these things if there were no authority. That is to say, there must be (for this purpose) some persons having the power to make laws and to impose penalties on those who violate them. To make good use of this authority, it is necessary to know what it compels [one] [to do] and to be persuaded that those who possess it must have as their purpose in employing it only [166] the procurement of the health and advantage of those who are their inferiors. Since women are no less capable of making this commitment than men, could men not submit themselves to women—and consent not only not to resist their orders, but even to contribute as much as they could to compelling the obedience of those men who might make difficulty for female rulers?

Thus, nothing should prevent a woman from sitting on a throne. In order to govern her people she could study their nature, interests, laws, customs, and habits, so that she might regard merit alone in the distribution of offices—that to the professions of the robe and the sword she might appoint only fair persons and to the offices of the church only enlightened, exemplary people. [167] Is it so difficult a thing that a woman could not do it—to teach herself the strength[s] and weakness[es] of a state and of those nations that surround it, to maintain secret intelligence agencies in foreign lands to uncover their plans and disrupt their measures, to have spies and faithful emissaries in all suspect places [and] to be informed precisely about everything that happens in those places in which we would take an interest? Would the conduct of a kingdom require more care and more vigilance than women have for their families and the nuns for their convents? Subtlety would no more be lacking to them in public negotiations than it fails them in private affairs. Since piety and sweetness [168] are natural to their sex, their rule

pour leurs familles, & les Religieuses pour leurs Couvens? Le rafinement ne leur manqueroit non plus dans les negotiations publiques, qu'il leur manque dans les affaires particulieres, & comme la pieté & la douceur [168] sont naturelles à leur Sexe, la domination en seroit moins rigoureuse, que n'a esté celle de plusieurs Princes, & l'on souhaiteroit sous leur regne, ce que l'on a craint sous tant d'autres, que les sujets se reglassent sur l'exemple des personnes qui les gouvernent.

Il est aisé de conclure que si les femmes sont capables de posseder souverainement toute l'authorité publique, elles le sont encore plus de n'en estre que les Ministres: comme d'estre Vicereynes, Gouvernantes, Secretaires, Conseilleres d'Estat, Intendantes des Finances.

[Elles peuvent estre Generalles d'Armée.] Pour moy je ne serois pas plus surpris de voir une femme le casque en teste, que de luy voir une Couronne; présider dans un Conseil de Guerre, comme dans celuy d'un Etat: Exercer elle-[169]-même ses soldats, ranger une armée en bataille, la partager en plusieurs corps, comme elle se divertiroit à le voir faire. L'Art Militaire n'a rien pardessus les autres, dont les femmes sont capables, sinon qu'il est plus rude & qu'il fait plus de bruit & plus de mal. Les yeux suffisent pour apprendre dans une Carte un peu exacte, toutes les routes d'un païs, les bons & les mauvais passages, les endroits les plus propres aux surprises & aux campemens. Il n'y a gueres de soldats qui ne sçachent bien qu'il faut occuper les défilez avant que d'y engager ses troupes, regler toutes ses entreprises sur les avis certains de bons Espions; tromper même son armée par des ruses & des contre-marches pour mieux cacher son dessein. Vne femme peut cela, & inventer des stra-[170]-tagêmes pour surprendre l'Ennenemy [*sic*], luy mettre le vent, la poussiere, le Soleil en face: & l'attaquant d'un costé, le faire envelopper par l'autre: luy donner de fausses alarmes, l'attirer dans une embuscade par une fuite simulée; livrer une bataille & monter la premiere à la brêche pour encourager ses soldats. La persuasion & la passion font tout: & les femmes ne témoignent pas moins d'ardeur & de resolution, lorsqu'il y va de l'honneur, qu'il en faut pour attaquer & pour defendre une place.

[Elles sont capables des Charges de Iudicature.] Que pourroit-on trouver raisonnablement à redire, qu'une femme

would be less harsh than the administration of many princes has been. And during their reign[s] we might wish for what we have feared during so many others: that subjects model themselves on the example of the persons who rule them.

It is easy to conclude that if women are capable of possessing all public authority supremely, they are even more [prepared] to be mere ministers of that authority (e.g., viceroys, governors, secretaries, counsellors of state, and comptrollers of finances).

As for me, I would be no more surprised to see a woman with a helmet on her head than to see her with a crown—presiding over a counsel of war as over a counsel of state, exercising [169] soldiers herself, arranging an army in battle formation, and dividing it into many corps (as she would please herself to see it done). The military art requires nothing more than the other [occupations] for which women are fit—except that it is ruder, makes more noise, and does more harm. Eyes suffice to learn all the roads of a country from a tolerably accurate map (i.e., the good and bad routes and the places best suited for surprise attacks and encampments). There are scarcely any soldiers who do not understand thoroughly that passes should be occupied before engaging their troops, [that] all enterprises should be directed utilizing the dependable advice of good spies, and [that]—the better to conceal their plan—their own army should be deceived by ruses and countermarches. A woman can do this and invent stratagems [170] to surprise the enemy (e.g., to put the wind, the dust, and the sun in [his] face; attacking him on one side to surround him on the other; to give him false alarms; to draw him into an ambush by simulated flight; to give battle and to mount first into the breach to encourage her soldiers). Persuasiveness and passion carry the day, and women do not display less ardor and resolution when honor is at stake than is needed to attack and to defend a place.

What reasonable objection could be found to a woman of good sense and enlightenment presiding at the head of a court and every other assembly. There are many able people who would have less trouble learning the laws and the customs [171] of a state than those of the games that women know so well. (It is as easy to remember these things as an

de bon sens, & éclairée, présidast à la teste d'un Parlement
& de toute autre Compagnie. Il y a quantité d'habiles
gens qui auroient moins de peine à apprendre les Loix &
les Coû-[171]-tumes d'un Etat, que celle des jeux, que les
femmes entendent si bien: il est aussi aisé de les retenir qu'un
Roman entier. Ne peut-on pas voir le point d'une affaire aussi
facilement, que le denoüement d'une Intrigue dans une piece
de Theatre, & faire aussi fidelement le rapport d'un procez
que le recit d'une Comedie. Toutes ces choses sont également
faciles à ceux qui s'y appliquent également.

Comme il n'y a ni charge ni employ dans la societé qui
ne soit renfermé dans ceux dont on vient de parler, ni où
l'on ait besoin de plus de science, ni de plus d'esprit: Il faut
reconnoitre que les femmes sont propres à tout.

Outre les dispositions naturelles de corps, & les idées que
l'on a des fonctions & des [172] devoirs de son Employ, il y a
encore un certain accessoire qui rend plus ou moins capable
de s'en acquiter dignement: la persuasion de ce qu'on est
obligé de faire, les considerations de Religion & d'interest,
l'émulation entre les pareils, le desir d'acquerir de la gloire,
de faire, de maintenir ou d'augmenter sa fortune. Selon qu'un
homme est plus ou moins touché de ces choses il agit tout
autrement: & les femmes n'y estant pas moins sensibles que
les hommes, elles leur sont à l'égard des Emplois, égales en
tout.

[Les femmes doivent s'appliquer à l'étude.] L'on peut donc
en assûrance exhorter les Dames à s'appliquer à l'étude, sans
avoir égard aux petites raisons de ceux qui entreprendroient
de les en détourner. Puisqu'elles ont un esprit comme nous
capable de con-[173]-noître la verité, qui est la seule chose
qui les puisse occuper dignement, elles doivent se mettre en
état d'éviter le reproche d'avoir enfermé un talent qu'elles
pouvoient faire valoir, & d'avoir retenu la verité dans l'oisiveté
& dans la molesse. Il n'y a pas d'autre moyen pour elles
de se garantir de l'erreur & de la surprise, à quoy sont si
exposées les personnes qui n'apprennent rien, que par la voye
des Gazettes, c'est à dire, par le simple rapport d'autruy, & il
n'y en a point d'autre non plus pour estre heureuses en cette
vie, en pratiquant la vertu, avec connoissance.

entire novel). Can we not see the point of a court action as easily as the outcome of a plot in a theater piece—and as faithfully make the report on a lawsuit as the narration of a comedy? All these things are equally easy for those who apply themselves equally to them.

As there is neither an office nor a profession in society that is not included in those of which we have just spoken (nor in which there is need of more education or intelligence), it must be acknowledged that women are fit for all [jobs].

Beyond the natural dispositions of the body and the ideas that we have about the functions and the [172] duties of our professions, there is yet a certain something additional that renders [us] more or less capable of acquitting ourselves worthily: the conviction of what it is our duty to do, considerations of religion and self-interest, the emulation between [us and our] fellows, [our] desire to acquire glory, [and] to make, to maintain or to increase our fortune[s]. According as a man is more or less affected by these things, he acts very differently, and women—being no less sensitive to them than men—are with respect to the professions equal to men in everything.

We can then with assurance urge ladies to apply themselves to study without taking notice of the petty arguments of those who would try to divert them from it. Since women have minds like ours—capable of knowing [173] truth (the only thing that can worthily occupy them), they must put themselves in position to avoid the reproach of having suppressed a talent that they could turn to account (and of having retarded the truth by their idleness and indolence). There is no other way for them to protect themselves against the error and surprise to which persons are so much exposed who learn nothing but by reading newspapers (that is to say, by [hearing] the simple testimony of others). And there is no other way, either, for them to be happy in this life while practicing virtue with understanding.

Whatever interest women pursue beyond this, they will find it in study. If their tea parties were turned into academies, the conversations that take place in them would be more profound, agreeable, and [174] elevated. And each woman can gauge the satisfaction that she would take in conversing

[L'utilité de l'étude pour les femmes.] Quelque interest qu'elles cherchent outre celuy-là elles le rencontreront dans l'étude. Si les Cercles étoient changez en Academies, les entretiens y seroient plus solides, plus agreables, & [174] plus grands: Et chacune peut juger de la satisfaction qu'elle auroit à parler des plus belles choses, par celle qu'elle ressent quelquefois à en entendre parler les autres. Quelques legeres que fussent les sujets de conversation, elles auroient le plaisir de les traiter plus spirituellement que le commun: Et les manieres delicates qui sont si particulieres à leur Sexe, estant fortifiées de raisonnemens solides, en toucheroient bien davantage.

Celles qui ne cherchent qu'à plaire y trouveroient admirablement leur compte; & l'éclat de la beauté du corps relevé par celuy de l'esprit, en seroit cent fois plus vif. Et comme les femmes les moins belles, sont toûjours regardées de bon oeil, lorsqu'elles sont spirituelles, les avantages de l'esprit cultivez par [175] l'étude, leur donneroient moyen de suppléer abondamment, à ce que la nature, ou la fortune leur auroient dénié. Elles auroient part aux entretiens des sçavans, & regneroient parmy eux doublement: Elles entreroient dans les affaires: les maris ne pourroient s'exempter de leur abandonner la conduite des familles, & de prendre en tout leurs conseils; & si les choses sont dans un état qu'elles ne peuvent plus estre admises aux Emplois, elles pourroient au moins en connoître les fonctions, & juger si on les remplit dignement.

La difficulté d'arriver à ce point ne doit pas épouvanter. Elle n'est pas si grande qu'on la fait. Ce qui est cause qu'on croit qu'il faut tant de peine pour acquerir quelques connoissance, [176] c'est que l'on fait pour cela apprendre quantité de choses qui sont tres-inutiles, à la pluspart de ceux qui y aspirent. Toute la science n'ayant jusques à present presque consisté qu'à posseder l'histoire des sentimens de ceux qui nous ont precedé, & les hommes s'en estant trop rapportez à la coûtume & à la bonne foy de leurs Maîtres, tres-peu ont eu le bonheur de trouver la methode naturelle. L'on pourra y travailler, & faire voir qu'on peut rendre les hommes habiles en bien moins de temps, & avec plus de plaisir qu'on ne s'imagine.

about the most exalted subjects from the pleasure that she sometimes feels to hear others talk about them. However light might be the subjects of conversation, these women would have the pleasure of treating them more intelligently than the ordinary person. And the delicate manners that are so characteristic of their sex—being backed up by solid arguments, they would reach even deeper.

Those women who only seek to please would find education admirably to be to their advantage, and the brilliance of the beauty of the body would be a hundred times more vivid if heightened by the beauty of the mind. And since less beautiful women are always looked on with favor when they are intelligent, the resources of a mind cultivated by [175] education would give them a way to abundantly supply what nature or fortune had denied them. They could take part in the conversations of educated men and reign among them in two ways: they could enter into public life, [and] their husbands would have no excuse not to relinquish to them the management of their families and [no excuse not] to take their advice about everything. And if things are ever in a state where they can no longer be admitted to the professions, these women could at least understand the functions [of these posts] and decide whether we discharge them worthily.

The difficulty of achieving this goal must not frighten [women]. It is not as great as we make it out to be. What causes us to believe that so much effort is needed to acquire a bit of knowledge [176] is that we force (to that end) those who aspire to learning to learn a great many things that are extremely useless to most of them. Since all education until now has consisted almost only of the possession of the history of the thoughts of those who have preceded us, very few people (men having put too much trust in custom and in the good faith of their masters) have had the good fortune to find the natural method [for acquiring knowledge]. We might work at this and show that we could train people in much less time and (much more pleasantly) than we now imagine.

[177] Que les femmes ont une disposition avantageuse pour les sciences, & que les idées justes de perfection, de Noblesse & d'honnesteté leur conviennent comme aux hommes.

Iusques icy nous n'avons encore regardé que la teste dans les femmes, & l'on a vue que cette partie considerée en general, a en elles autant de proportion, que dans les hommes, avec toutes les sciences, dont elle est l'organe. Neanmoins, parceque cét organe n'est pas entierement semblable, même dans tous les hommes, & qu'il y en a, en qui il est plus propre à certaines choses qu'à d'autres, il faut descendre plus dans le particulier, pour voir s'il n'y a rien dans les femmes, qui les rende **[178]** moins propres aux sciences que nous.

L'on peut remarquer qu'elles ont la Physionomie plus heureuse & plus grande que nous; elles ont le front haut, élevé, & large, ce qui est la marque ordinaire des personnes Imaginatives & spirituelles. Et on trouve en effet, que les femmes ont beaucoup de vivacité, d'imagination & de memoire: cela veut dire que leur cerveau est disposé de telle sorte, qu'il reçoit aisément les impressions des objets, & jusques aux plus foibles, & aux plus legeres, qui échapent à ceux qui ont une autre disposition, & qu'il les conserve sans peine & les presente à l'esprit au moment qu'il en a besoin.

[Que les femmes sont imaginatives.] Comme cette disposition est accompagnée de chaleur, elle fait que l'esprit est frappé plus **[179]** vivement par les objets; qu'il s'y attache & les pénetre davantage & qu'il en étend les images comme il luy plaist. D'où il arrive que ceux qui ont beaucoup d'Imagination considerant les choses par plus d'endroits & en moins de temps, sont fort ingenieux & inventifs, & découvrent plus d'une seule veuë, que beaucoup d'autres aprés une longue attention; ils sont propres à representer les choses d'une maniere agreable & insinuante, & à trouver sur le champ des biais & des expediens commodes; Ils s'expriment avec facilité & avec grace, & donnent à leurs pensées un plus beau jour.

Tout cela se remarque dans les femmes, & je ne vois rien dans cette disposition qui soit contraire au bon esprit. Le discernement & la justesse en sont **[180]** le caractere naturel:

[177] That women have disposition[s] well suited for education, and that accurate ideas about perfection, nobility, and honesty serve them as well as men.

Up to this point we have considered women only with respect to the head, and we have seen that this part (generally considered) is as fit in them as in men for all the fields of learning for which it is the organ. Nevertheless, because this organ is not exactly alike (even in all men) and there are some heads that are more fit for certain things than others, we must delve more deeply into the particular to see whether there is anything about women that renders them [178] less fit for learning than we are.

It can be seen that women have a happier, more open physiognomy than we [do]. They have the high, elevated, large forehead that is the ordinary mark of imaginative, intelligent persons. And we find, indeed, that women have much vivacity, much imagination, and good memory: and this indicates that their brains are arranged in such a way that they receive impressions of objects easily (even the weakest and the lightest impressions that escape persons who are constituted differently) and that they retain them without difficulty, and recall them to mind at the moment when they need them.

Since this propensity is accompanied by warmth, it causes the mind to be more quickly impressed [179] by objects—so that it better seizes on and penetrates them and enlarges images as it pleases. This means that people who have a lot of imagination are very ingenious and inventive (considering things from more perspectives in less time) and discover more from a single glance than many other people after a lengthy examination. They are skilled at presenting their thoughts in an agreeable, convincing manner and at instantly finding subterfuges and useful expedients. They express themselves with facility and grace and set forth their thoughts in the best light.

All this is to be found in women, and I see nothing in this disposition which is incompatible with a good mind. Discernment and precision are [180] its natural attributes. To acquire these qualities, we must become somewhat sedentary

pour acquerir ces qualitez, il faut se rendre un peu sedentaire, & s'arréter sur les objets, afin d'éviter l'erreur & la méprise où l'on tombe en voltigeant. Il est vray que la multitude des pensées dans les personnes vives, emporte quelquefois l'Imagination; mais il est vray aussi qu'on la peut fixer par l'exercice. Nous en avons l'experience dans les plus grands hommes de ce siecle, qui sont presque tous fort Imaginatifs.

L'on peut dire que ce Temperamment est le plus propre pour la societé, & que les hommes n'estant pas faits pour demeurer toûjours seuls & renfermez dans un cabinet, on doit en quelque façon plus estimer ceux qui ont plus de disposition à communiquer agreablement & utilement leurs pensées. Et ainsi [181] les femmes qui ont naturellement l'esprit beau, parce qu'elles ont de l'imagination, de la memoire & du brillant, peuvent avec un peu d'application acquerir les qualitez du bon esprit.

En voilà suffisamment pour montrer qu'à l'égard de la teste seule, les deux Sexes sont égaux. Il y a sur le reste du Corps des choses tres-curieuses, mais dont il ne faut parler qu'en passant. Les hommes ont toûjours eu ce malheur commun de réprendre, pour ainsi dire, leurs passions dans tous les ouvrages de la nature: & il n'y a gueres d'idées qu'ils n'ayent jointes avec quelque sentiment d'amour ou de haine, d'estime, ou de mépris; & celles qui concernent la distinction des deux Sexes, sont tellement materielles & tellement broüillées des sentimens d'imperfection, [182] de bassesse, de deshonnesteté & d'autres bagatelles, que ne pouvant estre touchées sans remuër quelque passion & sans exciter la chair contre l'esprit, il est souvent de la prudence de n'en rien dire.

Cependant, c'est sur ce mélange bizarre d'idées toûjours confuses, que sont fondées les pensées desavantageuses aux femmes, & dont les petits Esprits se se [*sic*] servent ridiculement pour les mortifier. Le plus juste temperament qu'il y ait entre la necessité de s'expliquer & la difficulté de le faire impunément, est de marquer ce qu'on doit raisonnablement entendre par perfection & imperfection, par noblesse & par bassesse, par honnesteté & par deshonnesteté.

[Idées de la perfection & de l'imperfection.] Concevant qu'il y a un Dieu, je conçois facilement que toutes [183] choses

and linger over objects for the purpose of avoiding the error[s] and mistake[s] into which we fall when fluttering about. It is true that the multitude of thoughts which lively persons have sometimes carries their imaginations away. But it is also true that we can correct this [problem] with practice. We have an example of this in the greatest men of this century, who are almost all very imaginative.

We might claim that this temperament is the one that most fits us for society. And since people have not been made always to live alone shut up in a study, we ought somehow to prefer those who have the greater gift for communicating their thoughts pleasantly and usefully. Consequently, **[181]** women who naturally have quick minds can—because they have imagination, memory and brilliance—with a little application acquire the qualities of intelligence.

This is enough to demonstrate that with regard to the head alone the two sexes are equal. With respect to the rest of the body, there are very curious things—but of which we must speak only in passing. Men have always had the common misfortune of reproducing, in a manner of speaking, their passions in all the works of nature. And there are scarcely any ideas that they have not mixed up with some feeling of love or hate, esteem or contempt. The things that relate to the distinctions between the two sexes are so physical and so blended with feelings of imperfection, **[182]** baseness, indecency, and other frivolities that—since they cannot be touched on without stirring up some passion and without exciting the flesh against the spirit—it is often prudent to say nothing about them.

However, it is certain that this bizarre mix of perpetually confused notions is the basis for the ideas prejudicial to women that small minds employ (ridiculously) to humiliate them. The most just compromise between the necessity of explaining oneself and the difficulty of doing so honestly is to note what we ought reasonably to understand by [the terms] "perfection" and "imperfection," "nobility" and "baseness," "decency" and "indecency."

Once I have comprehended that there is a God, I readily comprehend that all **[183]** things depend on Him. And if after having considered the natural, interior state of creatures

dépendent de luy; & si aprés avoir consideré l'état naturel &
interieur des Creatures, qui consiste, si se [*sic*] [ce] sont des
corps, dans la disposition de leurs parties à l'égard les unes
des autres, & leur état exterieur qui est le rapport qu'ils ont
pour agir ou pour souffrir avec ceux qui les environnent, si,
dis-je; je cherche la raison de ces deux états, je n'en trouve
point d'autre que la volonté de celuy qui en est l'Autheur.
I'observe ensuite, que ces corps ont d'ordinaire une certaine
disposition qui les rend capables de produire & de recevoir
certains effets; par exemple, que l'homme peut entendre par
les oreilles les pensées de ses semblables, & leur faire entendre
les siennes par les organes de la voix. Et je remarque que
les corps sont incapables de ces [184] effets, lorsqu'ils sont
autrement disposez. D'où je me forme deux idées, dont l'une
me represente le premier état des choses avec toutes ses suites
necessaires, & je l'appelle état de perfection: Et l'autre idée
me represente l'état contraire que je nomme imperfection.

Ainsi un homme est parfait à mon égard, lorsqu'il a
tout ce qu'il luy faut selon l'institution divine pour produire
& pour recevoir les effets ausquels il est destiné; & il
est imparfait, lorsqu'il a plus ou moins de parties, qu'il
n'est necessaire, ou quelque indisposition qui l'éloigne de
sa fin. C'est pourquoy ayant esté formé de sorte qu'il a
besoin d'alimens pour subsister, je ne conçois pas ce besoin,
comme une imperfection, non plus que la necessité attachée à
l'usage [185] des alimens, que le superflus sorte du corps. Ie
trouve ainsi que toutes les creatures sont également parfaites,
lorsqu'elles sont dans leur état naturel & ordinaire.

Il ne faut pas confondre la perfection avec la noblesse. Ce
sont deux choses bien differentes. Deux Creatures peuvent
estre égales en perfection, & inégales en noblesse.

En faisant reflexion sur moy-même, il me semble que mon
Esprit étant seul capable de connoissance, doit estre préferé
au Corps, & consideré comme le plus noble: mais lorsque je
regarde les corps, sans avoir égard à moy, c'est à dire, sans
songer qu'ils me peuvent estre utiles, ou nuisibles, agreables,
ou désagreables, je ne puis me persuader que les uns soient
plus nobles que les [186] autres, n'estant tous que de la
matiere diversement figurée. Au lieu que si je me mêle avec
les corps, considerant le bien & le mal qu'ils me peuvent

(which consists, if they are corporeal, in the disposition of their parts with respect to each other) and their exterior state (which is the affinity they have to act or suffer with those around them)—if, I say, I seek the reason for these two conditions, I find none other than the will of Him who is their author. Next, I observe that these bodies usually have a certain disposition that renders them capable of producing and receiving impressions of a certain kind. (For example, a man can hear the thoughts of his fellows through his ears and make them understand his thoughts using the organs of his voice.) And I notice that bodies are incapable of these [184] performances when they are arranged in some other manner. From this I derive two ideas: of which the one represents for me the first state of things with all that necessarily follows from it (I call it the state of perfection), and the other idea represents for me the contrary state (which I call imperfection).

Thus a man is perfect (in my view) when he has all that is necessary—according to divine institution—[for him] to produce and to receive the impressions for which he is destined. And he is imperfect when he has more or fewer parts than are necessary or some indisposition that keeps him from his end. This is why, having been made in such a way that food is necessary for sustenance, I do not see this need as an imperfection—no more than is the necessity (linked with the use [185] of food) that the excess depart the body. I, therefore, find that all creatures are equally perfect when they are in their natural and ordinary state.

Perfection must not be confused with nobility. These are two very different things. Two creatures can be equal in perfection and unequal in nobility.

In reflecting on myself, it seems that my mind—since it alone is capable of knowledge—must be preferred to my body and held to be the nobler thing. But when I consider bodies without having reference to myself (that is to say, without taking into account whether they can be useful or injurious, agreeable or disagreeable to me), I cannot persuade myself that some are more noble than [186] others—all being but variously formed from matter. Whereas, if I involve myself with bodies [and] consider the good and the evil that they

faire; je viens à les estimer differemment. Encore que ma
teste regardée sans interest ne me touche pas plus que les
autres parties, je la prefere neanmoins à toutes quand je viens
à penser qu'elle m'importe davantage dans l'union de mon
Esprit avec le Corps.

 C'est pour la même raison qu'encore que tous les endroits
du Corps soient également parfaits, on a neanmoins pour
eux des regards differens; ceux mêmes dont l'usage est plus
necessaire estant considerez souvent avec quelque sorte de
mépris & d'aversion, parce que cét usage est moins agreable
ou autrement. Il en est de même de tout ce qui [187] nous
environne & nous touche, car ce qui fait qu'une chose plaist à
l'un & déplaist à l'autre, c'est qu'elle les a frappez differement.

 [L'Idée de l'honesteté.] L'Engagement des hommes dans
la societé, est ce qui produit en eux l'idée de l'honnesteté.
Ainsi quoy qu'il n'y ait ny imperfection ny bassesse à soulager
le corps, & que ce soit même une necessité & une suite
indispensable de sa disposition naturelle, & que toutes les
manieres de le faire soient égales, il y en a neanmoins que l'on
considere comme moins honnestes, parce qu'elles choquent
davantage les personnes en presence desquelles on les fait.

 Comme toutes les Creatures & toutes leurs actions
considerées en elles mêmes, & sans aucun rapport à l'usage
ny à l'esti-[188]-me qu'on en fait, sont aussi parfaites &
aussi nobles les unes que les autres, elles sont aussi également
honnétes, étant considerées de la même façon. C'est pourquoy
l'on peut dire que les regards d'honnesteté & de deshonnesteté
sont presque tous dans leur origine, les effets de l'imagination,
& du caprice des hommes. Cela paroist en ce qu'une chose
qui est honneste en un païs, ne l'est pas dans l'autre; & que
dans un même Royaume, mais en divers temps, ou bien en un
même temps, mais entre des personnes d'état, de condition &
d'humeur differente, une même action est tantost conforme,
tantost contraire à l'honnesteté. C'est pourquoy l'honnesteté
n'est autre chose que la maniere d'user des choses naturelles,
selon l'estime que les hommes en font, [189] & à quoy il est de
la prudence de s'accommoder.

 Nous sommes tous tellement pénétrez de cette idée, quoy
que nous n'y fassions pas de refléxion, que les personnes
ou amies, ou spirituelles & judicieuses, qui s'assujettissent

can do me, I come to value them differently. Although my head (regarded disinterestedly) does not affect me more than the other parts [of my body], I nevertheless prefer it to all of them when I come to realize that it is more important to me in the union of my mind with the body.

For the same reason, although all the parts of the body are equally perfect, we nevertheless regard them differently. (Even those parts whose use is most necessary are often considered with some kind of contempt and aversion because this use is less pleasant or otherwise.) It is the same with everything that [187] surrounds and affects us, for what makes a thing please one person and displease another is the fact that it strikes them differently.

The involvement of people in society is what produces in them the idea of decency. Thus, although there is neither imperfection nor baseness in the process of relieving the body (and this is even a necessity and an indispensable consequence of its natural disposition) and all methods for doing so are equally effective, there are nevertheless some means that are considered to be less decent [than others]—because they are more displeasing to the people in whose presence they are done.

Since all creatures and all their actions (when considered in themselves and without any reference to the use that can be made of them or the value [188] that can be put on them) are one as perfect and as noble as the others, they are also, when considered in the same way, equally decent. Therefore, we can say that judgments of decency and indecency are almost all originally the result of people's imagination and caprice. This is confirmed by the fact that a thing that is decent in one country is not in another—and that in the same kingdom at various times (or even at the same time, but between persons of different estate, condition and humor) one and the same action sometimes conforms to and sometimes violates standards of decency. Consequently, [a sense of] decency (to which it is prudent to accommodate oneself) is nothing other than a way of using the things of nature according to the values people assign them.

[189] We are all so steeped in this idea (although we have not reflected on it) that people (either [as] friends or

en public & avec le vulgaire aux façons de l'honnesteté, s'en délivrent en particulier, comme des charges autant importunes que bizarres.

Il en est de même de la Noblesse. En quelques Provinces des Indes, les Laboureurs ont le même rang que les Nobles parmy nous: en certains païs on préfere les gens d'épée à ceux de robe; en d'autres on pratique tout le contraire: Chacun selon qu'il a plus d'inclination pour ces états, ou qu'il les estime plus importans.

En comparant ces idées là, [190] avec les pensées que le vulgaire a sur les femmes, l'on reconnoîtra sans peine, en quoy consiste son erreur.

persons of intelligence and discretion) who in public conform with the common man to the fashions [defining] decency, free themselves from these things in private as from baggage [that is] as burdensome as [it is] bizarre.

It is the same with respect to [the concept of] "nobility." In some provinces of the Indies laborers have the same rank as nobles [do] among us. In certain countries men of the sword are preferred to those of the robe, and in others quite the contrary is the case—each according as he has more propensity for these estates or as he esteems them more important.

If the thoughts that [190] ordinary people have about women are compared with these points [we have made], the source of their error will easily be identified.

D'où vient la distinction des Sexes: jusques où elle
s'étend: & qu'elle ne met point de difference entre
les hommes & les femmes, par rapport au vice & à
la vertu; & que le temperamment en general n'est ny
bon ny mauvais en soy.

[D'où vient la difference de Sexes.] Dieu voulant produire les
hommes dépendemment les uns des autres, par le concours
de deux personnes, fabriqua pour cét usage deux corps qui
estoient differens. Chacun estoit parfait en sa maniere, & ils
devoient estre tous deux disposez comme ils sont à present:
Et tout ce qui dépend de leur constitution par-[191]-ticuliere
doit estre consideré comme faisant partie de leur perfection.
C'est donc sans raison que quelques-uns s'imaginent que les
femmes ne sont pas si parfaites que les hommes, & qu'ils
regardent en elles comme un défaut, ce qui est un Appanage
essentiel à leur Sexe, sans quoy il seroit inutile à la fin
pour laquelle il a esté formé; qui commence & cesse avec la
fecondité, & qui est destiné au plus excellent usage du monde;
c'est à dire, à nous former & à nous nourrir dans leur sein.
      [Les Femmes contribuent plus que les hommes à
generation.] Les deux Sexes sont necessaires pour produire ensemble leur pareil: & si l'on sçavoit comment le
nostre y contribuë, l'on trouveroit bien du méconte pour
nous. Il est difficile de comprendre sur quoy se fondent ceux
qui soûtiennent que les hommes sont [192] plus nobles que
les femmes, en ce qui regarde les enfans. Ce sont proprement
celles-cy qui nous conçoivent, qui nous forment, qui nous
donnent l'Estre, la naissance, & l'éducation. Il est vray que
cela leur coûte plus qu'à nous : mais il ne faut pas que
cette peine leur soit préjudiciable, & leur attire le mépris, au
lieu de l'estime qu'elles en meritent. Qui voudroit dire, que
les peres & les meres, qui travaillent à élever leurs enfans,
les bons Princes à gouverner leurs sujets, & les Magistrats
à leur rendre la justice, soient moins estimables, que ceux
de l'entremise & du secours desquels ils se servent, pour
s'acquiter de leur devoir?
      [Sur le temperamment.] Il y a des Medecins, qui se sont
fort étendus, sur le Temperamment des Sexes aux desavantage
[*sic*] des femmes, & ont fait des [193] discours à perte de veuë,

Whence comes the distinction between the sexes: how
far it extends, that it does not create a difference
between men and women with respect to vice and
virtue, and that the general character [of a sex] is
neither good nor bad in itself.

God, wishing to produce human beings [by making them]
depend on each other (through the union of two persons),
made (for this purpose) two different bodies. Each is perfect
in its way, and both must be set up as they are now. And
everything that springs from their characteristic structure[s]
[191] must be considered as constituting part of their
perfection. There is no reason, therefore, for some people to
imagine that women are not as perfect as men and for these
people to regard as a fault in women what is an essential lot
of their sex—without which their sex would be useless for the
purpose for which it was made ([a purpose] that begins and
ends with a fecundity that is destined for the best use in [all]
the world—i.e., to form and nourish us in their womb[s]).
    The two sexes are necessary for the production (together)
of their own kind. And if we understand how our [sex]
contributes to this, we will find much to be displeased with
in ourselves. It is difficult to comprehend on what those
who maintain that, with respect to children, men are **[192]**
more noble than women base their argument. Women are,
appropriately, the ones who conceive us, form us, and give us
being, birth, and training. It is true that this costs them more
than it does us, but their suffering should not be counted
against them and earn them contempt in place of the respect
they deserve. Who would want to claim that the fathers and
mothers who work to raise their children, the good princes
[who labor] to govern their subjects, and the magistrates who
[strive] to render them justice are less worthy than those
whose mediation and assistance they use to acquit themselves
of their duty?
    There are physicians who have elaborated extensively
on [the subject of] the constitution of the sexes (to the
disadvantage of women) and [who] have **[193]** lectured
endlessly to demonstrate that the female sex must have a
character totally different from ours (a character that renders

pour montrer que leur Sexe doit avoir un temperamment tout
à fait different du nôtre, & qui le rend inferieur en tout. Mais
leurs raisons ne sont que des conjectures legeres, qui viennent
dans l'esprit de ceux qui ne jugent des choses que par préjugé
& sur de simples apparences.

Voyant les deux Sexes plus distinguez pour ce qui regarde
les fonctions Civiles, que celles qui leur sont particulieres,
ils se sont imaginez, qu'ils devoient estre de la sorte; & ne
discernant pas assez exactement ce qui vient de la coûtume
& de l'education d'avec ce que donne la nature; ils ont
attribué à une même cause, tout ce qu'ils voyoient dans la
societé, se figurant que Dieu en creant l'homme & la femme
les avoit disposez d'une façon qui [194] doit produire toute la
distinction que nous remarquons entr'eux.

C'est porter trop loin la difference des Sexes. On la
doit restreindre dans le dessein que Dieu a eu de former
les hommes par le concours des deux personnes, & n'en
admettre qu'autant qu'il est necessaire pour cét effet. Aussi
voyons-nous que les hommes & les femmes sont semblables
presque en tout pour la constitution interieure & exterieure
du corps, & que les fonctions naturelles, & desquelles dépend
nôtre conservation, se font en eux de la méme maniere. C'est
donc assez afin qu'ils donnent naissance à un troisiéme, qu'il
y ait quelques organes dans l'un qui ne soient pas dans
l'autre. Il n'est pas besoin pour cela, comme on se le figure,
que les femmes ayent moins de force & [195] de vigueur que
les hommes: Et comme il n'y a que l'experience qui puisse
bien faire juger de cette distinction, ne trouve-t-on pas que
les femmes sont mélées comme nous; il y en a de fortes &
de foibles dans les deux parties: les hommes élevez dans la
molesse sont souvent pires que les femmes, & ployent d'abord
sous le travail: mais quand ils y sont endurcis par necessité
ou autrement, ils deviennent égaux, & quelquefois superieurs
aux autres.

Il en est de même des femmes. Celles qui s'occupent à
des exercices penibles, sont plus robustes que les Dames qui
ne manient qu'une aiguille. Ce qui peut faire penser que si
l'on exerçoit également les deux Sexes, l'un acquereroit peut
estre autant de vigueur que l'autre; ce que l'on a veu autre
fois dans [196] une Republique, où la Lutte & les exercices

it inferior in all things). But their arguments are but light conjectures that arise in the mind[s] of those who judge things only on the basis of prejudice and simple appearances.

Seeing that there is more distinction between the two sexes in what concerns their civil functions than in the functions that are specific to them [in nature], these men [i.e., those who judge things casually] have surmised that things must be this way. And not discerning with enough exactitude what derives from custom and education and what nature provides, they have attributed to the same cause everything they see in society—imagining that God in creating man and woman arranged them in a way that **[194]** must produce all the distinction[s] that we observe between them.

This is to carry the difference between the sexes too far. We should restrict it to the plan that God had to form human beings through the union of two persons, and [we should] only admit as much [distinction between them] as is necessary for this purpose. Also: we see that men and women are almost alike in everything relating to the interior and exterior of the body and that their natural functions (on which our preservation) depends are the same. It is, therefore, enough in order that men and women give birth to a third being that there be some organs in the one that are not in the other. This creates no need, as is imagined, for women to have less strength and **[195]** vigor than men. And since experience alone can provide a basis for accurately judging differences [of strength], do we not find that women are as varied as we [are]—[that] there are some strong and weak persons in both camps? Men raised in softness are often worse than women, and bend first under a burden. But when they are hardened by necessity or otherwise, they become equal and sometimes superior to other men.

It is the same with women. Those who occupy themselves with difficult exercises are more robust than the ladies who handle nothing but a needle. This may suggest that if the two sexes exercised equally, one might perhaps acquire as much vigor as the other. This has been seen in other ages in **[196]** a republic where wrestling and exercises were common to both [sexes]. The same is reported of the Amazons of South America.

leurs estoient communs: on rapporte le même des Amazones qui sont au Midy de l'Amerique.

[Il ne faut point avoir égard à quelques expressions desavantageuses aux femmes.] L'on ne doit donc faire aucun fond sur certaines expressions ordinaires tirées de l'état present des deux Sexes. Losqu'on veut blâmer un homme avec moquerie, comme ayant peu de courage, de resolution & de fermeté, on l'appelle effeminé, comme si on vouloit dire, qu'il est aussi lâche, & aussi mou qu'une femme. Au contraire, pour loüer une femme qui n'est pas du commun à cause de son courage, de sa force, ou de son esprit, on dit, que c'est un homme. Ces expressions si avantageuxes aux hommes ne contribuënt pas peu à entretenir la haute idée qu'on a d'eux; faute de sçavoir qu'elles ne [197] sont que vrai semblables; & que leur verité suppose indifferemment la nature, ou la coûtume, & qu'ainsi elles sont purement contingentes & arbitraires. La vertu, la douceur & l'honnesteté estant si particulieres aux femmes, si leur Sexe n'avoit pas esté si peu consideré, lorsqu'on auroit voulu signifier avec éloge qu'un homme a ces qualitez en un degré éminent, on auroit dit, c'est une femme, s'il avoit plû aux hommes d'établir cét usage dans le discours.

Quoy qu'il en soit, ce n'est pas la force du corps, qui doit distinguer les hommes; autrement les bestes auroient l'avantage pardessus eux, & entre nous ceux qui sont les plus robustes. Cependant l'on reconnoît par experience que ceux qui ont tant de force, ne sont gueres propres [198] à autre chose qu'aux ouvrages materiels, & que ceux au contraire qui en ont moins, ont ordinairement plus de teste. Les plus habiles Philosophes & les plus grands Princes ont esté assez delicats, & les plus grands Capitaines, n'eussent peut-estre pas voulu lutter contre les moindres de leurs soldats. Qu'on aille dans le Parlement, on verra si les plus grands Iuges égalent toûjours en force le dernier de leurs Huissiers.

Il est donc inutile de s'apuyer tant sur la constitution du corps, pour rendre raison de la difference qui se voit entre les deux Sexes, par rapport à l'esprit.

Le temperamment ne consiste pas dans un point indivisible: comme on ne peut trouver deux personnes en qui il soit tout semblable, on ne peut non plus déterminer précisément

We must not then rely on certain common figures of speech derived from the present state of the two sexes. When we mockingly want to reprimand a man for having little courage, resolution, and firmness, we call him "effeminate"— as if we would say that he was as cowardly and as weak as a woman. On the other hand, to praise a woman who (because of her courage, strength, or intellect) is not of the common [type], we say that she is a "man." These expressions (so complimentary to men) contribute not a little to upholding the high opinion that we have of men—since we are not aware that these figures of speech **[197]** are only conjectural (that their truth supposes nature or custom [as their cause] without discriminating [between these things] and that they are, therefore, purely contingent and arbitrary). If the female sex had not been so little appreciated (virtue, sweetness, and decency being so characteristic of women), when we wanted to note—with a compliment—that a man had these qualities to an eminent degree, we should have said, "He is a woman" (if it had pleased people to establish this custom in discourse).

However that may be, it is not the strength of the body that ought to accord eminence among human beings (otherwise beasts would have supremacy over them and, among us, those of us who are the most robust [would rule]). However, we discover from experience that those who have such strength are scarcely fit **[198]** for anything other than physical labor and that those, on the other hand, who have less strength ordinarily have more intelligence. The most skilled philosophers and the greatest princes have been somewhat frail men, and the greatest captains would not perhaps have wanted to wrestle against the least of their soldiers. Let us go into the court—we will see if the greatest judges always equal the least of their bailiffs in strength.

It is useless, therefore, to rely so much on the structure of the body to supply a reason for the difference that is seen between the two sexes with respect to the mind.

Character does not consist of an indivisible point. As we cannot find two persons in whom it is completely the same, we cannot, either, determine precisely in what they **[199]** differ. There are many sorts of the short-tempered, the sanguine, and the melancholy. And all these diversities

en quoy ils [199] different. Il y a plusieurs sortes de bilieux, de sanguins, & de melancholiques: & toute ces diversitez n'empeschent pas qu'ils ne soient souvent aussi capables les uns que les autres, & qu'il n'y ait d'excellens hommes de toute sorte de temperamment: & supposant même, que celuy des deux Sexes soit aussi different qu'on le pretend, il se trouve encore plus de difference entre plusieurs hommes qu'on croit neanmoins capables des mêmes choses. Le plus & le moins estant si peu considerables, il n'y a que l'esprit de chicane qui y fasse avoir égard.

Il y a apparence que ce qui grossit tant en idée la distinction, dont nous parlons, c'est qu'on n'examine pas avec assez de précision tout ce que l'on remarque dans les femmes & ce défaut fait tomber dans l'erreur de ceux qui [200] ayant l'esprit confus, ne distinguent pas assez ce qui appartient à chaque chose, & attribuënt à l'une ce qui ne convient qu'à l'autre, parce qu'ils les trouvent ensemble dans un même sujet. C'est pourquoy voyant dans les femmes tant de difference pour les manieres, & pour les fonctions, on l'a transportée au temperamment, faute d'en sçavoir la cause.

[Les femmes peuvent prétendre l'avantage pour le corps.] Quoy qu'il en soit, si on vouloit examiner quel est le plus excellent des deux Sexes, par la comparaison du corps, les femmes pourroient prétendre l'avantage, & sans parler de la fabrique interieure de leur corps, & que c'est en elles que se passe ce qu'il y a au monde de plus curieux à connoître, sçavoir, comment se produit l'homme qui est la plus belle, & la pus [*sic*] admirable de tou-[201]-tes les Creatures; qui les empécheroit de dire, que ce qui paroist au dehors leur doit donner le dessus: que la grace & la beauté leur sont naturelles & particulieres, & que tout cela produit des effets autant sensibles qu'ordinaires, & que si ce qu'elles peuvent par le dedans de la teste, les rend au moins égales aux hommes, le dehors ne manque presque jamais de les en rendre les Maîtresses.

La beauté estant un avantage aussi réel que la force & la santé, la raison ne deffend pas de s'en prévaloir plûtost que des autres; & si on vouloit juger de son prix par les sentimens & par les passions qu'elle excite, comme l'on juge presque de toutes choses, on trouveroit qu'il n'y a rien de plus estimable,

do not prevent them often from being one as competent as another—and [do not prevent] there being excellent men of all sorts of temperament[s]. Even supposing that the characters of the two sexes is as different as we pretend, an even greater difference is found among many men who are, nevertheless, believed [to be] capable of the same things—the differences of degree being of so little account [among them that] only quibbling would make us pay attention to it.

There is a likelihood that the thing that exaggerates the idea [of] the distinction [between the sexes] of which we are speaking is our failure to examine all that we see in women with enough precision. This shortcoming causes [us] to fall into the error of those who, [200] having a confused mind, do not adequately distinguish what belongs to each thing and [who] attribute to one what accords only with another (because they find these two things together in the same subject). This is why, seeing in women such a great difference [with us] in manners and functions, we have credited it to the account of temperament—for want of knowing its cause.

Be that as it may, if we should want, by a comparison of body, to inquire into which is the more excellent of the two sexes, women could claim the advantage. (And [they could do so] without mentioning the interior structure of their bodies and [the fact] that the thing transpires in them that in all the world is most intriguing to the understanding—the knowledge of how man, the most beautiful and most admirable of all [201] creatures, originates). Since grace and beauty are natural to and characteristic of women and all [these things] produce effects [that are] as acute as [they are] common, who would prevent women from claiming that outward appearance must give them the upper hand? If what they can do with the inside of the head makes them at least men's equals, the outside almost never fails to render them men's rulers.

Beauty being an advantage as real as strength and health, reason does not forbid deriving advantage for oneself from it rather than from the others. And if we should wish to judge its worth (as we judge almost all things) by the feelings and the passions that it excites, we would find that there is nothing more estimable—nothing having more effect. That is to say, nothing stirs [202] and agitates more passions [and]

n'y ayant rien de plus effectif, c'est à dire, qui remuë [202] & agite plus de passions, qui les méle, & les fortifie plus diversement, que les impressions de la beauté

Il ne seroit pas necessaire de parler davantage sur le temperamment des femmes, si un Autheur autant celebre que poly ne s'étoit avisé de le considerer comme la source des défauts qu'on leur attribuë vulgairement; ce qui aide beaucoup à confirmer les gens dans la pensée qu'elles sont moins estimables que nous. [Tous les temperammens sont presque égaux.] Sans rapporter son sentiment, je diray que pour bien examiner le temperamment des deux Sexes par rapport au vice & à la vertu, il le faut considerer dans un état indifferent, où il n'y ait encore ni vertu ni vice en nature: & alors on trouve que ce qu'on appelle vertu dans un temps, pouvant devenir vice en un autre, se-[203]-lon l'usage qu'on en fait, tous les temperammens sont égaux en ce point là.

[Ce que c'est que la vertu.] Pour mieux entendre cette pensée, il faut remarquer qu'il n'y a que nôtre ame qui soit capable de vertu, laquelle consiste en general dans la resolution ferme & constante de faire ce qu'on juge le meilleur selon les diverses occurrances. Le Corps n'est proprement que l'organe & l'instrument de cette resolution, comme une épée entre les mains pour l'attaque & pour la defense: & toutes les differentes dispositions qui le rendent plus ou moins propre à cét usage, ne doivent estre appellées bonnes ou mauvaises, que selon que leurs effets sont plus ordinaires, & plus importans pour le bien & pour le mal; par exemple, la disposition à la fuite pour s'éloigner des maux qui [204] menacent, est indifferente, parce qu'il y en a qu'on ne peut éviter autrement; & alors il est de la prudence de s'enfuir: au lieu que c'est une timidité blâmable de se laisser emporter à la fuite, lorsque le mal est surmontable par une genereuse resistance qui produit plus de bien que de mal.

[Les femmes ne sont pas plus portées au vice que les hommes.] Or l'esprit n'est pas moins capable dans les femmes que dans les hommes, de cette ferme resolution qui fait la vertu, ni de connoïtre les rencontres où il la faut exercer. Elles peuvent regler leurs passions aussi-bien que nous, & elles ne sont pas plus portées au vice qu'au bien. On pourroit même faire pencher la balance en leur faveur de ce costé cy:

mixes and strengthens them more diversely than impressions of beauty.

It would not be necessary to say more about women's character if an author,[1] as famous as [he is] cultured, had not ventured to consider it the source of the faults that we commonly attribute to women (which action on his part helps a great deal to confirm people in the notion that women are less admirable than we [are]). Without relating his opinion, I will say that in order better to examine the character[s] of the two sexes (with respect to vice and virtue) they must be considered in a neutral state in which neither virtue nor vice yet exists in nature. And then we find that, since what we call virtue at one time becomes vice at another **[203]** (depending on the use that we make of it), all characters are equal in that respect.

To understand this thought better, it is necessary to realize that our souls alone are capable of virtue (which generally consists in the firm and constant resolution to do what we judge best with respect to different situations). The body is, properly [speaking], only the organ and the instrument of this resolution—like a sword in hand for attack and defense. All the different dispositions that render it more or less fit for this use should be called good or bad only according to whether their consequences lead most ordinarily and importantly to good or evil. For example: the disposition to flee so as to distance oneself from the threat of evil **[204]** is indifferent, for there are some dangers that we cannot otherwise avoid (and, then, it is prudent to flee). On the other hand, it is culpable timidity to allow oneself to be swept into flight when evil can be surmounted by a courageous resistance that yields more good than bad.

But the mind[s] of women are not less capable than those of men of this firm resolution that constitutes virtue—nor of understanding the situations in which it is necessary to exercise it. Women can rule their passions as well as we [can], and they are not more inclined to vice than to the good. We might even tip the balance in their favor on this side, since

---

[1]Marie Louise Stock (p. 121, n. 2) claims that Poullain's reference is to Cureau de la Chambre (1594?–1675), author of *Les Charactères des Passions*.

puisque l'affection pour les enfans, sans comparaison plus
forte dans les femmes que dans les hommes, est naturellement
atta-[205]-chée à la compassion, qu'on peut appeler la vertu
& le lien de la societé civile: n'étant pas possible de concevoir
que la societé soit raisonnablement établie pour autre chose,
que pour survenir aux besoins, & aux necessitez communes
les uns des autres. Et si on regarde de prés comment se
forment en nous les passions, on trouvera que de la façon que
les femmes contribuënt à la production & à l'éducation des
hommes, c'est comme une suite naturelle, qu'elles les traitent
dans leurs afflictions, en quelque maniere comme leurs enfans.

affection for infants (without comparison, stronger in women than in men) is linked naturally **[205]** with compassion. [And compassion] might be called the virtue and the bond of civil society—it not being possible to conceive that society is established rationally for any other thing than to serve the needs and necessities common to all. And if we closely examine how the passions are formed in us, we will find that from the way women contribute to the production and to the education of men, it is a natural consequence that they treat them in their afflictions in some way like their children.

[206] Que la difference qui se remarque entre les hommes & les femmes pour ce qui regarde les moeurs vient de l'Education qu'on leur donne.

Et il est d'autant plus important de remarquer que les dispositions que nous apportons en naissant, ne sont ny bonnes ny mauvaises, qu'on ne peut autrement éviter une erreur assez ordinaire par laquelle on rapporte souvent à la nature ce qui ne vient que de l'usage.

[Ce que peut l'estat exterieur.] L'on se tourmente l'esprit à chercher la raison pourquoy nous sommes sujets à certains défauts & avons des manieres particulieres; faute d'avoir observé ce que peuvent faire en nous l'habitude, l'exercice, l'éducation & l'état exterieur, c'est-à dire le rapport **[207]** de Sexe, d'age, de fortune, d'employ, où l'on se trouve dans la societé: Estant certain que toutes ces differentes veuës diversifiant en une infinité de manieres les pensées & les passions, disposent pareillement les esprits à regarder tout autrement les veritez qu'on leur presente. C'est pour cela qu'une même maxime proposée en même temps à des Bourgeois, à des Soldats, à des Iuges & à des Princes, les frappe & les fait agir si differemment: parce que les hommes ne se souciant gueres que de l'exterieur: le regardent comme la mesure & la regle de leurs sentimens: d'où vient que les uns laissent passer comme inutile ce qui occupe fortement les autres; que les gens d'épée se choquent de ce qui flatte les gens de robe: & que des personnes de même temperament **[208]** prennent quelquefois à contresens certaines choses, qui entrent du même biais dans l'esprit de personnes de constitution differente; mais qui ont la même fortune, ou la même éducation.

Ce n'est pas qu'on pretende que tous les hommes apportent au monde la même constitution corporelle. Ce seroit une pretention mal fondée: il y en a de vifs & de lents: mais il ne paroist pas que cette diversité empéche aucunement les esprits de reçevoir la même instruction: tout ce qu'elle fait c'est que les uns la reçoivent plus viste & plus heureusement que les autres. Ainsi quelque temperament qu'ayent les femmes, elles ne sont pas moins capables que nous de la verité & de l'étude. Et si l'on trouve à present

[206] That the difference in what concerns customs that is noticed between men and women comes from the education[s] we give them.

It is especially important to realize that the dispositions that we carry from birth are neither good nor bad—lest we not be able otherwise to avoid a rather common error by which things that derive from custom are frequently credited to nature.

We torment our minds searching for the reason why we are subject to certain faults and have particular ways of behaving—failing to have observed what can be worked in us by habit, practice, education, and the external environment (i.e., the context [207] of sex, age, fortune, and profession in which we find ourselves in society). It is certain that all these different points of view diversify the thoughts and passions in an infinite number of ways and, likewise, dispose minds to see the truths that we present to them in completely different fashions. This is the reason why one and the same precept presented at the same time to ordinary citizens, soldiers, judges, and princes strikes them (and causes them to act) so differently. Because people scarcely trouble themselves with anything but external[s], they take outward appearance as the measure and the rule of their thoughts—which is why some people allow to pass [them by] as useless what strongly occupies [the attention of] others, [and why] "men of the sword" take offence at what flatters "men of the robe," and [why] persons of the same temperament [208] sometimes take in a contrary sense certain things that (stated in the same way) are accepted by persons who have different constitution[s] but the same fortune or education.

It is not that we maintain that all men bring the same physical constitution into the world. (This would be a groundless claim.) There are some men who are quick and some slow, but it does not seem that this diversity in the least prevents minds from receiving the same instruction. All that it does is [to determine] that some receive it more rapidly and easily than others. Thus whatever character women have, they are not less capable than we are of truth and education. And if at present we find in several of them

en quelques-unes quelque deffaut, ou quelque obstacle, ou
[209] [Les defauts qui sont dans les femmes viennent de
l'éducation.] même que toutes n'envisagent pas les choses
solides comme les hommes, à quoy pourtant l'experience est
contraire, cela doit etre uniquement rejetté sur l'état exterieur
de leur Sexe, & sur l'éducation qu'on leur donne qui comprend
l'ignorance où on les laisse, les préjugez ou les erreurs qu'on
leur inspire, l'exemple qu'elles ont de leurs semblables &
toutes les manieres, à quoy la bien-seance, la contrainte, la
retenuë, la sujettion, & la timidité les reduisent.

[Quelle éducation on leur donne.] En effet on n'oublie
rien à leur égard qui serve à les persuader que cette grande
difference qu'elles voyent entre leur Sexe & le nostre, c'est un
ouvrage de la raison, ou d'institution divine. L'habillement,
l'éducation, & les exercices ne peuvent estre plus differens.
Une fille n'est en as-**[210]**-surance que sous les aisles de sa
mere, ou sous les yeux d'une gouvernante qui ne l'abandonne
point: on luy fait peur de tout: on la menace des esprits
dans tous les lieux de la maison, où elle se pourroit trouver
seule: Dans les grandes ruës & dans les temples mêmes il
y a quelque chose à craindre, si elle n'y est escortée. Le
grand soin que l'on prend de la parer y applique tout son
esprit: Tant de regards qu'on luy jette, & tant de discours
qu'elle entend sur la beauté y attache toutes ses pensées; &
les complimens qu'on luy rend sur ce sujet, font qu'elle y met
tout son bonheur. Comme on ne luy parle d'autre chose, elle
y borne tous ses desseins, & ne porte point ses veuës plus
haut. La danse, l'écriture, & la lecture sont les plus grands
exercices des femmes, tou-**[211]**-te leur Bibliotheque consiste
dans quelques petits Livres de devotion, avec ce qui est dans
la cassette.

Toute leur science se reduit à travailler de l'éguille [*sic*] [.]
Le miroir est le grand maistre, & l'oracle qu'elles consultent.
Les bals, les comedies, les modes sont le sujet de leurs
entretiens: elles regardent les cercles, comme de celebres
Academies, où-elles vont s'instruire de toutes les nouvelles de
leur Sexe. Et s'il arrive que quelques-unes se distinguent du
commun par la lecture de certains Livres, qu'elles auront eu
bien de la peine à attraper, à dessein de s'ouvrir l'esprit, elles
sont obligées souvent de s'en cacher: La pluspart de leurs

some fault or some obstacle or **[209]** even that all of them do not view serious subjects as men do (which is, however, disproved by experience), that must be credited solely to the external situation of their sex and to the education that we give them (which is comprised of the ignorance in which we leave them, the prejudice or the errors that we inspire in them, the example that they have of others of their own kind, and all the ways in which propriety, constraint, discretion, subjection, and timidity hold them back).

Indeed, we neglect nothing with respect to women that serves to persuade them that this great difference that they see between their sex and ours is a work of reason or a divine institution. Dress, education, and exercise cannot be more different. A young girl is **[210]** only safe under the wings of her mother or within sight of a governess who never leaves her. We make her fear everything. In the house we threaten her with ghosts everywhere where she might find herself alone. In the major streets and even in the temples there is something [for her] to fear if she is not escorted. The great care that we take to adorn her occupies her whole mind. So many glances are thrown her way and she hears so many discourses on her beauty that they take over all her thoughts. And she pins all her happiness on the compliments paid her on this subject. Since we speak to her of nothing else, she keys all her plans to this and never sets her sights higher. Dancing, writing, and reading are the major activities of women. **[211]** Their entire library consists of several small books of devotion along with what is [found] in their purse[s].

All women's knowledge comes down to working with a needle. The mirror is their great master and the oracle they consult. Balls, comedies, and fashions are the subjects of their conversations. They treat their tea parties like famous academies to which they come to instruct themselves in all the novelties of their sex. And if it happens that some of them distinguish themselves from the common herd by reading certain books (that they have taken substantial trouble to obtain—with the intention of broadening their minds), they are often obliged to conceal themselves. Most of their companions (through jealousy or something else) never fail to accuse them of wanting to flaunt affectations.

compagnes par jalousie ou autrement, ne manquant jamais de les accuser de vouloir faire les precieuses.

[212] Pour ce qui est des filles de condition roturiere, contraintes de gagner leur vie par leur travail, l'esprit leur est encore plus inutile. On a soin de leur faire apprendre un mestier convenable au Sexe, aussi tost qu'elles y sont propres, & la necessité de s'y employer sans cesse, les empéche de penser à autre chose: Et lorsque les unes & les autres élevées de cette façon ont atteint l'âge du mariage, on les y engage, ou b[i]en on les confine dans un cloître où elles continuent de vivre comme elles ont commencé.

En tout ce qu'on fait conoistre aux femmes void-on rien qui aille à les instruire solidement? Il semble au contraire qu'on soit convenu de cette sorte d'éducation pour leur abaisser le courage, pour obscurcir leur esprit, & ne le remplir que de vanité & de [213] sotises; pour y étoufer toutes les semences de vertu & de verité; pour rendre inutiles toutes les dispositions qu'elles pourroient avoir aux grandes choses, & pour leur oster le desir de se rendre parfaites, comme nous, en leur en ostant les moyens.

Lorsque je fais attention sur la maniere, dont on regarde, ce que l'on croit voir en elles de defectueux je trouve que cette conduite a quelque chose d'indigne de personnes doüées de raison. S'il y a également à redire dans les deux Sexes, celuy qui accuse l'autre peche contre l'équité naturelle; s'il y a plus de mal dans le nostre, & que nous ne le voyons pas, nous sommes des temeraires de parler de ceux d'autruy: si nous le voyons, & que nous n'en disions rien, nous sommes inustes de blâmer l'autre [214] qui en a moins. S'il y a plus de biens dans les femmes que dans les hommes, ceux-cy doivent estre accusez d'ignorance, ou d'envie de ne le pas reconnoître. Quand il y a plus de vertu, que de vice dans une personne, l'un doit servir à excuser l'autre, & lorsque les defauts qu'elle a sont insurmontables, & que les moyens de s'en deffaire, ou de s'en garentir, luy manquent, comme ils manquent aux femmes, elle est digne de compassion non de mepris. Enfin si ces défauts sont legers, ou seulement apparens, c'est imprudence, ou malice de s'y arrester; & il n'est pas difficile de montrer, qu'on en use ainsi vulgairement à l'égard des femmes.

[212] The mind is even more useless to young women of the plebeian class [who are] compelled to win their living by their labor. Care is taken, as soon as they are ready, to make them learn a trade appropriate to their sex, and the necessity of ceaseless labor prevents them from thinking of anything else. And when all [of those who have been] raised in this way have reached an age for marriage, we engage them in it or confine them in a cloister where they continue to live as they have begun.

In everything that we make women learn, do we see anything that would contribute to instructing them soundly? On the contrary, it seems that we have agreed on this kind of education in order to diminish their courage, cloud their intellect[s], and fill their minds with nothing but vanity and **[213]** foolishness—to stifle all the seeds of virtue and of truth in them, to render useless all the inclinations they might have to great things, and (by denying them the means) to deprive them of the desire to perfect themselves as we do.

When I think about the way in which we view what we believe [we] see [to be] defects in women, I find that this conduct is somewhat unworthy of persons endowed with reason. If there is equally [something] to criticize in the two sexes, the one that accuses the other sins against natural justice. If there is more wickedness in our [sex] and we do not see it, we are foolhardy to speak of [the sins] of others. If we see it and we say nothing about it, we are unjust in accusing the other [sex] **[214]** which has less [wickedness]. If there is more good in women than in men, men who do not recognize this must be accused of ignorance or envy. When there is more virtue than vice in a person, the one must serve to excuse the other. And when the faults that she has are insurmountable and the ways to rid herself of them (or to secure herself against them) are lacking to her (as they are lacking to women), she is worthy of compassion, not contempt. Finally, if these faults are light or only apparent, it is imprudent or malicious to dwell on them (and it is not hard to show that such use is commonly made of them with respect to women).

It is said that women are timid and incapable of defense, that their shadow[s] strike fear in them, that **[215]** the cry of

158 *Poullain*

[Que les defauts qu'on attribuë aux femmes sont imaginaires. La timidité.] On dit qu'elles sont timides, & incapables de deffense, que leur ombre leur fait peur, que **[215]** le cry d'un enfant les alarme, & que le bruit du vent les fait trembler. Cela n'est pas general. Il y a quantité de femmes aussi hardies, que des hommes, & l'on sçait que les plus timides font souvent de necessité vertu. La timidité est presqu'inséparable de la vertu, & tous les gens de bien en ont[. C]omme ils ne veulent faire mal à personne; & qu'ils n'ignorent pas combien il y a de méchanceté parmy les hommes, il faut peu de chose pour leur inspirer de la crainte. C'est une passion naturelle dont personne n'est exempt: tout le monde craint la mort, & les incommoditez de la vie, les Princes les plus puissans apprehendent la revolte de leur sujets & l'invasion de leurs ennemis, & les plus vaillans Capitaines d'estre pris au dépourveu.

La crainte est grande à pro-**[216]**-portion des forces qu'on croit avoir pour resister; & elle n'est blamable que dans ceux qui sont assez forts pour repousser le mal qui les menace: & l'on seroit aussi déraisonnable d'accuser de lâcheté un Iuge & un homme de lettre, qui n'auroient pensé qu'à l'étude de refuser de se battre en duel, que d'accuser un soldat qui auroit toûjours porté les armes, de ne vouloir pas entrer en dispute contre un sçavant Philosophe.

L'on éleve les femmes d'une maniere qu'elles ont sujet de tout apprehender. Elles n'ont point de lumieres pour éviter les surprises, dans les choses de l'esprit; Elles n'ont point de part aux exercises qui donnent l'adresse & la force pour l'attaque & pour la défense. Elles se voyent exposées à souffrir impunément les outrages d'un Sexe si sujet aux emporte-**[217]**-mens, qui les regarde avec mépris, & qui traite souvent ses semblables avec plus de cruauté & de rage, que ne font les loups à l'égard les uns des autres.

C'est pourquoy la timidité ne doit point passer dans les femmes pour un défaut, mais pour une passion raisonnable, à laquelle elles doivent la pudeur, qui leur est si particuliere, & les deux plus grands avantages de la vie, qui sont l'inclination à la vertu, & l'éloignement du vice, ce que la pluspart des hommes ne peuvent acquerir, avec toute l'éducation & toutes les lumieres qu'on leur donne.

an infant alarms them, and that the sound of the wind makes them tremble. This is not generally the case. There are a large number of women [who are] as intrepid as men, and we know that the most timid often rise to the occasion. Timidity is almost inseparable from virtue, and all sensible people have it. As they do not want to do harm to anyone and they are not unaware of how much spitefulness there is among men, only a small thing is needed to inspire them with fear. It is a natural passion from which no one is exempt. Everyone fears death and the infirmities of life. The most powerful princes are apprehensive of revolt by their subjects and invasion by their enemies—and the most valiant commanders of being taken unawares.

Fear is great in [216] proportion to the power that we believe [we] have to resist, and it is only culpable in those who are strong enough to repel the evil that threatens them. We would be as unreasonable to accuse a judge and a man of letters (who had thought only of studying) of cowardice for refusing to fight a duel as to reproach a soldier (who had always carried arms) for not wishing to enter into an argument against a learned philosopher.

We raise women in such a way that they have reason to be fearful of everything. They have no enlightenment to [help them] avoid deceit in the things of the mind. They have no share in the training that produces dexterity and strength for attacking and defending. They see themselves exposed to suffer with impunity the outrages of a sex (so subject to fits of passion) [217] that regards them with contempt and often treats its own kind with more cruelty and rage than wolves do each other.

This is why timidity in women should not count as a fault but as a reasonable emotion to which women owe both the modesty that is so characteristic of them and the two greatest advantages in life—which are the inclination to virtue and the aversion to vice (which most men, with all the education and all the insight that we give them, cannot acquire).

The fear of an insufficiency of goods is the ordinary cause of avarice. Men are no less subject to it than women. And if it comes down to a count, I do not know but the number of the former would be found [218] the greater and their avarice

[L'Avarice.] La crainte de manquer de bien est la cause ordinaire de l'Avarice. Les hommes n'y sont pas moins sujets que les femmes; & si l'on venoit à compter, je ne sçay si le nombre des premiers ne se trou-[218]-veroit pas le plus grand, & leur avarice la plus blâmable. Comme il n'y a pas loin des deux vices à la vertu qui tient le milieu, on prend assez souvent l'un pour l'autre, & on confond l'avarice avec une loüable épargne.

Vne même action pouvant estre bonne en l'un & mauvaise en l'autre, il arrive souvent, que ce qui est mal en nous, ne l'est point du tout dans les femmes. Elles sont privées de tous les moyens de faire fortune par leur esprit, l'entrée des sciences & des emplois leur estant fermée; & ainsi estant moins en état de se garentir des malheurs & des incommoditez de la vie, elles doivent en estre plus touchées. Il ne faut dont pas s'étonner; que voyant avec cela qu'on a tant de peine à acquerir vn peu de bien, elles ayent soin de le conserver.

[219] [La credulité.] Si elles reçoivent si aisément, ce qu'on leur dit, c'est un effet de leur simplicité, qui les empéche de croire, que ceux qui ont authorité sur elles, soient ignorans, ou interessez; & l'on peche contre la Iustice de les accuser de Credulité, puisqu'il y en a encore plus parmi nous. Les plus habiles ne se laissent que trop leurrer par une fausse apparence; & souvent toute leur science, n'est qu'une basse credulité, mais un peu plus étenduë que celle des femmes: je veux dire, qu'ils ne sont plus sçavans que les autres, que parce qu'ils ont donné plus legerement leur consentement à un plus grand nombre de choses, dont ils ont retenu les idées, telles quelles, à force de repasser pardessus.

[La superstition.] Ce qui fait la timidité des femmes, est ce qui produit la su-[220]-perstition que les sçavans mêmes leur attribuënt: mais il paroît qu'ils sont en cela semblables à ceux qui ayant plus de tort, se persuadent avoir plus de raison, parce qu'ils crient plus haut que les autres. Ils s'imaginent étre exempts eux-mêmes de superstition, parce qu'ils en voyent dans quelques femmes peu éclairées, pendant qu'ils y sont eux-mêmes plongez miserablement jusques aux yeux.

Quand tous les hommes seroient de veritables adorateurs de Dieu, en esprit & en verité, & que les femmes luy rendroient

the more culpable. As it is not far from two vices to the virtue that holds the middle ground [between them] we often take one for the other. Avarice is confused with praiseworthy thrift.

Since one [and the] same action can be a good deed for one person and a bad deed for another, it often happens that what is bad in us is not at all bad in women. Women are deprived of all the means to make a fortune through the use of their minds—entry into the fields of learning and the professions being closed to them. Since they are, consequently, in worse shape to protect themselves from misfortunes and the inconveniences of life, they should be more concerned about these things. There is no reason to be surprised that, seeing how much difficulty is entailed in acquiring a little property, women are careful to keep it.

[219] If they so easily accept whatever it said to them, this is a consequence of their simplicity (which prevents them from believing that those who have authority over them could be ignorant or self-interested). And we sin against justice to accuse them of credulity, since there are even more persons of this type among us. The most adept men allow themselves to be only too attracted by a false appearance, and often all their knowledge is only a low grade credulousness but a little more extensive than that of women. I mean to say that they are no more learned than others simply because they have more impulsively given their consent to a much greater number of things (of which they have retained the concepts, word for word, by dint of thinking them over and over).

What causes timidity in women is what produces the [220] superstitiousness that scholars also attribute to them. But it appears that in this case the scholars resemble men who, being most in the wrong, persuade themselves that they are most in the right because they shout louder than others. They fancy themselves to be exempt from superstition because they spot it in some scarcely enlightened women (meanwhile, they are themselves miserably plunged in it up to their eyes).

Though all men were genuine worshipers of God in spirit and in truth and women offered Him an entirely superstitious cult, women would be pardonable. They are not taught to learn about God by themselves. They know of Him only what

en tout un culte superstitieux, elles en seroient excusables. On ne leur apprend point à connoître Dieu par elles-mêmes: elles n'en sçavent que ce qu'on leur en dit: Et comme la pluspart des hommes en parlent d'une maniere si peu digne de ce qu'il est, & ne le [221] distingue [*sic*] de ses creatures, que par la qualité de Createur, il ne faut pas s'étonner que des femmes, ne le connoissant que sur leur rapport, l'adorent par Religion avec les mêmes sentimens qu'elles ont pour les hommes, qu'elles craignent & qu'elles reverent.

[Le Babil.] Il y a des gens qui croyent bien mortifier les femmes en leur disant, qu'elles ne sont toutes que des Babillardes. Elles ont raison de se fâcher d'un reproche si impertinent. Leur corps se trouve si heureusement disposé par le temperament qui leur est propre, qu'elles conservent distinctement les impressions des objects qui les ont frappées: elles se les representent sans peine, & s'expriment avec une facilité admirable: cela fait que les idées qu'elles ont se réveillant à la moindre occa-[222]-sion, elles commencent & continüent la conversation comme il leur plaît: & la penetration de leur esprit leur donnant moyen d'appercevoir aisément les rapports des choses elles passent sans peine d'un sujet à l'autre, & peuvent ainsi parler long temps, sans laisser mourir le discours.

L'avantage de la parole est naturellement accompagné d'un grand desir de s'en servir, dés que l'occasion s'en presente. C'est le seul lien des hommes dans la societé, & plusieurs trouvent qu'il n'y a point de plus grand plaisir, ni plus digne de l'esprit, que de communiquer ses pensées aux autres. C'est pourquoy les femmes pouvant parler aisément, & estant élevées avec leurs semblables, il y auroit à redire qu'elles manquassent de s'entretenir. Elles ne doivent donc passer pour [223] babillardes, que lorsqu'elles parlent mal à propos, & de choses qu'elles n'entendent point, sans dessein de s'en faire instruire.

Il ne faut pas s'imaginer qu'on ne babille que quand on parle sur des habits & sur des Modes. Le babil des Nouvelistes est souvent plus ridicule. Et cette quantité de mots entassez les uns sur les autres, & qui ne signifient rien dans la pluspart des ouvrages, sont un caquet bien plus sot que celuy des plus petites femmes. Au moins peut-on dire que les discours

we have told them of Him. And as most men speak of Him in a manner so little worthy of what He is (and [221] only distinguish Him from his creatures by the title of Creator), it is not surprising that women, knowing Him only from men's report, worship Him in religion with the same sentiments that they feel for the men whom they fear and revere.

There are men who think that they effectively shame women by declaring that women are all mere gossips. Women have reason to be offended by so impertinent a reproach. Their bodies find themselves so happily disposed by the character that is peculiar to women that women distinctly retain the sensations of objects that have impressed them. They describe these things without difficulty and express themselves with an admirable facility. This causes the ideas that they have to quicken at the least opportunity. [222] Women begin and continue conversation as it pleases them. And since their penetrating mind[s] give them the means easily to perceive the relationships of things, they pass without difficulty from one subject to another and can, therefore, speak for a long time without allowing the flow of words to die.

An advantage in speech is naturally accompanied by a great desire to avail oneself of it as soon as the occasion presents itself. Speech is the sole bond among people in society, and many find that there is no greater pleasure (nor one more worthy of the mind) than to communicate their thoughts to others. This is why women, being able to speak easily and being raised with their own kind, should be criticized were they to fail to converse. They ought, consequently, to be considered [223] gossips only when they speak poorly to the point and about things that they do not understand (without the intent to learn about them).

It should not be imagined that we gossip only when we talk about clothes and fashions. The gossip of journalists is often more ridiculous. And this quantity of words (heaped one upon another and signifying nothing in most works) is a much more foolish clatter than that of the most shallow-minded women. At least we can say that their speeches are real and intelligible and that they are not so vain as to imagine themselves (as most learned men [do]) cleverer than their

de celles-cy sont réels & intelligibles, & qu'elles ne sont pas
assez vaines, pour s'imaginer comme la pluspart des sçavans,
estre plus habiles que leurs voisines, parce qu'elles disent plus
de paroles qui n'ont point de sens. Si les hommes avoient
la langue aussi libre, il [224] seroit impossible de les faire
taire. Chacun s'entretient de ce qu'il sçait; les Marchands de
leur negoce, les Philosophes de leurs études, & les femmes
de ce qu'elles ont pû apprendre; & elles peuvent dire qu'elles
s'entretiendroient encore mieux & plus solidement que nous,
si on avoit pris autant de peine à les instruire.

[La Curiosité.] Ce qui choque certaines personnes dans les
entretiens des femmes, c'est qu'elles témoignent une grande
envie de sçavoir tout. Ie ne sçay pas quel est le goust des gens
ausquels il ne plaist pas que les femmes soient si curieuses:
pour moy je trouve bon qu'on ait de la curiosité; Et je conseille
seulement de faire en sorte qu'elle ne soit pas importune.

Ie regarde les conversations des femmes comme celles des
Philosophes, où il est permis égale-[225]-ment de s'entretenir
des choses dont on n'a point la connoissance, & il y a des
contre-temps, dans les unes & dans les autres.

C'est l'ordinaire de beaucoup de gens de traiter les curieux
comme des mandians. Lorsqu'ils sont en humeur de donner,
ils ne se fâchent point qu'on leur demande: & quand ils
ont envie de découvrir ce qu'ils sçavent, ils sont bien aises
qu'on les prie, sinon ils ne manquent pas de dire qu'on a
trop de curiosité. Parce qu'on s'est forgé que les femmes ne
doivent point étudier, on se formalise, qu'elles demandent
d'estre informées de ce qu'on apprend par l'étude. Ie les
estime d'estre curieuses, & je les plains de n'avoir pas les
moyens de se satisfaire en cela: n'en estant souvent empêchées
que par une juste apprehension de s'adresser à des [226]
[La Curiosité est marque d'esprit.] esprits sots & bourus,
de qui elles se verroient moquées, au lieu d'en recevoir de
l'instruction. Il me paroît que la curiosité est une marque des
plus certaines d'un bon esprit & plus capable de discipline.
C'est une connoissance commencée qui nous fait aller plus
vîte & plus loin dans le chemin de la verité. Lorsque de
deux personnes qui sont touchées d'une même chose, l'une la
regarde indifferemment, & que l'autre s'en approche à dessein
de la mieux voir; c'est signe que celle-cy a les yeux plus

neighbors because they utter more words that make no sense. If men had as much ease with language [as women do], it [224] would be impossible to shut them up. Each talks about what he knows: merchants about their deals, philosophers about their studies, and women about what they have been able to learn. And they can claim that they would converse even better and more seriously than we do, if as much trouble had been taken to instruct them.

What grates on some people in the conversations of women is that women show a great desire to know everything. I do not understand the taste of people who are displeased that women are so curious. For me, I find [it] good that a person has curiosity, and my advice is only to take care that such curiosity is not importunate.

I consider the conversations of women [to be] like those of philosophers—[conversations] in which [all parties] are permitted equally [225] to talk about things of which they have no knowledge. There are shortcomings in both [situations].

It is common for many people to treat the curious like beggars. When they are in a humor to give, they are not vexed that we ask [something] of them. And when they want to display what they know, they are very pleased that we entreat them. If not, they do not fail to claim that we are too curious. Because we have formed the opinion that women ought not to study, we take offense when women ask to be told about the things that we learn from study. I admire women because they are inquisitive people, and I am sorry they do not have the means to satisfy themselves in this regard (often being prevented only by a just apprehension of appealing [for help to] some [226] foolish, peevish spirits by whom they would see themselves mocked instead of gifted with instruction). It seems to me that curiosity is the most certain sign of a good mind most capable of education. Curiosity is a "knowledge begun" that makes us move more rapidly and farther along the road of truth. When [there are] two persons who are affected by the same thing [and] one regards it indifferently while the other advances on it with the intent of viewing it more clearly, this is an indication that the later has his eyes open wider. The mind in

ouverts. L'Esprit est dans les deux Sexes également propre
aux sciences; & le desir qu'il en peut avoir, n'est pas plus
blâmable en l'un qu'en l'autre. Lorsqu'il se sent frappé d'une
chose, qu'il ne voit qu'obscurément, il semble que c'est par un
droit naturel qu'il **[227]** veut en estre éclairci: & l'ignorance
estant le plus fâcheux esclavage où il se puisse trouver, il est
aussi déraisonnable de condamner une personne qui tâche de
s'en tirer, qu'un miserable qui s'efforceroit de sortir d'une
prison où on le tiendroit enfermé.

[Inconstance.] Entre tous les défauts que l'on donne aux
femmes, l'humeur inconstante & volage est celle qui fait plus
de mécontans. Cependant les hommes n'y sont pas moins
sujets, mais parce qu'ils se voyent les Maîtres, ils se figurent
que tout leur est permis: & qu'une femme s'étant une fois
attachée à eux, le lien ne doit estre indissoluble que de sa
part; quoy qu'ils soient tous deux égaux, & que chacun y soit
pour soy.

On ne s'accuseroit pas si souvent de legereté les uns &
les autres, si on observoit qu'elle est na[tu]-**[228]**-relle aux
hommes; & que qui dit mortel, dit inconstant: & que c'est
une necessité indispensable de l'estre de la maniere que nous
sommes faits. Nous ne jugeons des objets, nous ne les aimons
ou haïssons, que sur les apparences, qui ne dependent point de
nous. Les mêmes choses nous paroissent diversement, tantost
parce qu'elles ont souffert quelque changement, tantost parce
que nous en avons souffert nous-mêmes. La même viande
plus ou moins assaisonnée, chaude ou froide, nous cause
des sentimens tout differens: & demeurant là même, nous
en serions autrement touchez en maladie qu'en santé. Dans
l'Enfance, nous sommes indifferens pour des choses que nous
regardons dix ans aprés avec passion, parceque le corps est
changé.

[229] [Pourquoy il ne faut pas accuser les autres de ce
qu'ils ne nous aiment pas.] Si une personne a de l'amour pour
nous, c'est qu'elle nous croit aimables; & si une autre nous
haït, c'est que nous luy paroissons haïssables. Nous estimons
en un temps ceux que nous méprisions auparavant: parce
qu'ils ne nous ont pas toûjours parus de même, soit qu'eux
où [*sic*] nous ayons changé. Et tel objet s'étant presenté au

the two sexes is equally fit for education, and the desire that it can conceive for education is not more culpable in the one than in the other. When the mind senses itself struck by a thing that it sees only obscurely, it seems that it has a natural right **[227]** to want to be enlightened. Since ignorance is the most annoying slavery in which the mind can find itself, it is as unreasonable to condemn a person who tries to extract himself from ignorance as [to blame] a wretch who would exert himself to escape a prison where he has been held shut up.

Among all the faults of which we accuse women, an inconstant and frivolous humor is the one that causes most discontent. Men are, however, no less subject to this [failing]. But because they see themselves the masters, they imagine that everything is permitted to them. [They believe] that once a woman is attached to them, the bond ought to be indissoluble except from their side—although both are equal, and each one is in it for oneself.

Both sexes would cease to accuse each other of fickleness so often if we realized that fickleness is natural **[228]** to human beings. Who says "mortal," says "inconstant." [Inconstancy] is an indispensable necessity of beings constructed as we are. We judge objects [and] we love or hate them only on [the basis of] appearances that do not depend on us. The same things appear to us in different ways: sometimes because they have suffered some change; sometimes because we have suffered it ourselves. The same meat [when] more or less seasoned [or when] hot or cold causes totally different sensations in us. [Although it] remains the same, we will be otherwise affected [by it] in sickness than in heath. In infancy we are indifferent to the things that ten years later we look on with passion, for the body has changed.

[229] If a person loves us, it is because he or she believes us loveable. And if another one hates us, it is because we appear hateful to him or her. Because people do not always seem the same to us (be it that they or we have changed), we cherish at one time those whom we hated before. And such an object being presented to the heart, has found the door to it open which would have been closed to it a quarter of an hour sooner or later.

coeur, en a trouvé la porte ouverte, qui luy auroit été fermée un quart d'heure plûtost ou plus tard.

Le partage où nous nous trouvons souvent entre deux mouvemens contraires, que nous cause un même objet, nous convainc malgré nous, que les passions ne sont point libres, & qu'il est injuste de se plaindre d'estre consideré autrement que l'on voudroit. Comme il faut peu de chose pour donner de l'amour; il en faut peu [230] aussi pour le faire perdre, & cette passion ne dépend pas plus de nous dans son progrez, que dans sa naissance. De dix personnes qui aspirent à estre aimées, il arrive ordinairement, que celle qui aura moins de merite, moins de naissance & de bonne mine, l'emportera sur les autres: parce qu'elle aura l'air plus gay, ou quelque chose plus à la mode, ou à nostre goust, dans la disposition où nous nous trouvons alors.

[Artifice.] Bien loin de faire tort aux femmes en les accusant d'estre plus Artificieuses que les hommes, on parle pour elles, si on sçait ce que l'on dit, puisqu'on reconnoist par là, quelles [*sic*] sont aussi plus spirituelles & plus prudentes. L'Artifice est une voye secrette pour arriver à son but, sans en estre détourné. Il faut [231] de l'esprit pour découvrir cette voye, & de l'adresse pour s'y conduire: & l'on ne peut trouver à redire qu'une personne mette en usage l'artifice, pour éviter d'être trompée. La fourbe est bien plus pernicieuse, & plus ordinaire dans les hommes: ça [*sic*] toûjours esté le chemin le plus commun, pour entrer dans les Postes & dans les Emplois, où l'on peut faire plus de mal: & au lieu que les hommes qui veulent tromper, employent leurs biens, leurs lumieres, & leur puissance, dont on est rarement à couvert; les femmes ne peuvent se servir que des caresses, & de l'éloquence, qui sont des moyens naturels, dont on peut plus aisément se garantir, quand on a sujet de s'en défier.

[Plus grande malice.] Pour comble d'accusation & de défaut, on dit que les fem-[232]-mes sont plus malicieuses & plus méchantes que les hommes: & tout le mal dont on les peut charger, est renfermé dans cette pensée. Ie ne crois pas que ceux qui l'ont, prétendent qu'il y ait plus de femmes que d'hommes, qui fassent du mal. Ce seroit une fausseté manifeste. Elles n'ont point de part aux Emplois ny aux Charges dont l'abus est cause de toutes les calamitez

The quandary in which we often find ourselves ([torn] between two contrary movements that one and the same object causes in us) convinces us, despite ourselves, that the passions are not free and that it is unjust to complain of being looked on in some way other than we would wish. As it only takes a little thing to inspire love, little is also required [230] to make it perish. And this passion does not depend on us any more for its development than its birth. Of ten women who aspire to be loved, it commonly happens that the one who has least merit or least birth or good looks will win out over the others—because she has a cheerier attitude or something [that is] more in fashion or more to our taste in the frame of mind in which we find ourselves at the time.

Very far from doing an injustice to women by accusing them of being craftier than men, this argues in their favor (if we know what we are talking about—for, when we assert this, we acknowledge that women are also more intelligent and prudent [than men]). "Craft" is a hidden way to arrive at one's goal without being turned aside from it. [231] Intelligence is necessary to find this path and cleverness to conduct oneself along it. We cannot find [a basis] for criticizing a person who puts artifice to use to avoid being deceived. Cheating is much more pernicious—and more common among men. It has always been the most ordinary channel for entry into the posts and the professions where one can do most damage. Whereas men who want to deceive, employ their goods, their wits, and their power (from which we are rarely safe), women can only avail themselves of caresses and eloquence (which are natural means against which we can very easily defend ourselves when we have occasion to be distrustful).

To round out [the list of] accusation[s] and fault[s], women are said [232] to be more malicious and more spiteful than men. All the evil with which they can be charged is contained in this notion. I do not believe that those who maintain this pretend that more women than men do ill. This would be an obvious falsehood. Women take no part in the professions or the offices whose abuse is the cause of all public calamities. And women's virtue is too exemplary (and the disorder of men too well known) to call them into question.

publiques; & leur vertu est trop exemplaire, & le desordre des hommes trop connu pour les revoquer en doute.

Lors donc que l'on dit des femmes qu'elles ont plus de malice, cela ne peut signifier autre chose, sinon que quand elles se portent au mal, elles le font plus adroittement: & le poussent plus loin que les hommes: Soit. Cela marque en elles un tres so-[233]-lide avantage. On ne peut estre capable de beaucoup de mal, sans avoir beaucoup d'esprit & sans estre aussi par consequent capable de beaucoup de bien. Ainsi les femmes ne doivent pas tenir ce reproche plus injurieux, que celuy qu'on feroit aux riches, & aux puissans d'étre plus méchans que les pauvres, parce qu'ils ont plus de quoy nuire; & les femmes pourroient répondre comme eux, que si elles peuvent faire du mal, elles peuvent aussi faire du bien, & que si l'ignorance où on les laisse est cause qu'elles sont plus méchantes que nous, la science au contraire les rendroit beaucoup meilleures.

Cette petite discution des plus signalez défauts qu'on croit particuliers & naturels au beau Sexe fait voir deux choses, l'une, qu'ils ne sont pas si conside-[234]-rables que le vulgaire se l'imagine; & l'autre qu'ils peuvent estre rejettez sur le peu d'éducation qu'on donne aux femmes, & que tels qu'ils soient, ils peuvent estre corrigez par l'instruction dont elles ne sont pas moins capables que nous.

Si les Philosophes avoient suivy cette regle pour juger de tout ce qui concerne les femmes, ils en auroient parlé plus sainement: & ne seroient point tombez à leur égard dans des absurditez ridicules. Mais la pluspart des Anciens & des Modernes n'ayant basty leur Philsophie que sur des préjugez populaires, & ayant esté dans une grande ignorance d'eux-mêmes; ce n'est pas merveille qu'ils ayent si mal connu les autres. Sans nous mettre en peine des Anciens, on peut dire des Modernes, que la [235] maniere dont on les enseigne, leur faisant croire quoy que faussement, qu'ils ne peuvent devenir plus habiles que ceux qui les ont précedez, les rend esclaves de l'Antiquité, & les porte à embrasser aveuglément tout ce qu'ils y trouvent, comme des veritez constantes. Et parce que tout ce qu'ils disent contre les femmes, est fondé principalement sur ce qu'ils ont lû dans les Anciens, il ne sera pas inutile de rapporter icy quelques unes des plus curieuses

When, therefore, women are said to be more malicious [than men], that can indicate no other thing but that when women devote themselves to evil, they do it more adroitly and push it further than men. So be it. That marks a very substantial advantage **[233]** for them. One cannot be capable of great wickedness without also having great intelligence—and without being, as a consequence, capable of much good. Therefore, women should not consider this reproach to be more damaging than a charge that could be leveled against rich and powerful men: [i.e., that these men] are more wicked than the poor because they have more of what it takes to be harmful. Women could respond as these men [do]: that if they can do evil, they can also do good—and that if the ignorance in which we leave them is the reason why they are more wicked than we [are], education would, conversely, make them much better [than we are].

This brief discussion of the more conspicuous faults that are believed [to be] characteristic of and natural to the fair sex makes two things apparent: the one, that woman's defects are not as important **[234]** as the common man imagines; and the other, that they can be credited to the lack of education that we give women (and that such as they are, they can be corrected by instruction—of which women are not less capable than we are).

If the philosophers had followed this rule in evaluating everything concerning women, they would have spoken more judiciously and would not have fallen (with respect to women) into ridiculous absurdities. But most of the ancient and the modern thinkers having built their philosoph[ies] only on popular prejudices and having been in great ignorance of themselves, it is not surprising that they have so ill understood others. Without troubling ourselves about the ancient authors, we could say of the modern ones that the **[235]** way in which they are educated—making them believe (though falsely) that they cannot develop more expertise than those who have preceded them—makes them slaves of antiquity and leads them blindly to embrace as eternal truth everything that they find there. And because everything that they say against women is founded principally on what they have read in the [works of the] ancients, it will not be a waste

pensées sur ce sujet, que nous ont laissées ces illustres morts,
dont on revere tant aujourd'huy les cendres & la pourriture
même.

[Sentiment de Platon.] Platon le pere de la Philosophie
ancienne remercioit les Dieux de trois graces qu'ils luy avoient
faites; mais particulierement de ce qu'il estoit né hom-[236]-
me & non pas femme. S'il avoit en veuë leur condition
presente, je serois bien de son avis; mais ce qui fait juger
qu'il avoit autre chose dans l'esprit, c'est le doute qu'on dit
qu'il témoignoit souvent s'il faloit mettre les femmes de la
cathegorie des bestes. Cela suffiroit à des gens raisonnables
pour le condamner luy même d'ignorance ou de bétise, &
pour achever de le dégrader du tiltre de Divin qu'il n'a plus
que parmy les pedans.

[Sentiment d'Aristote.] Son disciple Aristote à qui l'on
conserve encore dans les Ecoles le nom glorieux de Genie
de la nature sur le préjugé qu'il l'a mieux connuë qu'aucun
autre Philosophe, prétend que les femmes, ne sont que des
Monstres. Qui ne le croiroit sur l'authorité d'un personnage
si celebre? De dire que c'est une impertinence, ce [237] seroit
trop ouvertement choquer ses supposts. Si une femme quelque
sçavante qu'elle fust, en avoit écrit autant des hommes, elle
perdroit tout son credit, & l'on s'imagineroit avoir assez fait
pour refuter une telle sottise que de répondre que ce seroit une
femme, ou une folle qui l'auroit dit. Cependant, elle n'auroit
pas moins de raison que ce Philosophe. Les femmes sont
aussi anciennes que les hommes: on les voit en aussi grand
nombre, & nul n'est surpris d'en rencontrer en son chemin.
Pour estre Monstre, selon la pensée même de cét homme, il
faut avoir quelque chose d'extraordinaire, & de surprenant.
Les femmes n'ont rien de tout cela: elles ont toûjours esté
faites de mêmes, toujours belles & spirituelles: & si elles ne
sont pas faites comme Ari-[238]-stote; elles peuvent dire aussi
qu'Aristote n'estoit pas fait comme elles.

Les disciples de cét Autheur, qui vivoient du temps de
Philon, tomberent dans une pensée, non moins grotesque à
l'égard des femmes; se figurant au rapport de cét Historien,
qu'elles sont des hommes ou des mâles imparfaits. C'est sans
doute parcequ'elles n'ont pas le menton garny de barbe: hors
de là je n'y comprend rien. Les deux Sexes pour estre parfaits,

of time to review here several of the more curious thoughts on the subject [of women] that these illustrious dead (whose cinders and, even, putrefaction are so revered today) have left us.

Plato, the father of ancient philosophy, thanked the gods for three favors that they had done him, but particularly for the fact that he was born a [236] man and not a woman. If he had in view women's present condition, I would very much share his way of thinking. But what makes me conclude that he had something else in mind is the doubt that he is said often to have expressed whether women should be assigned to the category of "animals." That should suffice for rational people to condemn him from his own lips for ignorance or stupidity and to complete his demotion from the title of "divine" (that he no longer holds except among pedants).

His disciple Aristotle, for whom is still reserved in the schools the glorious title of "genius of nature" (on the assumption that he understood nature better than any other philosopher), pretends that women are mere monsters. Who would not believe it on the authority of so famous a person? (To say that this thesis is a piece of insolence would [237] be too overtly to offend his supporters.) If a woman (however learned she be) had written as much about men, she would have lost all her credibility. And we would imagine ourselves to have done enough to refute such a silly thing to point out that it was a woman (or a fool) who had said it. However, this woman would not have had less reason than this philosopher. Women have been around as long as men. We see them in as great a number, and no one is surprised to encounter them in his path. To be a monster (even according to Aristotle's definition) something extraordinary and surprising would be required. Women have nothing of all that; they have always been formed the same way—always beautiful and intelligent. If women are not built like [238] Aristotle; they could say also that Aristotle was not built like them.

The disciples of this author, who lived at the time of Philo, fell into a [way of] thinking [that was] no less grotesque with respect to women—imagining (according to the report of this historian) that women are imperfect men or males. Without doubt, their reason is because women do not have

doivent estre comme nous les voyons. Si l'un estoit semblable à l'autre, ce ne seroit aucun des deux. Si les hommes sont les peres des femmes, les femmes sont meres des hommes, ce qui les rend au moins égaux: & on auroit autant de raison que ces Philosophes, de dire que les hommes sont des femmes imparfaites.

[239] [Pensée plaisante de Socrate.] Socrate, qui estoit pour la Morale l'Oracle de l'Antiquité, parlant de la beauté du Sexe, avoit accoûtumé de la comparer à un Temple bien apparent, mais basti sur un cloaque.

Il ne faut que rire de cette pensée, si elle ne fait pas mal au coeur. Il y a apparence qu'il jugeoit du corps des autres par le sien, ou par celuy de sa femme, qui étoit une diablesse, qui le faisoit detester; & qu'il luy parloit ainsi de son Sexe, à dessein de la faire bouquer, & qu'il enrageoit dans son ame d'estre laid comme un magot.

[Pensée de Diogene.] Diogene surnommé le chien, parce qu'il ne sçavoit que mordre, voyant un jour en passant deux femmes, qui s'entretenoient ensemble, dit à ceux de sa compagnie que c'étoient-là deux serpens, un Aspic & un Vipere, qui [240] se communiquoient leur venin. Cét * [*C'est à dire Sentence d'un homme illustre.] Apophtegme est digne d'un honneste homme; & je ne m'étonne pas qu'on le mette au rang des belles Sentences Philosophiques. Si Tabarin, Verboquet & l'Espiegle, eussent vécu de son temps, il est certain que nous trouverions leurs rencontres plus spirituelles. Le bon homme estoit un peu blessé, & ceux qui le connoissent un peu, jugent bien qu'il n'avoit alors autre chose à dire.

[Democrite.] Pour l'admirable & plaisant Démocrite, comme il aimoit un peu à rire, il ne faut pas prendre au pied de la lettre tout ce qui est sorty de sa bouche. Il avoit la taille fort grande, & sa femme des plus petites. Estant un jour interrogé pourquoy il s'estoit si mal assorty, il répondit en raillant à son ordinaire, que lors-[241]-qu'on est obligé de choisir, & qu'il n'y a rien de bon à prendre, le moindre est toûjours le meilleur. Si on eût fait la même demande à sa femme, elle eût pû repartir avec autant de raison, qu'un petit & un grand mary ne valant gueres mieux l'un que l'autre, elle avoit pris le sien comme à la blanque, de peur de prendre le pire en choisissant.

chin[s] garnished with beards (apart from that I do not understand it). To be perfect, the two sexes must be as we see them. If the one were like the other, there would not be "either of them." If men are the fathers of women, women are mothers of men—which renders them at least equals. And we would have as much reason as these philosophers to say that men are imperfect women.

[239] Socrates (who would be antiquity's oracle in the field of ethics), [when] speaking of the beauty of the feminine sex, was accustomed to compare it to a temple that looked fine, but was built over a sewer.

We would only have to laugh at this idea if it did not make us sick at heart. It seems that Socrates judged the bodies of other people by his own or by that of his wife—who was a demon (which made him hate it)—and that he spoke so about her gender with the intent of enraging her (and that in the depth of his soul he was furious that he was ugly as a maggot).

One day, Diogenes (surnamed the "dog" because he only knew how to bite) saw two women passing by who were talking together. He said to those in his company that there were two serpents, an asp and a viper, who **[240]** shared their venom. This apophthegm is worthy of an honest man, and I am not astonished that it ranks with the beautiful philosophical maxims. If Tabarin, Verboquet, and l'Espiegle[1] had lived in his day, it is certain that we would find their tales more ingenious. The good man was a bit put out, and those who knew him somewhat concluded correctly that he did not have anything else to say in this situation.

As for the admirable, pleasant Democritus—since he loved to laugh a bit, we need not take literally everything that crossed his lips. He was very tall, and his wife was very small. Being asked one day why he had matched himself so badly, he answered (jokingly, according to his custom) that

---

[1] Tabarin (Antoine Girard, 1584–1633) was a noted comedian and entertainer; Verboquet, the "Generous," was the pseudonym of the author of a popular collection of amusing stories (*Les Delices*) published in 1625, and l'Espiegle (Till Eulenspiegel) was a legendary jokester whose escapades were narrated in the folk literature of several nations.

[Pensée de Caton.] Caton ce sage & severe Critique prioit souvent les Dieux de luy pardonner s'il avoit esté assez imprudent pour confier le moindre secret à une femme. Le bon homme avoit à coeur un fait fameux de l'Histoire Romaine; dont les Antiquaires * [*Les Amateurs de l'Antiquité.] se servent comme d'un grand argument pour montrer le peu de retenuë des femmes. Un enfant de douze ans pressé par sa mere de luy dire la resolution du Se-[242]-nat, où il avoit assisté, inventa pour sa défaité, qu'on avoit arrété de donner plusieures femmes à chaque mary. Elle l'alla dire aussi tost à ses voisines, pour prendre des mesures avec elles; & toute la Ville le sçeut au bout d'une demie-heure. Ie voudrois bien sçavoir, ce que feroit un pauvre mary, si dans un Etat où les femmes seroient les Maîtresses, comme dans celuy des Amazones, on luy venoit rapporter, qu'il auroit esté resolu au Conseil, de donner à chaque homme un compagnon: Sans doute qu'il n'en diroit mot.

Voila quelques-unes des grandes & sublimes pensées, que ceux que les sçavans étudient comme des Oracles, ont euës sur le sujet du beau Sexe: Et ce qu'il y a de plaisant, & de bizarre tout ensemble, c'est que des gens gra-[243]-ves se servent serieusement, de ce que ces fameux Anciens n'ont dit souvent que par raillerie. Tant il est vray que les préjugez & la préoccupation font faire de bevuës à ceux mêmes, qui passent pour les plus raisonnables, les plus judicieux, & les plus sages.

FIN

when [241] one is forced to choose and there is nothing good to take, the least is always the best. If someone had posed the same question to his wife, she would have been able to retort with as much reason that: since a small or a large husband is neither one scarcely worth more than the other, she had picked him randomly for fear of taking the worse by making a choice.

Cato, (the wise, severe censor) often prayed to the gods to pardon him if he had been so imprudent as to confide the least secret to a woman. The good man had in mind a famous event from Roman history—which antiquaries use as a great argument for demonstrating women's lack of discretion. A child of twelve years, [being] pressed by his mother to tell her about a resolution of the Senate [242] (where he had assisted), invented—to put her off—[the story] that it had been decided to give each husband many wives. She immediately went to tell the tale to the ladies of the neighborhood to plot a strategy with them, and the whole town knew the story within half an hour. I would very much like to know what a poor husband would do if in a state where women were the rulers (as in the nation of the Amazons), it had just been reported to him that a resolution had been passed in council giving each man a "fellow workman." Without doubt he would not say a word about it.

These are some of the great, sublime thoughts that the ancient authors (whom our experts study like oracles) have had on the subject of the fair sex. And what is amusing and bizarre both at the same time is that serious men make [243] serious use of what these famous ancients often said only in jest. So true is it that prejudices and preoccupation cause blunders even among those who pass for the most reasonable, most judicious, and wisest [of men].

The End

Poullain

Avertissement

Les plus fortes Objections qu'on nous peut faire; se tirent de l'Authorité des grands hommes, & de l'Ecriture-sainte. Pour ce qui est des premieres, on croit y satisfaire suffisamment, en disant qu'on ne reconnoist point icy d'autre Authorité, que celle de la Raison & du bon Sens.

Pour ce qui regarde l'Ecriture, elle n'est contraire en aucune façon, au dessein de cét Ouvrage, si l'on prend bien l'un & l'autre. On prétend icy qu'il y a une égalité entie-[re entre les deux Sexes con-][1]siderez indépendemment de la Coûtume qui met souvent ceux qui ont plus d'Esprit & de merite; dans la dépendance des autres. Et l'Ecriture ne dit pas un mot d'Inégalité; & comme elle n'est que pour servir de regle aux hommes dans leur conduite, selon les idées qu'elle donne de la iustice, elle laisse à chacun la liberté de juger comme il peut de l'état naturel & veritable des choses. Et si l'on y prend garde, toutes les Objections qu'on en tire, ne sont que des Sophismes de préjugé, par lesquels, tantôt on entend de toutes les femmes des passages qui ne conviennent qu'à quelques unes en particulier; tantost on rejette sur la nature ce qui ne vient que de l'Education ou de la Coûtume, & ce qu'ont dit les Autheurs Sacrez par rapport aux Usages de leurs temps.

---

[1]The material within brackets is proposed as a reconstruction of a gap in the text of the original edition

A Notice

The strongest objections that can be made against us derive from the authority of great men and the Holy Scriptures. As to the first, we believe that we have countered it adequately by stating that we do not here recognize any authority other than that of reason and common sense.

With respect to Scripture: it is in no way contrary to the intent of this work—if we understand both correctly. We maintain here that there is a complete equality [between the two sexes]—if they are considered independently of the custom that often forces those who have more intelligence and merit to submit to others. The Scriptures do not say a word about inequality. And as Scripture is only to serve as a guide for people in their conduct (according to the ideas of justice it provides), it allows each person the freedom to decide as [best] he can the natural and true state of things. If we read the Bible carefully, all the objections [to our thesis] that are drawn from it are but sophisms of prejudice by which, sometimes, passages that pertain only to certain women in particular are applied to all women and, at other times, nature is blamed for something that derives only from education or from custom and from what the sacred authors have said relative to the practices of their day.

BIBLIOGRAPHY

Works by François Poullain de la Barre:

Les Rapports de la langue Latine à la Françoise pour traduire elegamment et sans peine. Paris: 1672.

De l'Egalité des deux Sexes, Discours physique et moral, où l'on voit l'importance de se défaire des préjugez. Paris: 1673.

  [*The Woman as Good as the Man, or the Equality of Both Sexes*, trans. by A.L. London, 1676]

De l'Education des Dames pour la conduite de l'esprit dans les sciences et dans les moeurs. Paris: 1674.

De l'excellence des hommes contres l'égalité des sexes. Paris: 1675.

Essai des Remarques particulières sur la langue Françoise pour la ville de Genève. Geneva: 1691.

La Doctrine des Protestans sur la liberté de lire l'Ecriture Sainte, le Service divin en langue entendue, l'Invocation des Saints, le Sacrement de l'Eucharistie–Justifiée par le Missel Romain & par des réflexions sur chaque point, avec un Comentaire philosophique sur ces Paroles de Jesus-Christ: "Ceci est mon corps; Ceci est mon sang," Math. chap. xxvi, v. 26. Geneva: 1720.

Works relating to François Poullain de la Barre:

Abensour, Léon. *Histoire générale du féminisme des origines à nos jours.* Paris: Delagrave, 1921.

_____ . *La femme et le féminism avant la Révolution.* Paris: Leroux, 1923.

_____ . *Le Problème féministe: Un cas d'aspiration collective vers l'égalité.* Paris: Radot, 1927.

Albistur, Maire, and Daniel Armogathe. *Histoire du féminisme français du moyen-âge à nos jours.* Paris: Des Femmes, 1977.

Alcover, Madeleine. *Poullain de la Barre: Une aventure philosophique.* Papers on French Seventeenth Century Literature/Biblio 17: Paris, Seattle, Tübingen, 1981.

_____ . "The Indecency of Knowledge." *Rice University Studies*, 64, 1 (Winter, 1978): 25–39.

Angenot, Marc. *Les champions des femmes: Examen du discours sur la supériorité des femmes (1400–1800).* Montréal: Les Presses de l'Université du Québec, 1977.

Ascoli, George. "Essai sur l'histoire des idées féministes en France du seizième siècle à la Révolution." *Revue de synthèse historique*, XIII (1906): 25–57, 161–184.

Bayle, Pierre. *A General Dictionary, Historical and Critical*, VII. London: 1738: 448.

Caffiaux, Philippe Joseph. *Défenses du beau sexe ou Mémoires historiques, philosophiques et critiques pour servir d'apologie aux femmes.* Amsterdam: 1753.

Dictionnaire historique et biographique de la Suisse. Ed. by Marcel Godet, *et al.* Neuchâtel: 1921–1934.

Goujet, Claude Pierre. *Bibliothèque Françoise ou histoire de la litérature Françoise*, I. Paris: 1740.

Grappin, Henri. "Notes sur un féministe oublié: le Cartésian Poullain de la Barre." *Revue d'histoire littéraire de la France*, XX (1913): 852–867.

_____ , "A Propos du féministe Poullain de la Barre." *Revue d'histoire littéraire de la France*, XXI (1914): 387–389.

Haag, Eugène, and Emile Haag. *La France Protestante*, VIII. Paris: J. Cherbuliez, 1846–1859.

Hine, Ellen McNiven. "The Woman Question in Early Eighteenth Century French Literature: The Influence of François Poullain de la Barre." *Studies on Voltaire and the Eighteenth Century*, CXVI (1973): 65–79.

Hoffmann, Paul. *La femme dans la pensée des lumières*. Paris: Editions Ophrys, 1977.

Journal des Sçavans. (April 8, 1675; March 16, 1676).

Lefèvre, G. "Poullain de la Barre et le Féminisme au XVIIe siècle." *Revue pédagogique*, LXIV (1914): 101–113.

LeFranc, Abel. "Lettre, au Rédacteur." *Le Temps* (25 May 1906).

Maclean, Ian. *Woman Triumphant: Feminism in French Literature*, 1610–1652. Oxford: Clarendon Press, 1977.

Magné, Bernard. "Education des femmes et féminisme chez Poullain de la Barre (1647–1723)." *Marseille*, 1 (1972): 117–127.

_____ . *Le féminisme de Poullain de la Barre, origine et signification*. Ph.D. Dissertation, University of Toulouse, 1964.

_____ . "Une source de la lettre persane XXXVIII? *L'Egalité des deux sexes* de Poullain de la Barre." *Revue d'histoire littéraire de la France*, 3, 4 (May-August, 1968): 407–414.

Moréri, Louis. *Le grand dictionnaire historique ou le mélange curieux de l'histoire sacrée et profane,* VI. (Basel: 1733): 1101.

Natsch, Clara. "Poulain de la Barres Bemerkungen zum Genfer-Französische." Ph.D. Dissertation, University of Zurick, 1927.

Piéron, Henri. "De L'influence sociale des principes Cartésiens: Un précurseur inconnu de féminisme et de la Révolution: François Poulain de la Barre." *Revue de synthèse historique,* V (1902): 153–185, 270–282.

Reynier, Gustave. *La femme au XVIIe siècle.* Paris: Plon, 1933.

Richards, S.A. *Feminist Writers of the 17th Century, with Special Reference to François Poullain de la Barre.* London: David Nutt, 1914.

Ronzeaud, Pierre. "La femme au pouvoir ou le monde à l'envers." *XVIIème siècle,* 108 (1975): 9–33.

Rossat-Mignot, S. "Poullain de la Barre, un féministe du XVIIème siècle." *Cahiers rationalistes,* 322 (March, 1976): 156–160.

Seidel, Michael. "Poulain de la Barre's *The Woman as Good as the Man.*" *Journal of the History of Ideas,* XXV (July-Sept., 1974): 499–508.

Senebier, Jan. *Histoire Littéraire de Genève,* II. (Geneva: 1786): 282–283.

Stock, Marie Louise. "*Poullain de la Barre: A Seventeenth-Century Feminist.*" Ph.D. Dissertation, Columbia University, 1961.

Index to English Texts

Theologian: 47
Theology: xli 73, 91, 101
Thomas Aquinas: 47
Titus Livy: 101
Truth, 107, 113, 117, 127, 157, 171;
 Relativity of: 153
Turk: 51, 77
Turkey: xxxii, 19
Tyranny: 27
Unitarian: xvii
University: 121
Verboquet: 175
Vice: 67, 69, 71, 99, 109, 119, 141,
 149, 157
Virgil: 67 n. 2
Virtue: xli, xlii, 53, 59, 61, 67, 69,
 71, 73, 95, 99, 101, 107, 109, 115,
 119, 127, 141, 149, 151, 157, 159,
 169
Wife: 23, 75, 77, 103, 177
Woman as Good as the Man: xvi
Women
 Advancement of: 9, 11
 Anti-feminist: 7, 21
 Avarice of: xlvii, 159
 Body and: xl, xliv, 17, 21
 Business and: 47, 59
 Characteristics of: xxix, xxxiii, xlii,
  xliii, xlv, 27, 31, 43, 47, 53, 59,
  69, 73, 121, 123, 129, 131, 133,
  133, 145, 147, 151, 159, 171
 Children and: 17, 19, 23, 25, 43, 59,
  69, 71, 77, 141, 151
 Craftiness of: xlvii, 169
 Credulity of: 161
 Curiosity of: 165
 Education of: xxv, xxvii, xxxi,
  xxxiii, xxxv, xxxvi, xli, xlii, xliii,xlvi,
  xlviii, 7, 9, 11, 19, 29, 31, 35, 37,
  41, 43, 51, 53, 73, 85, 86–117,119,
  121, 129, 131, 153, 155
 Female Readers: xliii, 9
 Fickleness of: xlvii, 67
 Gossips: xlvii, 163, 177

Housekeeping and: xxxvi, xliii, 19,
 47, 57, 59
Hypocrisy of: 65
Inconstancy of: 167
Inferiority of: xxiii, xxx, xxxviii, 15,
 17, 25, 33, 55, 63
Language and: xxvi
Maliciousness of: xlvii, 169, 171
Marriage and: xxxvi, xlvi, 25, 57
Military and: xxxiii, xliii, 17, 73,
 125
Mind and: xxv, xxxix, xl, 17, 21, 61
Misanthropic: 11
Modesty of: 159
Monarchy and: xxxiv, xliii, 17, 29,
 73, 119, 121, 123, 125
Pregnancy and: xxiv, xxxii, 23,
 141, 147
Professions and: xxiii, xxx, xli, xlii,
 17, 19, 23, 119, 121, 125
Rage of: 65
Regents: 29
Religion and: xliii, 29, 39, 41, 47,
 53, 55, 73, 95, 121, 123, 161, 163
 "School of:" xxxv, 37
State and: xxx, 25, 29, 73, 97, 99,
 119, 123
Strength of: 143, 159
Subjugation of: xxiv, xxvi, xxxi,
 xxxviii–xxxix, 7, 15, 19, 21, 23,
 67, 75
Superiority of: xxvi, xliv, 7, 31, 35,
 37, 45, 53, 57, 59, 87, 89, 93, 105,
 147
Superstitiousness of: xlvii, 161
Timidity of: xlvii, 157, 159
Vanity of: 31, 155, 157
Verbal Fluency of: xxxvi, xliii, 39,
 43, 45, 47, 93, 121, 163, 169
Vices of: 51, 53, 61, 113
Working: xlvi, 39, 49, 61, 157
Writers: 45, 47, 51

STUDIES IN THE HISTORY OF PHILOSOPHY